SEVENTY YEARS OF THE
SOUTH WESTERN

SEVENTY YEARS OF THE SOUTH WESTERN
A RAILWAY JOURNEY THROUGH TIME

COLIN BOOCOCK

AN IMPRINT OF PEN & SWORD BOOKS LTD.
YORKSHIRE – PHILADELPHIA

Cover Images:

Front cover: Rebuilt 'Merchant Navy' 4-6-2 35018 *British India Line* makes a sure-footed start from Bournemouth West with the Bournemouth Belle on 21 April 1956.

Back cover: Stagecoach-liveried EMU 2409 stands at London Waterloo in summer 2009.

The magnificent signal gantry at Southampton Central's west end on 10 April 1956 frames 34039 *Boscastle* and 30850 *Lord Nelson* on fast services to Plymouth and Bournemouth, while 30851 *Sir Francis Drake* rests in the bay.

Waterloo is London's busiest terminus station with 24 platforms.

First published in Great Britain in 2022 by
Pen and Sword Transport
An imprint of
Pen & Sword Books Ltd.
Yorkshire - Philadelphia

Copyright © Colin Boocock, 2022

ISBN 978 1 52678 088 1

The right of Colin Boocock to be identified as author of this work has been asserted by him in accordance with the Copyright, Designs and Patents Act 1988.

A CIP catalogue record for this book is available from the British Library.

All rights reserved. No part of this book may be reproduced or transmitted in any form or by any means, electronic or mechanical including photocopying, recording or by any information storage and retrieval system, without permission from the Publisher in writing.

Typeset in 11/13.5 by SJmagic DESIGN SERVICES, India.

Printed and bound in India by Replika Press Pvt. Ltd.

Pen & Sword Books Ltd incorporates the imprints of Pen & Sword Books Archaeology, Atlas, Aviation, Battleground, Discovery, Family History, History, Maritime, Military, Naval, Politics, Railways, Select, Transport, True Crime, Fiction, Frontline Books, Leo Cooper, Praetorian Press, Seaforth Publishing, Wharncliffe and White Owl.

For a complete list of Pen & Sword titles please contact

PEN & SWORD BOOKS LIMITED
47 Church Street, Barnsley, South Yorkshire, S70 2AS, England
E-mail: enquiries@pen-and-sword.co.uk
Website: www.pen-and-sword.co.uk

or

PEN AND SWORD BOOKS
1950 Lawrence Rd, Havertown, PA 19083, USA
E-mail: Uspen-and-sword@casematepublishers.com
Website: www.penandswordbooks.com

CONTENTS

The Author 7
Acknowledgements 8
Introduction 9

Chapter 1: Joseph Locke's main line 17
Chapter 2: Castleman's corkscrew 27
Chapter 3: To the west of England 39
Chapter 4: Direct to Portsmouth 50
Chapter 5: An amazing terminus (Waterloo) 59
Chapter 6: Order out of chaos (Clapham Junction) 68
Chapter 7: Suburban south 75
Chapter 8: Suburban north 82
Chapter 9: Railway hub – Southampton 91
Chapter 10: Railway hub – Eastleigh 103
Chapter 11: Railway hub – Bournemouth 112
Chapter 12: Railway hub – Salisbury 123
Chapter 13: Railway hub – Exeter 129
Chapter 14: Way out west 135
Chapter 15: Somerset & Dorset hills 147
Chapter 16: Cross-country 157
Chapter 17: Hampshire by-ways 166
Chapter 18: Dorset and Devon branches 175
Chapter 19: The islands 186
Chapter 20: Hampshire diesels 197
Chapter 21: Electrification advances 205
Chapter 22: New trains 214
Chapter 23: Franchisees 222
Chapter 24: The future? 228

Index **232**

THE AUTHOR

For twenty-seven years of his early life, Colin Boocock lived or worked in the area covered by the South Western railway, mainly at Addlestone, Bournemouth, Eastleigh and Romsey. It was only in 1969 at the age of thirty-one that he finally left the area in a career move, and even then, for just over a year in 1985-1986, he had to commute to London Waterloo from a flat in Raynes Park while working on a project for the British Railways Board. He had joined the then Bournemouth Junior Railway Club in 1949 and was a member when it amended its name to the Bournemouth Railway Club in 1953. He has remained a member ever since, attending the Club's annual dinner and the occasional meeting, travelling from wherever he lived at the time, be it Romsey, Cardiff, Doncaster, Glasgow, Stockport or Derby. He even edits the Club's bi-monthly magazine, *BRC News*, and so is still well-placed to write in this book about the progress and changes made to what he has always regarded as his 'home' railway.

His times at Eastleigh, from 1954 to 1959 as an engineering apprentice in the locomotive works, and a further spell in works management there from 1965 to 1969, taught him much about the local railways at those times of change. Later in his career he was in senior management during the fundamental changes up to and including railway privatisation. Thus, he can write with authority on the processes that have turned what some politicians now call our 'dismembered railways' into one of the safest railway systems in the world.

ACKNOWLEDGEMENTS

Throughout this book, the photographs that are not credited after their captions were taken by the author. Photo credits acknowledge the copyright holders of the other photographs. I am extremely grateful to all those who have helped illustrate this book with such a comprehensive and quality range of photographs.

INTRODUCTION

The South Western[1] has several claims to fame, not all of which are fully understood within the railway enthusiast fraternity.

- The South Western was the last railway in the UK to operate main line express trains with steam locomotives, continuing with steam until July 1967.
- Its principal main line is the superbly aligned London to Southampton route engineered by the outstanding civil engineer Joseph Locke and opened in 1838 to 1840.
- The South Western also ran one of the most exciting main lines for steam performance in the hilly but speedy Atlantic Coast Express route to Exeter, as well as an interesting

The prime main line of the South Western is one of the best aligned main lines in the country, ideal for fast running. On the four-track section near Hersham, rebuilt 'Merchant Navy' class 4-6-2 35013 *Blue Funnel* Certum Pete Finem, heads an express bound for Exeter and beyond. (*Tony Sterndale, courtesy of the Bournemouth Railway Club Trust*)

---

1. In this book, the South Western is defined as the railways of the Western Section of the Southern Region of British Railways and its successors from 1948 to the present day (2021 at the time of writing).

10 • SEVENTY YEARS OF THE SOUTH WESTERN

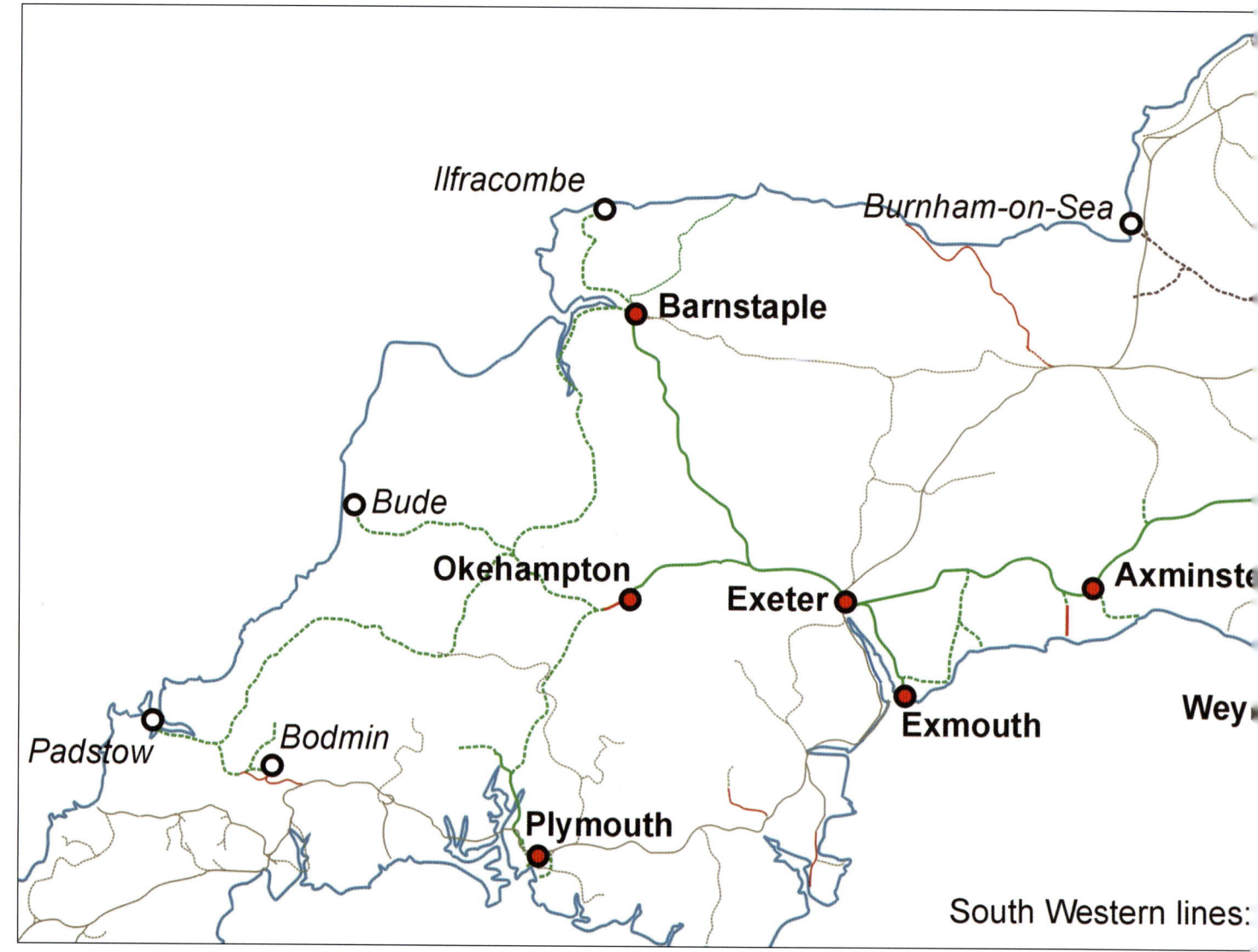

Map 1 – The South Western system.

collection of straggling routes in the far south-west.
- The South Western once owned some of the busiest docks in the United Kingdom at Southampton.
- It was the first in the UK to use diesel electric multiple units on local and rural stopping trains with the Hampshire diesel scheme of 1957.
- It was the first railway in the UK to operate push-pull trains up to twelve coaches in length at 90mph speeds, from late 1966.
- As a former part of the Southern Railway, the South Western operates a fully electrified network of London suburban lines heading out of Waterloo.
- It owns and operates London's biggest terminus station at Waterloo.
- It is a partner with other railways in Britain's busiest interchange station, Clapham Junction.

The main period covered by this book is the past seventy-odd years from the formation of British Railways in 1948.

INTRODUCTION • 11

London Waterloo

The third of O.V. Bulleid's three main line diesel locomotives, 10203, pulls away from Basingstoke with the Down Atlantic Coast Express on 2 April 1955, shortly before being transferred to the London Midland Region. On the left, a WR 'Hall' 4-6-0 is backing towards the depot. (*Philip J. Kelley/David Peel collection*)

Electrification of the Bournemouth line brought a novel form of push-pull operation to the Weymouth line. Entering Poole station in April 1983 is an Up fast service composed of two four-car trailer units propelled by a class 33/1 diesel locomotive. On arrival at Bournemouth, the carriages would be coupled to the rear of the next fast train to London, electric unit hauled.

At the busy Vauxhall station, South West Trains class 455 unit 5707 calls with a suburban service from Guildford via Epsom to Waterloo on 15 September 2005.

This includes 1963, when the British Railways Board transferred all Southern Region lines west of Salisbury to the Western Region; the electrifications of the Bournemouth and Weymouth lines and those from Eastleigh and Southampton to Portsmouth; the creation of Network SouthEast in 1986; and the effects of privatisation that introduced Stagecoach and South West Trains to the scene in 1996 and First Group/MTR with their South Western Railway franchise that took over in 2017.

For train lovers, the book illustrates some of the ancient, inherited steam locomotives through the Maunsell and Bulleid engines, to dieselisation and electrification. The varieties of coaching stock seen in these eras are not neglected either.

Freight, for which the Southern Railway was less well-known, has changed in character dramatically during the last seventy years or so. Slow lumbering steam-hauled sixty-wagon freights plying between Southampton Docks and Feltham, from where wagons were distributed all over the UK, have evolved into long container trains that now head north via Basingstoke and Oxford. The era of trainloads of crude or refined oil is largely over now, but it was fascinating while it lasted.

Boat trains for sea-faring passengers were a feature of the South Western for many decades. Nowadays, the much more frequent train services suffice with bus connections to the docks or ferry terminals, other than at Lymington and Portsmouth where there still are direct ferry links to the Isle of Wight.

The author also takes the liberty of including the Somerset & Dorset line, Portland Bill, the Isle of Wight and

Symbolic of the increasing freight traffic handled by Southampton Docks was the need in the late 1940s to replace pre-grouping 0-4-0Ts by more modern USA 0-6-0Ts that were available as the war ended. These in turn were replaced in the early 1960s by diesels. USA No 30063 pauses between duties in the Eastern Docks in 1955.

The Somerset & Dorset line was a cross-country route that climbed over the Mendip Hills on its way from Broadstone Junction to Bath. Its prime daily train was the Pines Express from Bournemouth West to Manchester. At Evercreech Junction this heavy train took on a 2P 4-4-0 as pilot to its BR or LMS class 5 4-6-0. In 1957, 40569 double-heads 73051 which is taking on water. Later the 2Ps were replaced by BR class 4 4-6-0s, and Bulleid Pacifics and 9Fs shared the main duties with the class 5s. The S&D route closed in 1966.

Hayling Island in the South Western area, just because they are or were so interesting and near at hand.

Going behind the scenes, we take a look inside the cavernous shops of the main works at Eastleigh where carriages and locomotives were repaired and overhauled, and in one or two of the area's depots that maintained the locomotive fleet.

The period covered by this book includes most of the railway closures that so upset local people, Members of Parliament and railway enthusiasts alike in the 1950s and 1960s. The railway we have today is in most respects very different from that on which I, as a young railway enthusiast and photographer, grew up. In many respects it is much better now, but there are features of the old railway that we miss – the luxury of Pullman cars, quality dining in the Surrey Rooms at Waterloo, deep-cushioned seats in all trains, boat trains crossing Canute Road and into the docks at Southampton, the occasional chaos as trains met cars on

BR inherited an interesting network of railways on the Isle of Wight. The island's southernmost station was at Ventnor, where class O2 0-4-4T 18 *Ningwood* has its smokebox cleared of ash after taking water for its return trip to Ryde Pier Head on 24 June 1956.

Weymouth Quay, the reassuring slams of train doors as commuters joined or left old electric units, the heavy climbs over the Mendip Hills on the S&D line, and the leisurely speeds in the short push-pull trains meandering alongside the River Test between Stockbridge and Andover. These are in the past now, but they do live on in people's memories. Hopefully this book can stimulate some of this nostalgia while bringing our knowledge of the South Western up to date.

Even more antiquated was the branch line from Axminster to Lyme Regis which for much of its life used nineteenth-century locomotives of the Adam 0415 class. 4-4-2T 30582 approaches the only intermediate station, Combpyne, in 1956.

CHAPTER 1

JOSEPH LOCKE'S MAIN LINE
AN APOCRYPHAL TALE

Enthusiasts who have travelled widely will have heard the story about the high-ranking Russian who was shown the then new railway station at Vauxhall. He allegedly returned to his home country with the exciting news that he had seen a Vauxhall, the word that sounds the same as the word that is now used for a railway station in the Russian language and pronounced Vokzal, though in Cyrillic script the latter is usually expressed as ВОКЗАЛ. I think the story is actually apocryphal because the London & Southampton Railway (L&SR) originally terminated at Nine Elms at the London end, and its extension to Waterloo which passed through Vauxhall was not opened until 1848. Russia had been operating passenger railways since 1837, so in the intervening eleven years it must have invented a word for a railway station well before 1848!

The south London district of Nine Elms featured large in the first decades of the L&SWR because not only was its terminus there, but the railway also set up its depots and main workshops at Nine Elms on both sides of the main line. Indeed, Nine Elms works built 814 steam locomotives and much rolling stock up to the time when the two main works there closed in 1894 and 1909, as described in a later chapter.

While the railway to Southampton was built and opened in stages, and then extended at each end to better-located termini, it was conceived from the start as a high speed, easily graded railway that had potential for centuries of development. Joseph Locke, civil engineer, is credited with the railway's excellent alignment, the only curves of note outside

The first station out of London Waterloo is Vauxhall, seen here on 4 July 2018 as a pair of Siemens class 707 EMUs operated by South West Trains passes through on the westbound suburban lines.

18 • SEVENTY YEARS OF THE SOUTH WESTERN

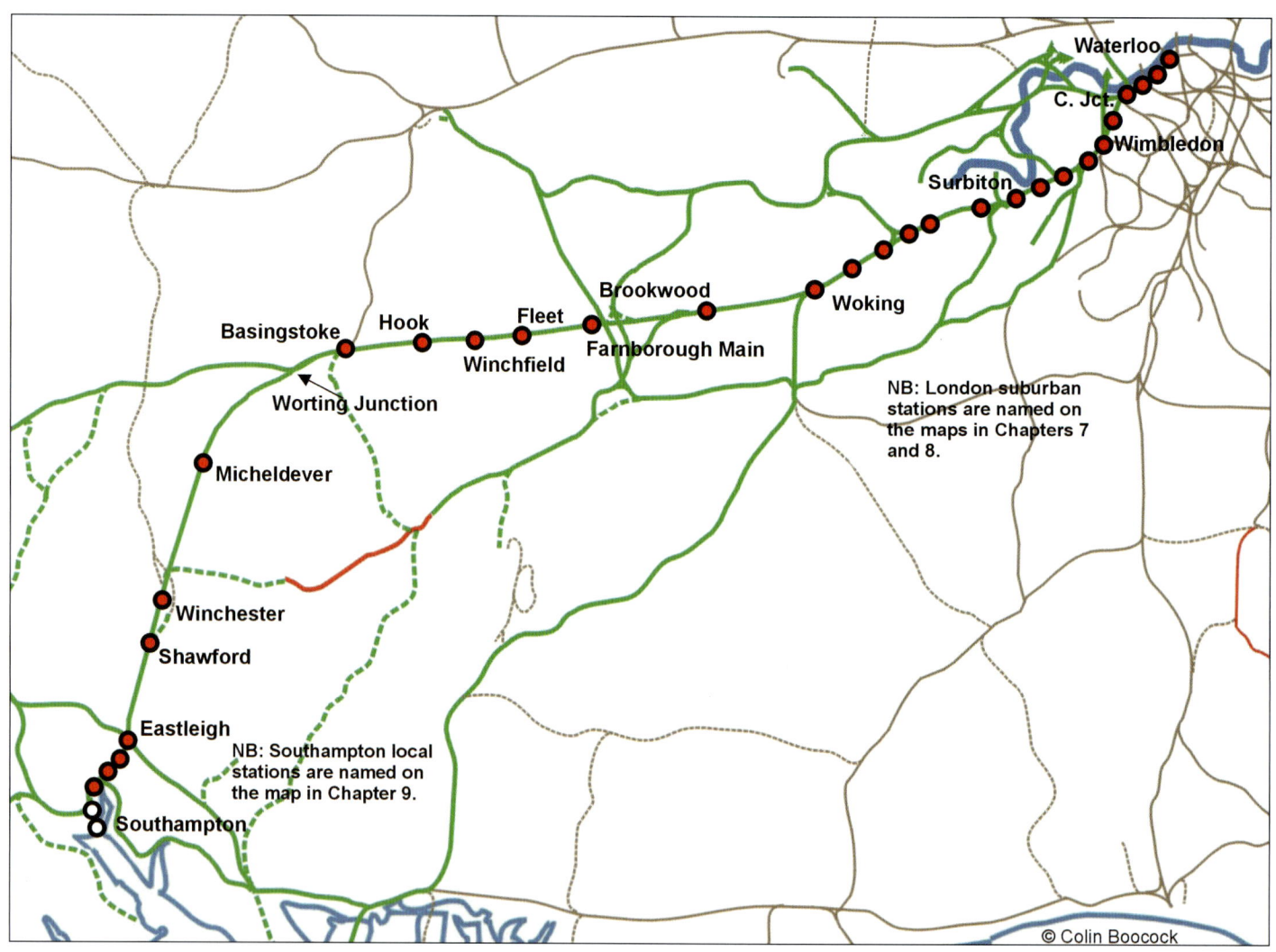

Map 2 – Joseph Locke's main line.

the terminal cities being through the stations at Farnborough and Micheldever. Its longest gradient, calling for excellent enginemanship in the Up direction, was sixteen miles at 1 in 252 from Eastleigh up to the tunnel at Litchfield, between Micheldever and Basingstoke. Wanting to build extensions to other places such as Portsmouth, Salisbury and Dorchester, the L&SR renamed itself in 1839 as the London & South Western Railway (L&SWR).

Towns of note on the London to Southampton main line were Woking, Basingstoke, and Winchester (the old capital of Wessex and host to the longest medieval cathedral in Europe). Virtually all other calling places were at first little more than large villages, though most managed to grow into sizeable towns as the railway brought prosperity westwards. Its first terminus in Southampton was at Northam, known then as Northam Bridge, presumably because that was where the road between Southampton and the Woolston ferry crossed the railway. The railway took only a short time to extend to its rather grand Southampton Terminus station, a location close to the old St Mary's quarter and just across the road from the docks.

Initially, the main line was all double track. The L&SWR later accommodated growth by enlarging long sections to four tracks, particularly from Waterloo through to beyond Basingstoke where the newer line to Salisbury and the west country veered off at Worting Junction and the two double tracks resumed. A longish section of four tracks was also developed between just beyond Shawford to Eastleigh to reduce conflict between passenger trains and the several freight trains in and around that area, and there were four tracks between St Denys and the Terminus, too. The L&SWR pattern on the main line four track sections was Up slow, Up main, Down main and Down slow. At the London end, pressure on the railway from increasing traffic led to the widening of the railway still further to six tracks between Clapham Junction and the approaches to Waterloo. From Wimbledon inwards the slow lines are on the south of the main line formation. From Clapham Junction inwards, the 'Windsor' lines join and stay on the north side.

And, of course, there were many other lines thrown off from the main line as the L&SWR expanded its reach. Key to this story is the winding route that peeled off on a sharp curve just missing Northam station. We now know this line as going to Bournemouth and Weymouth, but originally it by-passed Bournemouth altogether in its drive to reach Dorchester and beyond, an unusual story that is taken up in the next chapter.

The L&SWR and the Southern Railway prioritised the London to Southampton main line with investment to reduce the impacts of flat junctions. Almost all lines turning off it, as far as and including Worting Junction, were rebuilt with flyovers or flyunders, a major exception being the junction with the Portsmouth Direct line that turned south off the main line just after Woking station. Quite why a grade-separated junction was not built there is a puzzle because it is an intensively used junction and movements conflicts occur when trains are not on time. Network Rail is being encouraged to think about this, assuming funds could be eventually made available and enough land acquired to make it possible.

Another feature that was inherited by British Railways at nationalisation in 1948 was the automatic signalling along the long stretch of fast four trackage between Woking and Basingstoke. At set intervals on gantries that spanned the four tracks stood the semaphore arms of the section signals and their related distant signals. These were activated via pneumatic cylinders and acted automatically as the trains progressed, returning to danger as soon as each train had passed, and clearing again when the train had left the next section. Initially lower quadrants, these signals were replaced by BR with upper quadrants, still in auto mode. Only later did multiple aspect colour light signals take over.

That the SR had been a forward-looking railway was evidenced also by its push to electrify its London suburban lines, and then some of the shorter main lines. Later chapters detail the suburban lines from Waterloo that are relevant to the South Western story, and the drive to reach Portsmouth more directly.

A journey today along this line to Southampton begins on the concourse of the recently refurbished and extended Waterloo station, one of the big stations that Network Rail manages. At the time of writing, First Group/MTR's South Western Railway franchise is the principal operator there, and the Southampton-bound 'fast' trains are destined for Bournemouth, most going on from there to Dorchester and Weymouth. Our train is likely to be a class 444 electric multiple unit of five or ten cars built by Siemens' factory in Austria. A slow passage across the points and crossings in the station throat is followed by gentle acceleration on viaducts at roof-top level towards Vauxhall, and soon we pass Queenstown Road (formerly Queens Road Battersea) on our right and need to slow down for (or even stop at) Clapham Junction before any really fast running can happen.

Steady running takes us past Earlsfield and the electric multiple unit maintenance depot at Wimbledon before we reach the station of that name, by which time the Up slow line has crossed over on a concrete flyover. Just before the station, a line curves in from the left, a suburban line from the Streatham direction that now brings in trains from the Thameslink line that soon branches off again for Sutton. Immediately after Wimbledon are two flat junctions, both on the left. The first is now part of the Croydon tramway but it used to handle short EMUs bound for West Croydon. The second is the double track flat junction taking the Thameslink Sutton trains. Then comes Raynes Park, a station with staggered platforms that embrace a flyunder arrangement to get the Chessington branch away to the left. Another grade separated junction leads off to the right at New Malden where the Shepperton and Twickenham trains head away. Then we pass through Berrylands and Surbiton stations in close succession, losing after them the short branch to Hampton Court on the right, and then to the left is the L&SWR suburban route to Guildford which ran via Effingham Junction. Apart from the Wimbledon junctions, which were links from and to the SR's Central Section (ex-London, Brighton & South Coast Railway), all these junctions are grade separated.

Speed rises through Esher (for Sandown racecourse), Hersham and

Just east of Wimbledon used to be the SR's Durnsford Road power station which was built to feed power to the suburban electric network through its system of sub-stations, switching stations and conductor rails. The coal for the power station arrived in wagons that were shunted into position by this home-built Bo-Bo electric locomotive numbered 74S. (*Colin J. Marsden*)

A stunning feature of Joseph Locke's excellent main line was the long, almost straight stretch of four tracks that led through Woking all the way to beyond Basingstoke. 'King Arthur' class 4-6-0 30784 *Sir Nerovens* speeds a Waterloo-Basingstoke semi-fast westwards near Hersham in Surrey. (*Tony Sterndale, courtesy of the Bournemouth Railway Club Trust*)

Walton-on-Thames before we pass through the centre tracks at Weybridge where there is another flat junction to the right, though the trains that head off from the bay platform there do not conflict with the main line as they move off north-west to double back to Waterloo via Staines. There is a trailing burrowing junction from this branch before Byfleet & New Haw, which used to be called West Weybridge[2]. Beyond West Byfleet, we reach the busy junction station at Woking, after which there is quite a clatter as our train crosses the tracks heading off left towards Guildford and Portsmouth on the so-called 'Direct' route.

We have now left the rather scrubby lands of Surrey and into more leafy Hampshire. The 444 is quite capable of speeding up the long climb towards milepost 31 that includes the divergence by flyover of the branch from Brookwood towards Alton, by which time we have passed on the left the large cemetery that was laid out as an overflow for London burials in the nineteenth century and which is again referred to in Chapter 5 when I discuss Waterloo station. Now we are on the long fast stretch that has a slight curve through Farnborough (now called Farnborough Main, a rather unusual name, in deference to the former South Eastern line's station at Farnborough North) and then we speed up towards the modern line speed of 100mph through Fleet, Winchfield and Hook before slowing for the junction at Basingstoke where the former Great Western line from Reading trails in on the right, a flat junction. Cross-Country DEMUs join our route here, one every hour, with occasional extras in between.

---

2. This was one of a group of six stations in succession that all began with a W before its name was changed by BR to begin with a B. Imagine: Walton-on-Thames, Weybridge, West Weybridge, West Byfleet, Woking and (if you go down the Portsmouth Direct line) Worplesdon!

Worting Junction was the parting of the ways where the Salisbury and Exeter route diverged from the Southampton main line. The L&SWR provided this flyover junction to reduce conflictions. Rebuilt 'Merchant Navy' 4-6-2 35014 *Nederland Line* takes an Up Bournemouth to London train over the Battledown flyover on 8 August 1964. (*Alan Trickett*)

As far as Basingstoke, the slow lines have hosted outer-suburban trains formed of class 450 Siemens four-car EMUs, usually in eight-car formations. Beyond Basingstoke, the four tracks peel apart at Worting Junction with its often-photographed Battledown flyover, the Salisbury and Exeter trains, nowadays exclusively classes 159 and 158 DMUs, heading off to the right and leaving our train to climb on the double track up and over Roundwood summit to the tunnel at Litchfield. The descent of the sixteen miles of 1 in 252 is interrupted by braking for the speed restriction through Micheldever after passing through two more tunnels, and later there is another shorter tunnel at Wallers Ash where there are long loops on both sides of the railway to enable freights to keep out of the way of expresses.

There used to be a junction called Winchester Junction, but there is no sight of it today. Here the secondary line from Alton came in on the left, while the temporary link from the former Didcot, Newbury & Southampton line that was worked by the GWR came in on the right, the DN&S line proper diving underneath our main line to call at its own Winchester Chesil station in the city centre. This line therefore by-passed the L&SWR's Winchester City station, joining the main line after calling at the outside of an almost independent platform at the

next station, Shawford. After Shawford, the next four-track section begins, as we continue along the valley of the River Itchen, passing the extensive freight yards at Allbrook before thumping across the junction under the road bridge at the approach to Eastleigh station where the line comes in from Salisbury and Romsey before it heads off left towards Fareham and (nowadays) Portsmouth. Originally, this line went straight to Gosport, which was closed to rail passenger trains from 1952 and to freight from 1969.

On the left after the Portsmouth line has disappeared is the former Eastleigh Locomotive Works that still survives, then we pass the flat field that now includes a runway for airliners, but which used to be just a field on which propeller-driven planes for Paris or the Channel Islands would splash their way on take-off or landing. All trains now stop at Southampton Airport Parkway station, that station having been given priority now at the expense of Eastleigh; Eastleigh station nowadays sees only half-hourly stopping train EMUs and the 'Romsey rocket' DMUs calling there. Southampton Airport station was new in 1966, before which BR didn't consider the old Eastleigh Airport worthy of a train service[3]. It has expanded massively since then, as has the adjacent airport, and is now a Parkway station with car parks and a few hotels nearby. It still has just two often very busy platforms, however.

In modern times there are many heavy trains of containers from Southampton Docks that have to thread their way between the frequent electric train service. 57006, a former 47 rebuilt with General Motors power unit, brings a northbound container train through Winchester station on 19 July 2005.

---

3. There was a halt there from 1929 for just a few years called Atlantic Park Hostel Halt. It was closed well before the 1950s.

In earlier years the Southampton main line's freight was dominated by the heavy loads taken from Southampton Old Docks towards London, usually Feltham yard. One of these trains approaches Eastleigh behind Urie H15 4-6-0 30487 on 23 May 1955.

The train now enters the suburbs of the city of Southampton, and passes through Swaythling station, a typical L&SWR two-platform station that is dwarfed by the next one at St Denys. Here the line from Portsmouth and Fareham trails in on the left round a sharp curve that leads it into its own pair of platforms before the two double-track lines intermingle to form a four-track section in full view of an arm of Southampton Water. Bevois Park yard passes by on the right, followed by the wide level crossing at Mount Pleasant and Northam yards on the left, a space now occupied by the Siemens rolling stock maintenance depot.

If we were to follow the original main line at Northam (not for our 444 unit as it is not electrified), we would go straight ahead through the former two-platform station there and head about a mile south to the Docks. A sharp curve to the right would take us into Southampton Terminus station, a moderate but quite grand affair with a typical large L&SWR station building fronting the road that formed a reasonably impressive entrance for local people to access the railway. The line that by-passes this terminus crosses Canute Road and enters the docks area. This crossing has hosted boat trains and banana trains (steam-heated to help the fruit ripen) and many freights, all of which had to be waved across the road from the docks by a man with a red flag, there ostensibly to hold back the road traffic while trains from the docks slowly crossed into railway civilisation.

In the 1950s and early 1960s, the hourly Alton push-pull trains were the regular trains at the Terminus, headed by L&SWR M7 0-4-4Ts until they were

On 9 July 1967, the day steam traction finished on the Southern Region, class 47 D1924 approaches St Denys in the Southampton outskirts with the very last Bournemouth Belle Pullman train from Bournemouth to London Waterloo. The railway here skirts one edge of Southampton Water.

Joseph Locke's main line terminated here. This used to be Southampton Terminus, the platforms of which lay behind and to the left of the building. Beyond them were tracks that crossed Canute Road and into the Eastern (Old) Docks.

replaced by Ivatt class 2 2-6-2Ts not long before the service was dieselised. Other services were stopping trains to Portsmouth and to Bournemouth, often with T9 'Greyhound' 4-4-0s, plus a few services to and from the Didcot, Newbury & Southampton line. These latter regularly brought Great Western engines into the Terminus station. The DNS line south of Newbury closed in 1960. The Alton services soldiered on long enough to be dieselised with two-car diesel electric multiple units from 1959.

In the Beeching era, the passenger services to Southampton Terminus were withdrawn at about the same time as the Winchester to Alton branch line was completely closed.

Had our train turned sharply to the right on the approach to Northam station it would have followed the totally different main line that is the subject of the next chapter. Joseph Locke's London & Southampton main line was superbly aligned, vertically and laterally. What follows is a different story altogether!

CHAPTER 2

CASTLEMAN'S CORKSCREW
MISSING THE POINT

The railway west of Southampton got its nickname 'Castleman's corkscrew' because on the map it wandered widely during its course towards Dorchester. Some called it 'Castleman's snake', an equally apt name.

In steam days, the sharp double-track curve to the right from the junction just before Northam station was restricted to 15mph. Electrification in 1967 and the elimination of the third side of the triangle there enabled the curve's speed limit to be raised. Curves are just part of the nemesis of this part of the railway. The two-track cutting through the centre of Southampton wriggled between the streets of houses before plunging into Southampton tunnel, situated under road junctions and the landscaping in front of Southampton's grand Guildhall with its tall, square Italianate tower. Folklore has it that German bombers during the Second World War mistook this tower for that of St Mary's church and bombed the city centre more than the docks that were the main target. Hence the 'modern' city centre shopping area is rather like that at Plymouth, and for similar reasons, namely it had to be rebuilt from scratch after the war.

Emerging from the tunnel, our train runs into Southampton Central station. It was not always called this, having started out as Southampton West, logical in view of its geographical position. It was renamed in the early twentieth century

Castleman's 'corkscrew' begins where the line to Southampton Central and points west turns sharply off the London to Southampton Terminus line just short of the former Northam station. Until electrification, the curve imposed a speed restriction to 15mph. 'King Arthur' 4-6-0 30765 *Sir Gareth* takes the Newcastle to Bournemouth West train round the curve on 2 August 1957.

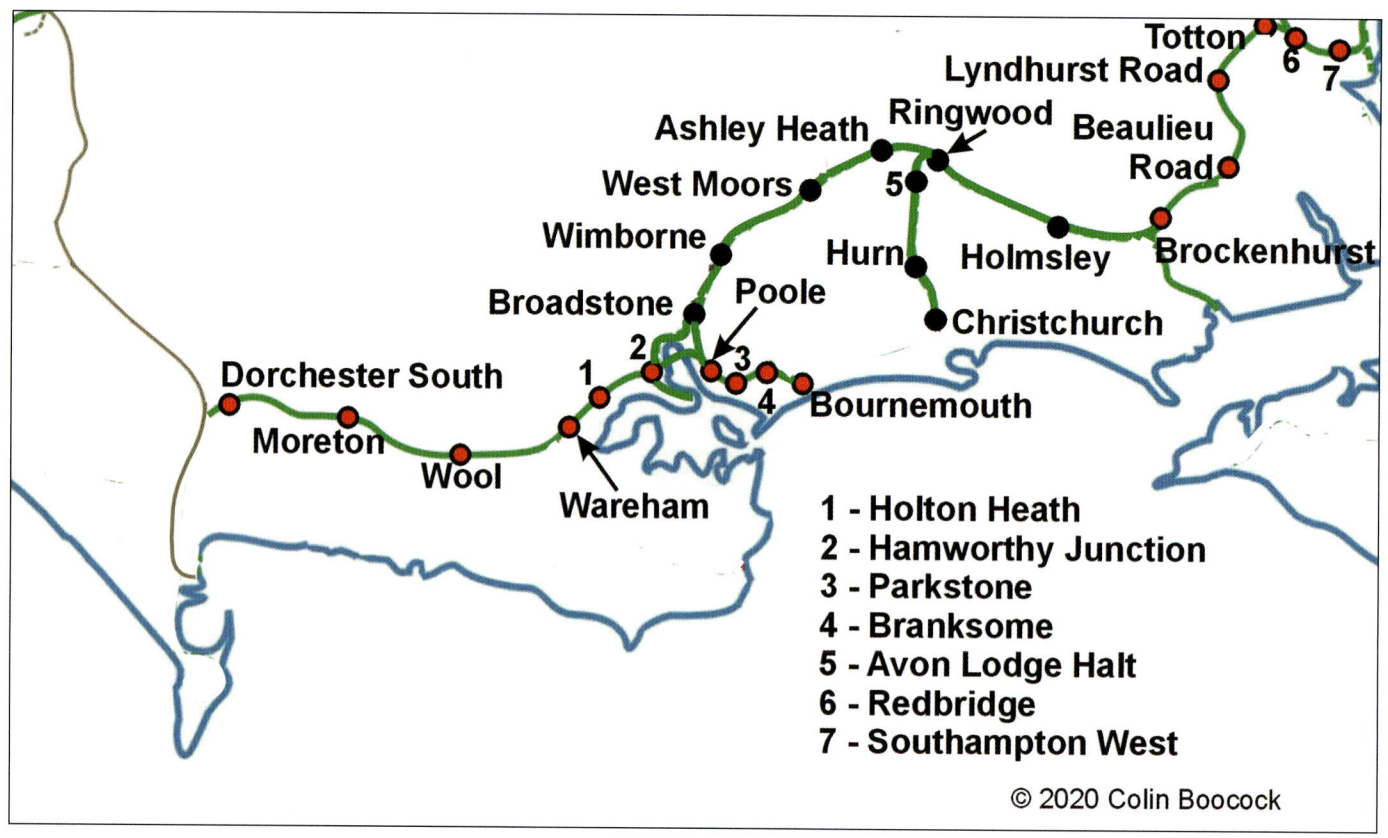

Map 3 – Castleman's corkscrew (early days).

when the Terminus became mainly a stop for local trains. When the Terminus was closed, the word Central was dropped; but to avoid later confusion with Southampton Airport Parkway station it has once again become Southampton Central. The Southern Railway widened the station to four tracks and built 'Art Deco' buildings on the Down side, which have recently been refurbished to good effect. On the Up side of this station, BR replaced the old buildings by a rectangular 1960s office block incorporating the station facilities.

On leaving Southampton, the railway remains as four tracks. Towards Millbrook the Western Docks are visible for a couple of miles; this area was reclaimed land, Southampton Water having been adjacent to the railway in L&SWR days. The main traffic nowadays is containers. Millbrook station is an island platform flanked by the slow lines, this being an odd arrangement where the fast lines are outboard of the slow ones, until all become two tracks again before Redbridge station.

Redbridge has a civil engineering depot passed on the left that for decades had its own shunting locomotive, for many years a dumpy C14 0-4-0T numbered 77S. Just after the ends of the platforms at Redbridge is a double-track junction; lines on the right head northwards bound for Romsey and Salisbury, and in times past also Andover Junction. Our train curves left at 50mph onto a causeway crossing the end of Southampton Water before curving right into Totton, once of timber merchant fame. A single lead junction on the left takes freights round to the west side of the Water to reach Marchwood and Fawley. Locals would love the passenger service there to be restored; it seems a long way off, but moves are afoot.

We accelerate now into the New Forest, passing the station of Ashurst, formerly

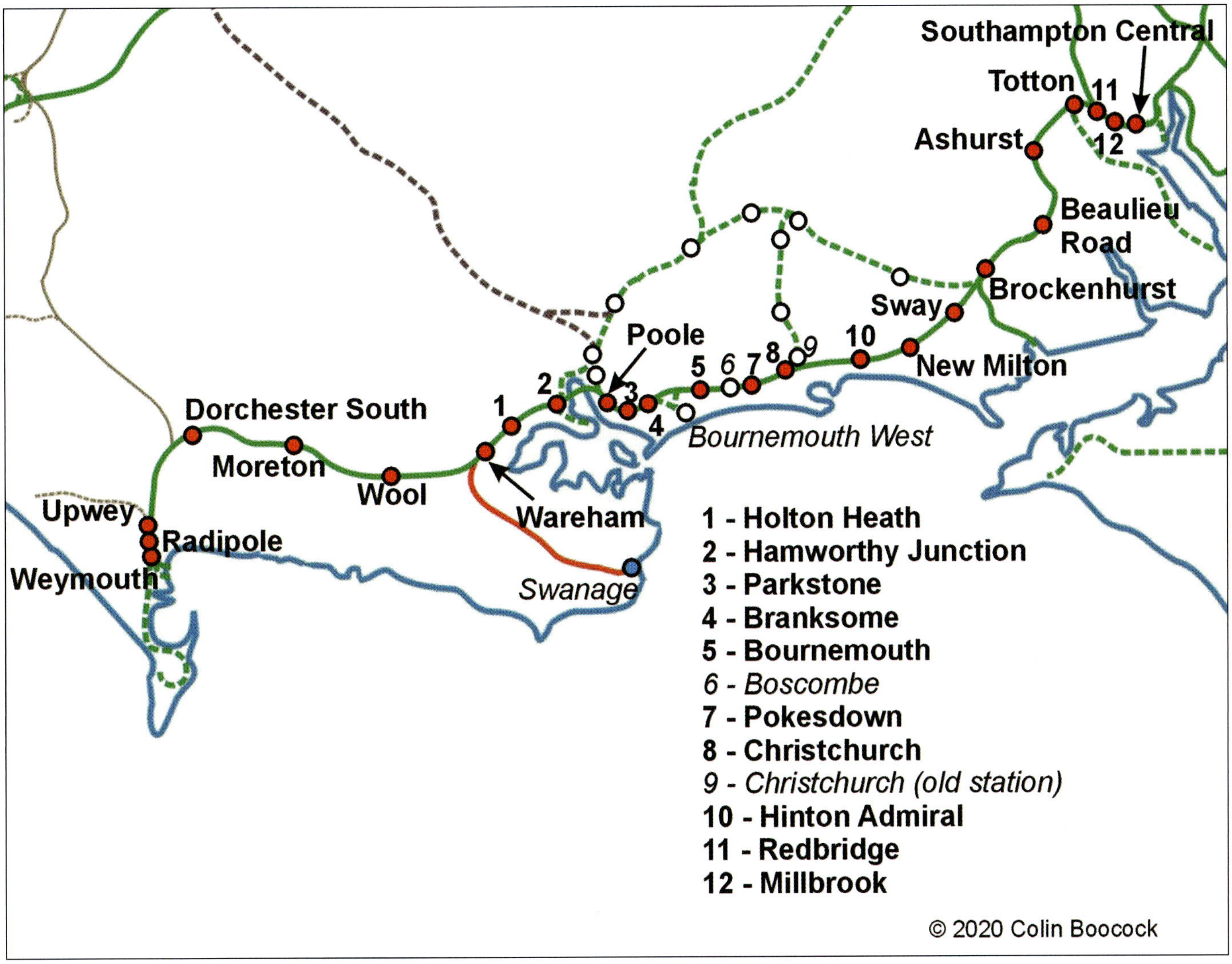

CASTLEMAN'S CORKSCREW • 29

Map 4 – Southampton to Weymouth.

On what the Scots would call a dreich day in 1968, a semi-fast Waterloo-Bournemouth train crosses the causeway at Redbridge. The train is formed, from the front, of a 4TC unit, powered by a 4REP in the middle of the train, with a 3TC at the rear.

The small station of West Moors was next to a junction on the Brockenhurst to Hamworthy Junction section that ran via Ringwood and Wimborne. The line from Salisbury via Fordingbridge joined the 'corkscrew' here. The line was being used as a diversion route on 27 March 1960 and 34020 *Seaton* passes through with the 11.16am from Bournemouth Central via Poole to London Waterloo.

Lyndhurst Road. That older name, dropped in BR's late years, harked back to the L&SWR's treatment of communities that Castleman's railway deigned only loosely to serve. Lyndhurst Road wasn't in Lyndhurst, not even close. One got out there hoping for onward transport to be provided by a local person with horse and attached conveyance. Our train, after climbing and meandering through the Forest, mainly open heath around here, blasts through Beaulieu Road with its nearby hotel (not much else and quite a distance from Beaulieu village) and continues through woodland, maybe passing wild ponies and deer as it holds 75mph round Woodfidley curve towards Brockenhurst.

Nowadays, every train calls at Brockenhurst, justifying its four platforms formed in two islands. It is the junction for the Lymington branch which nowadays has a four-car EMU shuttling half hourly to and from Lymington Pier where ferries leave for Yarmouth in the Isle of Wight. Brockenhurst is in a sort of railway dip – all trains have to climb to go anywhere from Brockenhurst. Castleman's railway veered north-west as the Lymington branch turned off southwards; the 'corkscrew' meandered with minimal earthworks across the New Forest, with a station at Holmsley, originally called Christchurch Road, albeit some six miles from that town. This route after Lymington Junction succumbed to the Beeching rationalisation of our railways; its last passenger trains ran in 1964. In its early days, however, it was the main line to Dorchester, aiming at further west. Exeter for example was in its sights, but never reached, at least not that way. The next station was Ringwood and beyond Ringwood the L&SWR threw off southwards a single-track unimportant branch line along the Avon valley to reach the village of Christchurch and later the edge of that at Bournemouth. The Southern Railway closed this branch in 1935.

Back to Castleman and his corkscrew main line, which was soon galloping across flat country towards West Moors, junction for Salisbury, a single track from that city trailing in on the right, and then onwards to the busy market town of Wimborne. All these stations were standard two-platform structures with associated yards and goods facilities. After Wimborne, a line to the north veered off. This was the Somerset & Dorset Joint Railway, managed by the Midland and L&SW Railways, not the fastest railway to the north but busy at summer weekends with extra traffic. The necessary reversal at Wimborne taxed both railways, so a third side to the triangle was laid that brought the S&D line to join Castleman's facing south at the next station, Broadstone, enabling the Wimborne link to be abandoned. The single line from the S&D linked with the L&SWR's double track main line on the approach to Broadstone. The main line immediately split there to four tracks through the platforms, the right-hand pair being the line for Dorchester. To the left was the line for Poole, the port on the edge of the world's second largest natural harbour according to some sources.

We will firstly take the right-hand tracks and head towards Dorchester, calling at Hamworthy (with its junction leading to Hamworthy Quay, opposite Poole Quay), Holton Heath and Wareham. About a mile beyond Wareham, then a station with four platform faces, one of which was the bay for Swanage trains, was Worgret Junction where the aforesaid branch trains would head off on a single line to Corfe Castle and Swanage. Our two main line tracks continue over undulating land through Wool and Moreton before terminating in Dorchester.

Of course, this account is at variance with what happens today. Hindsight is a wonderful thing. We can sit in our armchairs and be amazed that the L&SWR didn't think to include the seaside resorts of Bournemouth and Weymouth in its initial plans. But we forget that, in the mid-nineteenth century, these places

Up trains had to reverse to get alongside their designated platform at Dorchester South. 34107 *Blandford* (later renamed *Blandford Forum* at the local council's request) has just done that with the Weymouth portion of a train for Waterloo in April 1952. The foreground track is the Up main line. (*T.B. Owen/Colour-Rail BRS585*)

On 28 April 2006, handsome class 442 express unit 2424 in full Stagecoach colours calls at the 'new' Up platform at Dorchester South on a Weymouth to London working. This through platform was opened in 1970, at which time the platform into which trains used to reverse was closed.

were mere coastal villages with no claim to fame. The idea of travelling by train long distances to enjoy sea bathing only developed as that century progressed, and it needed the economic buoyancy of the Victorian era to fund such pleasures.

However, Bournemouth and Weymouth did develop to become prosperous seaside resorts. The Great Western was the first into Weymouth, but the L&SWR got a foothold into Bournemouth in two directions, one by extending its Broadstone to Poole line up a steep 1 in 60/50 gradient through Parkstone to Branksome and then down to a neat five-platformed terminus called Bournemouth West, reached in 1874. That was admittedly a long way round, involving approaching the resort from the west with trains that had started their journeys from London about 110 miles to the east 'as the crow flies' and a lot further by rail! Four years earlier the Ringwood to Christchurch branch had been extended to a site on the then northern edge of Bournemouth just short of Holdenhurst Road and a station called Bournemouth East opened with goods facilities. However, the last miles of that more direct route were slow, with inadequate capacity for expansion to meet the growing needs of what was fast becoming the conurbation of Bournemouth, Poole and Christchurch. (Only in spring 2019, however, did the three town councils at last agree to merge as a joint council for the BCP conurbation!)

By 1888, the L&SWR had made complete amends to these omissions. A new stretch of double-track main line was opened that bisected Lymington Junction, headed uphill towards a new station at Sway, a village with an odd tower folly nearby, and pushed on through the town of New Milton, quite a magnet for the surrounding villages, and called at Hinton Admiral before emerging on a long embankment that spanned the floodplain of the River Avon on its approach to Christchurch. The branch from Ringwood off the 'corkscrew' was re-joined just past the original station at Christchurch, so a replacement, larger station was built on a speed-restricted curve (60mph) between the two river bridges, the second bridge crossing the River Stour at the foot of a steady uphill railway climb at 1 in 99 towards Pokesdown and the station intended to serve that area, Boscombe. The Southern Railway much later built a separate station to serve Pokesdown; Dr Beeching's efforts closed Boscombe and its goods yard in the early 1960s, the only station between Waterloo and Bournemouth Central to close in those cuts.

At the approach to Bournemouth East yard, the new railway took a slightly more northern alignment and dived under Holdenhurst Road to emerge into the grand station of Bournemouth Central with its fine overall roof. This was linked to Bournemouth West station by a three-and-a-half mile double track line that ventured briefly across the borough boundary into Poole, turned sharply left at Gas Works Junction from where it crossed the Bourne valley on one of two fine brick viaducts, whereafter it joined the well-established line from Poole and dropped down into Bournemouth West (only the second

Approaching Christchurch with a Down stopping train on 31 March 1957 is 'Scotch Arthur' 4-6-0 30789 *Sir Guy*. The building on the left is the former station where the platform used to be on the branch line from Ringwood that first gave trains access to Bournemouth. The Ringwood to Christchurch section closed in 1935.

Two 4TC units form a Weymouth to Waterloo portion being propelled by a class 33/1 diesel up the foot of the 1 in 60/50 bank towards Parkstone and Branksome in April 1983. Poole Park lake is on the right. The land on the left had recently been reclaimed from the sea and would be used later for housing.

station on the line from Waterloo to be closed by Dr Beeching). The other viaduct after Gas Works Junction linked across the valley to join the Bournemouth West to Poole line just before Branksome station, completing the triangle inside of which was a goods yard and locomotive sub-shed used largely by engines off the S&DJR. The main locomotive depot in the area was alongside Bournemouth Central station.

To get to Weymouth, the L&SWR had to swallow its pride. A short, sharply-curved pair of tracks turned left just before the terminus station at the county town of Dorchester, and a new through platform was built on the curve to serve the west-bound trains. This made a flat junction with the GWR about half a mile south of that railway's station. The L&SWR negotiated running rights over the GWR to Weymouth but sent its engines back to its own depot at Dorchester for anything more than coal and water. The GWR station became Dorchester West and the L&SWR's eventually became Dorchester South. There was ostensibly no room for a new platform for the Up line at Dorchester South, so Weymouth to Bournemouth trains had to reverse into the original platform, an inconvenience to trains that persisted for well over a hundred years right through to the 1980s when British Rail managed to fit a new platform on the Up curve in time for the inauguration of electric train working in 1988.

By this time, the line to Weymouth had been part of the Southern Region for a couple of decades. Trains to Weymouth climbed out of Dorchester with a final gradient of 1 in 91 up to Bincombe Tunnel, before the sharp descent starting at 1 in 52 down to Upwey, formerly Upwey Junction when the GWR once had a short branch to Abbotsbury, seen by the author around 1950 with a 14XX 0-4-2T and single auto coach. Radipole Halt followed, now just Radipole, a suburb of ever-expanding Weymouth. Arrival at Weymouth nowadays is perhaps an anti-climax. Weymouth station lost its timber

CASTLEMAN'S CORKSCREW • **35**

Leaving the west end of Poole station is the very last steam-hauled train on the Southern Region of BR on 9 July 1967. It is the evening parcels service from Bournemouth to Weymouth and is headed by the only BR class 3 2-6-0 ever to be allocated to the Southern, 77014; the possibly apocryphal story is that the engine had arrived on that region on a railtour the previous year and was never returned. (*Colin Stone/Anistr.com*)

Between Poole and Hamworthy Junction, the cut-off built to give Poole direct access to the west crosses Holes Bay on this causeway. Liquid petroleum gas tanks from Furzebrook (on the Swanage branch) head east behind Co-Co diesel 60024 on 31 July 1962. (*Patrick Fitz-Gerald*)

overall roof in the 1950s making its two long single platforms appear rather basic.

But back in early London & South Western Railway days, having managed to reach Weymouth, and with Exeter being well served by other routes, Dorchester Junction is where Castleman's snake died.

British Railways entered the scene in January 1948 and began slowly to grapple with the huge, agglomerated railway systems of the big four, plus some small railways which most commentators forget about as being absorbed into BR, though none of those affect this story[4]. Train services on the Waterloo to Bournemouth and Weymouth main line resumed after the war, mainly following the pre-war pattern from 1946. There was an approximately two-hourly service of fast trains from Waterloo, stopping only at Southampton Central to Bournemouth, with a Weymouth portion continuing from Bournemouth Central, the rest of the train dropping round to Bournemouth West behind whatever engine the local depot had available. These trains usually had six or seven coaches with a restaurant pair as the Bournemouth portion, and three to six coaches for the Weymouth portion. Between these trains were semi-fasts from Waterloo that mostly stopped at Basingstoke, Winchester, Eastleigh, Southampton Central, Brockenhurst, New Milton, Christchurch, Pokesdown, Boscombe and Bournemouth Central. The last ten miles or so seemed particularly slow to passengers who had spent nearly three hours covering just over 100 miles!

From 1946, Oliver Bulleid, the SR's Chief Mechanical Engineer, had provided this route with eleven very fine six-coach fixed sets with catering, to which were added other sets and additional carriages to make up the ten or eleven coaches on the semi-fasts and twelve or thirteen on the fasts.

Two 'star' trains emerged within this service pattern. In 1946, the SR reinstated the Pullman train the Bournemouth Belle, with up to twelve twelve-wheeled luxury cars including four or five first class vehicles. The whole train left Waterloo at 12.30pm and ran for two hours and ten minutes to reach Bournemouth Central at 2.40pm, calling at Southampton Central on the way. This was the train preferred by the more well-heeled of Bournemouth's citizens, and illustrated the high esteem in which that borough was by then regarded. A supplement on top of the normal train fare was payable to travel on the Bournemouth Belle and the cost of meals, served at all seats, added considerably to this. The return train left Bournemouth West at 4.34pm and Bournemouth Central at 4.45pm. In the later 1950s, all the expresses were retimed to do the 108 miles between Bournemouth Central and London Waterloo in two hours exactly, quite a task as they were all heavy trains, particularly the 'Belle' which often weighed over 500tons empty.

The other 'star' train was launched in 1951. Before the war, the SR had run a non-stop train between London and Bournemouth called the Bournemouth Limited which was the main two-hour train. In 1951 such a timing was not yet seen as feasible as the civil engineer was still recovering his permanent way from war-time maintenance arrears. However, British Railways wanted to launch a 'festival train' on each of the Regions to mark the excitement of the Festival of Britain, the big exhibition in

---

4. In case readers want to be reminded, these small railways absorbed into BR in 1948 were the Mersey Railway, the Cheshire Lines Committee, the Kent & East Sussex Railway and the East Kent Railway. There might well have been others.

London to raise Britain's business and manufacturing profile in the post-war era. Each Region was allocated a train of brand-new mark 1 BR standard corridor stock, the first I saw in regular service. The Southern Region's train carried a new name, the Royal Wessex. This took the breakfast slot from Weymouth, picking up a Swanage portion at Wareham, and the Bournemouth West portion at Bournemouth Central, making a thirteen-coach formation to head towards London from there at 8.40am, stopping at Southampton Central on the way. The Down train left London at 4.35pm.

British Railways allocated a pair of new class 7 'Britannia' 4-6-2s to each Region to work these festival trains. The SR side-stepped this requirement and instead allocated its 'Britannias' initially to Nine Elms and used 70009 *Alfred the Great* and 70014 *Iron Duke* on the Bournemouth Belle and one or two other trains. I did experience 70009 on the Up Royal Wessex just once, in August 1951, but otherwise the Up 'Wessex' was always a 'West Country' and the Down train a 'Merchant Navy' 4-6-2, both allocated to Bournemouth depot. 70009 left the SR after 1951 and 70014 went off to Stewart's Lane. On the Bournemouth line, Bulleid Pacifics reigned supreme again, for a while.

This BR mark 1 Royal Wessex train formation was not really suitable for its task. The six coaches of the Bournemouth West portion, for example, included a full-length kitchen car with no passenger seating, a first class restaurant car and a third class restaurant car, just to serve breakfast and afternoon tea. The third class carriages in the train seated three-a-side in compartments. So not only was there one more catering car than before which displaced a seating vehicle but there were fewer seats than in the Bulleid stock used on the other trains. And the mark 1 guard's brakes had long-length vans which didn't help either! Thus, it was not surprising that later coaches put into this train were mark 1 TSOs, open seconds[5] which seated four across. Bulleid stock also began to re-enter the formation to add more compartment seating and shorter luggage spaces.

It is worth dwelling a little more on the working of this train because of what it illustrates when compared with modern methods. On arrival at Waterloo, an M7 0-4-4T would take the empty Royal Wessex to the carriage sidings at Clapham Junction, not just for cleaning and servicing but also for reforming. The train had arrived in London with the five Weymouth coaches at the London end, followed by the two from Swanage, and the six Bournemouth West carriages at the rear. The train had to be shunted into the reverse formation before its Down journey that evening! The train had to have the Weymouth portion at the west end, the Swanage in the middle and the Bournemouth West six-set at the London end because the train engine went right through to Weymouth. So, this expensive train did just one return journey between Weymouth/Swanage/Bournemouth West and London each day. Likewise, the Bournemouth Belle stock did just one out-and-home journey daily. This was a common pattern in what some commentators still call 'the good old days'.

In addition to the expresses and semi-fasts, a series of stopping trains covered the intermediate stations at which the bigger trains didn't stop. There were regular 'semi-fasts' between Waterloo and Basingstoke that stopped at Clapham Junction and then all stations west of Woking. Other stopping trains

---

5. Second class replaced the designation third class on BR from June 1956.

served the smaller stations between Reading/Basingstoke and Southampton; Portsmouth or Southampton to Bournemouth; and Bournemouth to Weymouth. Some of the Bournemouth stopping trains originated at diverse points such as Andover Junction, Eastleigh or Southampton Terminus.

Bournemouth was also served by a couple of daily inter-Regional trains, one from the north-east and one from the Wirral. Chapter 16 details these trains.

Otherwise, the main motive power on the Bournemouth main line was Bulleid Pacifics, 'Lord Nelsons', 'King Arthurs' and on summer weekends H15s and S15s as well as the occasional 'Remembrance' N15X 4-6-0 and, from the mid-1950s, BR standard class 5s as well. After the Kent Coast electrification's two phases got under way from 1959 and 1962, 'Schools' class 4-4-0s began to appear on the Bournemouth line. As a schoolboy in the early 1950s I just recall seeing Drummond T14 4-6-0s working stopping trains in the Bournemouth area.

The 'Schools' became the favourite engines to work the Lymington boat trains from Waterloo. These operated on summer Saturdays to take holidaymakers bound for the Isle of Wight to join the ferries to Yarmouth in West Wight. Until the 'Schools' class became available again to the Western Section, the train engines, whether Pacifics or 4-6-0s, were all too big for the turntable at Brockenhurst and so, after handing over a Down boat train to a Q or Q1 0-6-0 for the branch run to Lymington, the train engine had to run light engine either to Bournemouth or Southampton/Eastleigh to be turned. The Schools had been designed to fit on 50ft turntables, and so could be turned at Brockenhurst.

The year 1967 saw the introduction of the first wave of electrification on the Bournemouth line. A later chapter tackles this important development in some detail.

CHAPTER 3

TO THE WEST OF ENGLAND
THE HILLY RACING TRACK

Worting Junction was the parting of the ways where the London to Southampton, Bournemouth and Weymouth main line separated from the line to Salisbury, Exeter and beyond. Twentieth-century railway photographers emphasised the large bow-girder Battledown flyover bridge as a visual icon at this junction.

Today, the Up Bournemouth trains cross this bridge before rattling fast downhill towards Basingstoke. Trains bound for the west country curve gracefully to the right, passing under the bridge. The original Worting Junction was from its 1854 beginning simply a flat one in which trains from the Southampton direction crossed the paths of trains coming from

Worting Junction west of Basingstoke is where the South Western main line to Salisbury and Exeter branches off the London to Southampton line. Leaning to the curve under the Battledown flyover bridge with an Up train from Exeter on 8 August 1964 is 'Battle of Britain' 4-6-2 34079 *141 Squadron*. (*Alan Trickett*)

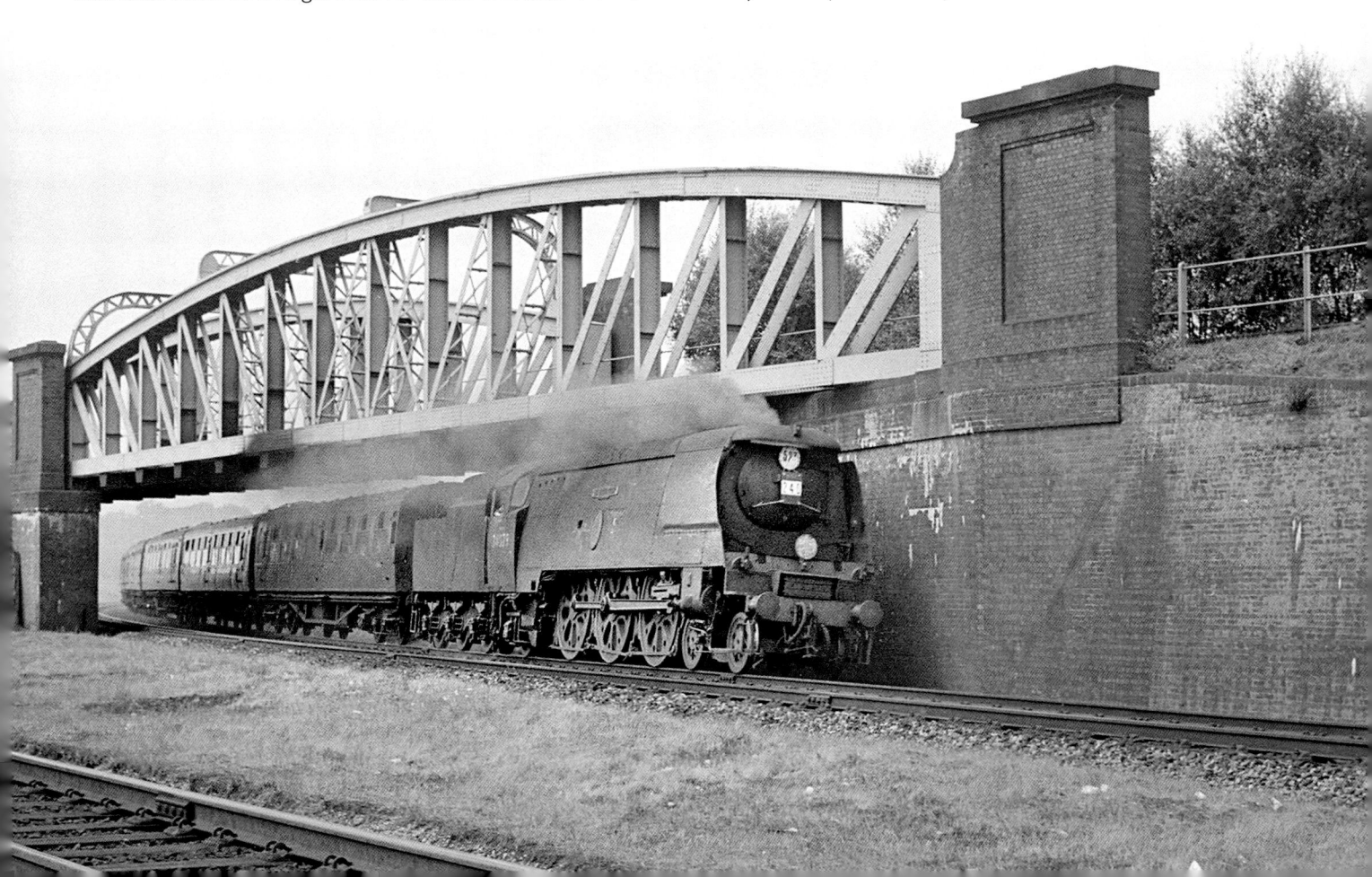

London towards Salisbury and the west. As rail traffic increased, this crossing became a constriction to the traffic flow and the L&SWR boldly constructed the flying junction with its impressive bridge as early as 1897. During electrification of the Bournemouth main line in 1966/67, the junction points that lead from the Down Main Line to the Bournemouth route were cleverly relaid as a 90mph turn-out with equal radius curves in both directions using standard track components innovatively.

Today the electric third rail continues only on the Bournemouth lines, the lines to the west still being without electric traction despite the Southern Railway having anticipated eventually taking the conductor rail at least as far west as Salisbury. The Western Region in its drive to reduce costs as much as possible during the late 1960s had actively singled the track west of Salisbury almost all the way to Exeter, with passing loops at principal stations. Thus, under the regime of diesel locomotive-hauled services that existed at that time, any unreliability caused by traction faults was multiplied because a late train in one direction held up opposite-direction trains at the passing loops. British Rail under its Network SouthEast business sector later built air-conditioned class 159 diesel multiple units (DMUs) for this route, confirming in travellers' eyes that it was no longer the principal main line that it used to be, even though these units are quality trains compared with earlier DMUs. Fortunately, the introduction of the 159s, based at the brand new maintenance depot at Salisbury, bequeathed to this railway the most reliable DMUs in the country, so services have been much more dependable nowadays. With their 90mph top speed and a limited-stop timetable, the 159s almost keep pace with

The 11.42 from Salisbury to Reading passes the site of the former station at Oakley on 10 May 1978. The unit is 'Hampshire' DEMU set 1124. (*Colin J. Marsden*)

the Bournemouth line's express electric multiple units (EMUs) that are able to run at up to 100mph on the main line between London and Basingstoke.

Now part of the South Western Railway franchise, our class 159 train of six or nine DMU cars is on high but level ground after passing under Battledown flyover, heading west as far as Overton station, then with easy gradients downhill past Whitchurch, where in earlier years one could glimpse the single track of the Didcot, Newbury & Southampton railway passing at right angles underneath. The downhill trend continues apace to Andover Junction, now plain Andover but formerly the point where the now-closed secondary line from Southampton, Eastleigh and Romsey trailed in from the south. A couple of miles after Andover there used to be a Great Western line that turned away northwards to serve Marlborough and Swindon. This was the former Midland & South Western Junction line, a meandering byway that took Southern Railway engines as far north as Cheltenham, and GWR ones to Southampton. It closed to passengers in 1961 and totally in 1965. Its main source of freight was a military establishment at Ludgershall.

Whitchurch used to have two stations but the one on the Didcot, Newbury & Southampton route closed in 1960. On the west of England main line, 47717, formerly named *Tayside Region* by ScotRail, pulls away from Whitchurch with the 06.46 Exeter to London Waterloo 10 October 1992. (*Patrick Fitz-Gerald*)

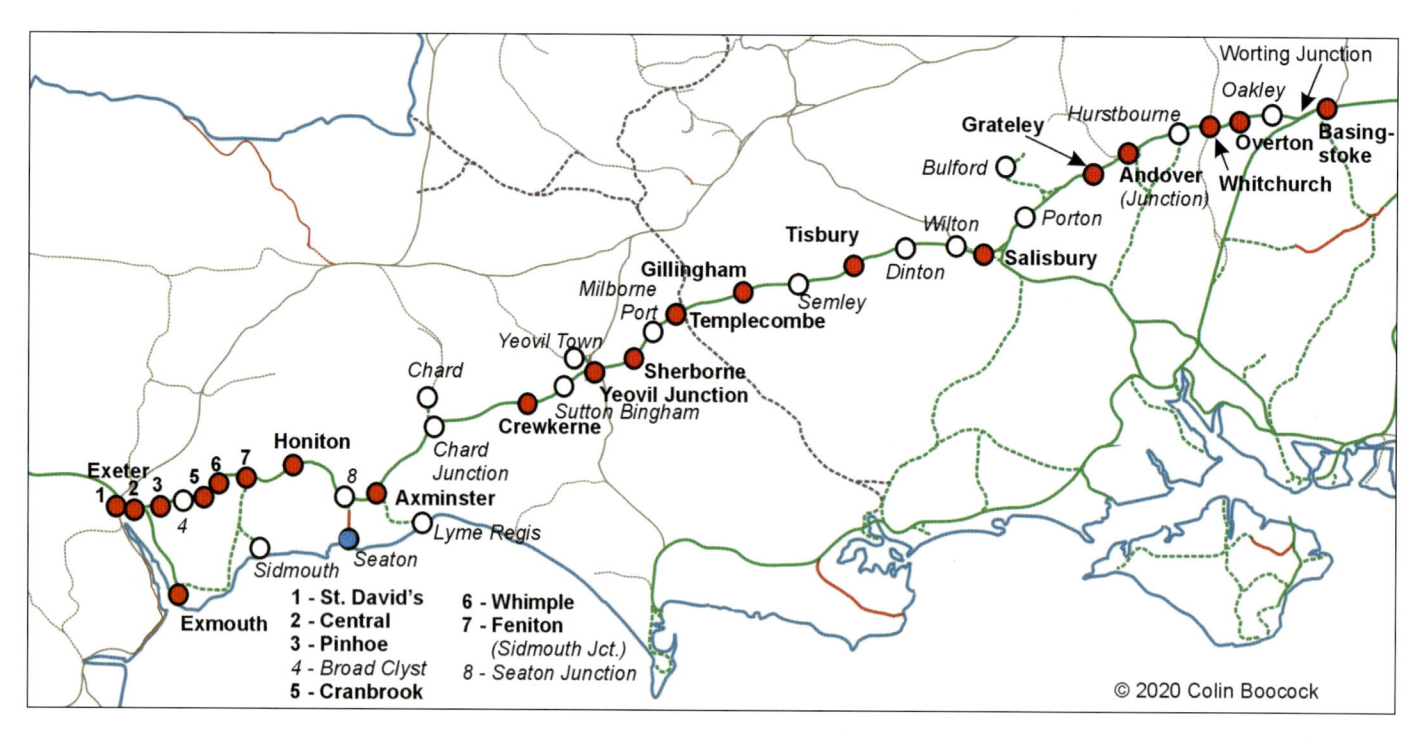

Map 5 – The West of England main line.

The present Andover station used to be Andover Junction. On 1 January 1956, 35021 *New Zealand Line* was restarting a Sunday morning express from Waterloo to the west country. At one side of the island platform sits ex-GWR 2-6-0 6320 with a train for Swindon Junction via the Midland & South Western Junction route.

Another military connection used to trail in to the west of England main line from the north about three miles after the summit station at Grateley. This was the link to Amesbury and Bulford, a line that had an extension to Bulford camp that was financed by the War Office and its successors. This railway also closed early, to passengers in 1952 and to goods and military trains in 1963.

Still on our downhill path, we pass through the site of the long-closed Porton station not long before slowing for Laverstock Junction and Tunnel Junction, both connecting the main line from opposite directions with the railway from Southampton via Romsey. The Laverstock curve was relaid from scratch in the 1980s to complete the triangle and to facilitate an alternative route for modern container trains travelling north from Southampton.

Emerging from Salisbury tunnel our train rounds the tight curve into the four-platform station, a curve that sounded the death knell of fast running of the L&SWR's Plymouth to London boat trains when one Up train running non-stop through Salisbury derailed here in 1906 with the loss of twenty-eight lives. Salisbury is the ancient city of Sarum and is famous for its cathedral, the one with the tallest spire in Britain at 404 feet. Salisbury also used to boast two engine sheds to look after steam locomotives. On the south side of the line west of the station was the Southern depot, the larger of the two, and to the north side, almost opposite, was that of the GWR. Great

Just east of Salisbury tunnel is Tunnel Junction where the line from Southampton and Eastleigh via Romsey joins the main line from London. Leaving the tunnel on 5 July 1991 is 50027 *Lion* with an Exeter to Waterloo train. (*Patrick Fitz-Gerald*)

On the eastern approach to Salisbury in summer 1991, 47710 rounds the curve with one of Network SouthEast's fast trains to Exeter, formed of mark 2b stock.

Western trains came into Salisbury from the direction of Bristol, Bath and Westbury on a double track line that paralleled the SR one for almost three miles from Wilton, where there were until the 1960s two parallel stations.

Some of those services were the Cardiff or Bristol to Portsmouth trains. In steam days these would change engines in Salisbury station. After dieselisation, each Region's locomotives or railcars worked through, as happens today. All this is history; the only depot at Salisbury now is the new one that BR built in 1992 for the class 159 DMUs that is sited alongside Salisbury station on its north side.

The site of Wilton station has a rather dubious claim to fame. When the Devon Belle Pullman train was introduced in 1947, the Southern Railway wanted to hoodwink the public that the train was non-stop from Waterloo to Exeter. Because the SR had no water troughs to replenish the locomotives' tender tanks and stopping the train at Salisbury to take water would be too obvious, management decided that the Pullman trains would change locomotives at Wilton during an unadvertised stop there. Curious passengers were told it was a signal check!

West of Wilton the first fifteen miles are steadily uphill through the small stations of Dinton (now closed) and Tisbury after which the gradient steepens to up to 1 in 145 on Semley bank, followed by a fall at 1 in 100, part of the saw-tooth racing profile of this fast route. A station in a dip is called Gillingham (a hard 'G' not a soft one which is reserved for Gillingham in Kent). Then the line undulates to Templecombe, a station that was once busy with interconnecting passenger and freight trains to and from the Somerset & Dorset Joint Railway, but which now has just one operating platform. That is actually better than the situation over fifty years ago. Templecombe station was closed in 1966 at the same time as the S&DJ line finally shut. A year later, the main line through Templecombe was singled. Pressure and some manpower effort from the local community resulted in the station being reopened in 1983, albeit in single-platform form.

Still climbing at around 1 in 100, our train tops the bank and passes the site of the former Milborne Port station and streaks down at 1 in 80 to reach the minster town of Sherborne, famed for its public school. The railway then undulates to reach Yeovil Junction. The Somerset town of Yeovil used to have three railway stations as well as a locomotive depot. In the days of steam your author recalls travelling on a push-pull train propelled by an M7 0-4-4T that ran faster than he expected from Yeovil Junction station to Yeovil Town, an SR station that was close to the town centre, beyond which a former GWR line continued to form a connection with the Berks & Hants line at Curry Rivel Junction to reach Taunton. Yeovil Town station had a small steam locomotive depot alongside. The station, the depot and the line towards Taunton all closed in the 1960s.

The other railway at Yeovil is the Castle Cary to Weymouth line that formerly brought GWR expresses, boat trains and stopping trains from Paddington or Bristol to Dorchester and Weymouth. Now singled south of Castle Cary, this route sees a service of DMU stopping

Templecombe was once a busy junction. In 1957, rebuilt 'Merchant Navy' 4-6-2 35014 *Nederland Line* arrives with an Up express. The Up yard hosts two S15 4-6-0s on freights and an ex-LMS 2P 4-4-0 off the nearby Somerset & Dorset line. This station was later closed, then reopened with just one platform.

Yeovil Town station and depot were linked by a short branch line to Yeovil Junction. Photographed on 25 August 1957, the M7 0-4-4T in the platform is working the push-pull shuttle to the Junction. The depot is hosting at least four Maunsell 4-6-0s, four 2-6-0s and a Bulleid light Pacific. The station was fed from the west by a secondary WR line from Taunton.

trains from Bristol to Weymouth that has several peculiar (to Southern eyes) three-hour gaps in it[6]. The line's station in Yeovil is at Pen Mill, close to the town centre. A separate line links Pen Mill and Junction stations. The Yeovil Railway Centre, a heritage organisation, has restored the former SR turntable near Yeovil Junction station. This sees use in the summer to turn steam locomotives that arrive at Weymouth on special trains and which then undertake light engine movements to and from Yeovil for turning and servicing.

After leaving Yeovil Junction our class 159 train, now reduced to one three-car set, begins the climb of Sutton Bingham bank and then the line undulates until the climb at 1 in 80 past Crewkerne station. If that station has any claim to fame from BR years it is the site where, in 1953, the crank axle of 'Merchant Navy' 4-6-2 35020 *Bibby Line* broke while passing through at 60mph; the locomotive's left side connecting rod broke free of its crank pin and flailed upwards to do damage to the Down platform awning. Fortunately for the passengers in the train behind it, the locomotive was not derailed, but the class was withdrawn for several weeks for axle examinations to be undertaken.

After Crewkerne the railway is still climbing and plunges through Hewish Tunnel, before beginning a long fast descent for over ten miles to Axminster, famous for carpets and cider. Axminster's railway interest lay in the lovely branch line that used to crawl uphill from there and ease back into Dorset to reach Lyme Regis. Oddly, the Lyme Regis bay platform at Axminster was at the west end of the Up platform, forcing connecting passengers to cross over by the footbridge to reach the branch train, and necessitating an overbridge to enable the branch line to climb over the main line. Axminster, being near the end of the

---

6. Weymouth has a two-trains-an-hour service from London via the South Western, so why the Great Western franchises have never seen fit to give it a good service to and from Bristol remains a mystery. The potential is there.

aforementioned fast downhill stretch, was also the site of a verified 104mph speed record by original 'Merchant Navy' 4-6-2 35022 *Holland America Line*.

Some time before reaching Axminster, our train passes on the right the site of the former branch line to Chard, a small town of 12,000 people that boasted two terminus stations, one L&SWR and one GWR, with a connecting link line between them that necessitated a reversal. The town lost its passenger service in 1962 and freight in 1966.

After Axminster, our train faces an eight mile climb at up to 1 in 80 to Honiton Tunnel, passing the station at Seaton Junction from which the former branch line trains to the seaside resort of Seaton set off. Descending from Honiton our train calls at Feniton station. This used to be known as Sidmouth Junction, from where the branch trains to seaside Sidmouth departed.

After Feniton, it is downhill most of the way through Whimple with a slight rise through Pinhoe up to Exmouth Junction where the Exmouth branch trails in on the left. On the right are industrial units that sit on the site of the former Exmouth Junction locomotive depot. Then we arrive at Exeter Central. Situated in the shopping district of the city, Exeter Central has two long main platforms with space between them that, before BR rationalised the layout, was occupied by two central tracks to enable locomotives to be exchanged or to run round their trains. There is also a bay platform at the east end of the Down one. Trains heading on to Exeter St David's need careful handling as the descent through the tunnel and subsequent curve is steep at 1 in 37. Steam-hauled trains were usually banked from St David's station up this incline. The DMUs today tackle this gradient in their stride.

Exeter Central station was called Exeter Queen Street until 1931 when the SR rebuilt the station into its current form.

Exeter St David's was the GWR station on its Paddington to Plymouth main line. Its claim to notoriety was that GWR and SR trains to London would call at the station facing opposite directions, an accident of railway geography. This feature also affected the same trains further west when they might pass each other again in Plymouth!

The SR's west of England main line star train used to be the Atlantic Coast Express. This was a complicated train that at different times had a main portion for Exeter and Plymouth and shorter portions, some of one or two coaches, variously to distant coastal places such as Ilfracombe, Bude, Torrington and Padstow. In some years there were also coaches in the train for one or two of the south Devon branches. On summer Saturdays, the 'ACE' as the train was colloquially known expanded to up to five separate trains in each direction with additional destination portions to, for example, Lyme Regis, Seaton and Sidmouth. In BR days, the 'ACE' was hauled by a 'Merchant Navy' Pacific because, at up to fifteen coaches, it was the South Western's longest passenger train.

I have already mentioned the Devon Belle. This had two portions from Waterloo, the front one for Plymouth and the rear for Ilfracombe. The train split at Exeter, the Ilfracombe portion continuing with the Pullman observation car at its rear. On arrival at Ilfracombe, that vehicle had to be shunted onto the local turntable so that it could be turned and then coupled to the other end of that portion ready for the next day's run back to London. This was yet another train that needed its formation switching round after arrival back in London.

Other trains along the west of England main line were largely in the hands of Bulleid Pacifics of both main types. Stopping trains were usually worked by

By 1964, the days of the Atlantic Coast Express were numbered. Light Pacific 34054 *Lord Beaverbrook* has just backed on to a portion of the ACE at Exeter Central; it carries the headcode for Padstow. The presence of ex-GWR pannier tanks reminds us that these 0-6-0Ts had taken over from SR types the task of banking heavy trains up from St David's. (*John H. Bird/Anistr.com*)

4-6-0s of Maunsell classes N15 or S15 or Maunsell Mogul 2-6-0s, and freights were almost totally handled by the competent S15s. Drummond 4-4-0s did stagger on for a time, but BR standard 4-6-0s and 2-6-0s took over from them until dieselisation swept even them aside. The SR line from Exeter to Plymouth curved left away from the GWR main line at Cowley Bridge Junction and ran on an inland route via Okehampton. With its hilly and curvaceous nature, it could not compete with the GWR route along the coast, neither for speed nor for scenic attraction. A later chapter in this book deals with these far-flung lines of the South Western.

Transfer of the railway west of Salisbury to the Western Region in 1963 resulted in a change of traction policy. I haven't found written evidence admittedly but I believe that the Southern Region had longer-term plans to electrify from Worting Junction to Salisbury and to use diesel locomotives beyond there.

That would have necessitated some steam locomotives running into the early 1970s, which would have been well within the competence of the rebuilt Bulleid engines. However, this was quite unacceptable to the British Railways Board. The move by the BRB to transfer the railways west of Salisbury to the Western Region in January 1963 almost without notice was probably intended to speed up the processes of railway rationalisation and of eliminating steam traction, whether or not Salisbury would ever be added to the electric network. Certainly, it was not long before the WR was using surplus diesel hydraulic locomotives on the expresses to Waterloo, surplus because the on-going rationalisation of secondary routes of that period and the fall in freight volumes were beginning to release many relatively new diesels that would otherwise have become surplus to the Western Region's requirements.

Initially the diesel class used on Waterloo to Exeter trains was the 'Warship' type B-B. These could deliver 2,200bhp power from their twin engines, and so could handle trains timed for 8P power group steam locomotives with competence. Later, the WR adopted the BRB's policy of replacing diesel hydraulics with diesel electrics, which brought the more powerful English Electric class 50s on to this route. These proved to be good runners, but locomotive unreliability did not help, and the presence of long sections of single track west of Salisbury was sometimes a distinct hindrance to good timekeeping. Later, the route became part of Network SouthEast, ironic in view of its geographic location. When the 50s proved to be a liability, that sector replaced them with class 47 diesel electric Co-Cos to work the trains of air-braked, electrically heated mark 1 and 2 stock.

One working in the early electrification era deserves special mention. In the 1970s there was a morning peak hour service that brought a four-car VEP electric multiple unit from Southampton to Basingstoke. Meanwhile, a diesel-worked push-pull train formed of a 4TC unit (no traction motors) propelled by a class 33/1 Bo-Bo diesel locomotive worked Up from Salisbury and coupled to the rear of the EMU at Basingstoke. The Southern Region's engineers had provided a common form of train control on its push-pull diesel electric and electro-diesel locomotives that would multiple with its standard EMUs. So this formation of 4VEP+4TC+33/1 could be seen speeding towards London being driven from the front cab of the EMU with the diesel pushing away happily at the rear with no-one in either of its cabs! Later in the day, the westbound train had the diesel in the lead with the EMU at the rear, both being driven from the front cab of the locomotive.

Dieselisation of the west of England main line however brought to an end the reign of the last star train on this route – the Devon Belle had been relatively short-lived, having already been withdrawn in 1954. The Atlantic Coast Express lost its name and prestige in 1964.

Today on the internet, the entry in Wikipedia for what we used to know as the 'west of England main line' identifies it as 'Suburban rail, Heavy rail'. How are the mighty fallen!

CHAPTER 4

DIRECT TO PORTSMOUTH
DIRECT…..IN A MANNER OF SPEAKING

Rather like its attempts to get to Dorchester and beyond as described in Chapter 2, the L&SWR was not fully successful in reaching the docks and dockyards in the Portsmouth and Gosport areas, at least when seen with the benefits of hindsight. For example, at first it set its sights on Gosport, a town that would later succumb to playing second fiddle to the growing port of Portsmouth, just across the mouth of the dockyard basin. The railway reached Gosport by laying a branch line from the London & Southampton main line that started southwards at Bishopstoke, the village later to be swamped by the town of Eastleigh which eventually gave its name to the junction station there.

An Up Portsmouth Harbour to London Waterloo express passes through Havant on 26 May 1958 formed of two 4COR units (No 3116 leading) flanking a 4RES. These trains were introduced in 1937 and lasted for three decades before being replaced by 4CIG and 4BIG units. The platform tracks at Havant were on loops off the main line. The junction for the South Western's 'Direct' line was east of the station. Brighton line trains headed straight on along the coast line.

The branch line was later joined at Fareham by a particularly curvaceous line from Southampton. Arrival at Gosport for passengers was in the quite impressive if small terminus station with its overall roof and porticoed entrance building. The Gosport line was opened in 1841.

Meanwhile, the London, Brighton & South Coast Railway also had eyes on the Portsmouth area as a traffic magnet, and approached it from nearly the opposite direction, sending a coastal route westwards from Hove and turning south onto Portsea Island to reach a terminus station at Portsmouth Town, which it did in 1847. Meanwhile, the L&SWR built two lines linking London with the central Hampshire town of Guildford, one via Epsom and one as a branch from the Southampton main line at Woking.

Another company proposed and began to build a rather sinuous railway south from Guildford that was also aiming at the Portsmouth area. Although in theory this would provide a ready-made link to Portsmouth and its docks, the L&SWR hesitated to buy it out because of its lower potential for fast running, but with the LB&SCR making such progress towards improving its own Portsmouth services, the L&SWR relented and took over the new railway. Having thus established its railway from London via Woking and Guildford as far as the approach to Havant, things began to get nasty. The LB&SCR flatly refused to let the L&SWR have running rights over its last few miles to Portsmouth and reportedly physically blocked the South Western's line at the junction at Havant by removing a switch blade. The L&SWR sent an early morning train along the new line and arrived at Havant carrying navvies who attempted to reinstate the switch blade and gain access for the train on to the LB&SCR's line to Portsmouth. The LB&SCR retaliated by removing another track section. This temporary impasse gained the name 'the battle of Havant', around which many a probably apocryphal tale has been woven. Eventually, the railways did agree to share the railway into the LB&SCR's terminus station at Portsmouth, and the Portsmouth 'Direct' line was born, generally agreed to have been in 1859.

A railway extension to the harbour in 1876 gave passengers direct access from the new Portsmouth Harbour station to the landing stage from which paddle steamer ferries to Ryde in the Isle of Wight were able to connect with trains. The station in the town then became Portsmouth Town. The deviation to the Harbour added two high level through platform faces flanking a long, curved island alongside the Town station. For several decades there had been a branch line from Fratton to the beach resort of Southsea, but local trams took much of its business away and the Southsea branch closed in 1915. Portsmouth Town station was thereafter known as Portsmouth & Southsea, the name it retains today.

The Southern Railway electrified the Portsmouth Direct main line in 1937 using the 660V dc conductor rail system with top contact that the SR had inherited from the L&SWR and had made standard for all its electrifications. This was effectively only the second principal main line in the country to be electrified, the London to Brighton main line and key branches off it having been the first, in 1933. British Rail Southern Region raised the traction voltage of its electrified main lines to 750V dc during the 1960s and 1970s.

The Portsmouth electrification was an immediate 'hit' with the public in general, particularly as it led to a very high standard of train timekeeping. A tale which sounds apocryphal today, but which has the ring of truth in it tells of a house owner whose property backed on to the Direct railway just south of the junction at Woking. When entertaining

52 • SEVENTY YEARS OF THE SOUTH WESTERN

1 - Gosport
2 - Portsmouth Harbour
3 - Portsmouth & Southsea
4 - Fratton
5 - Hilsea
6 - *Southsea*

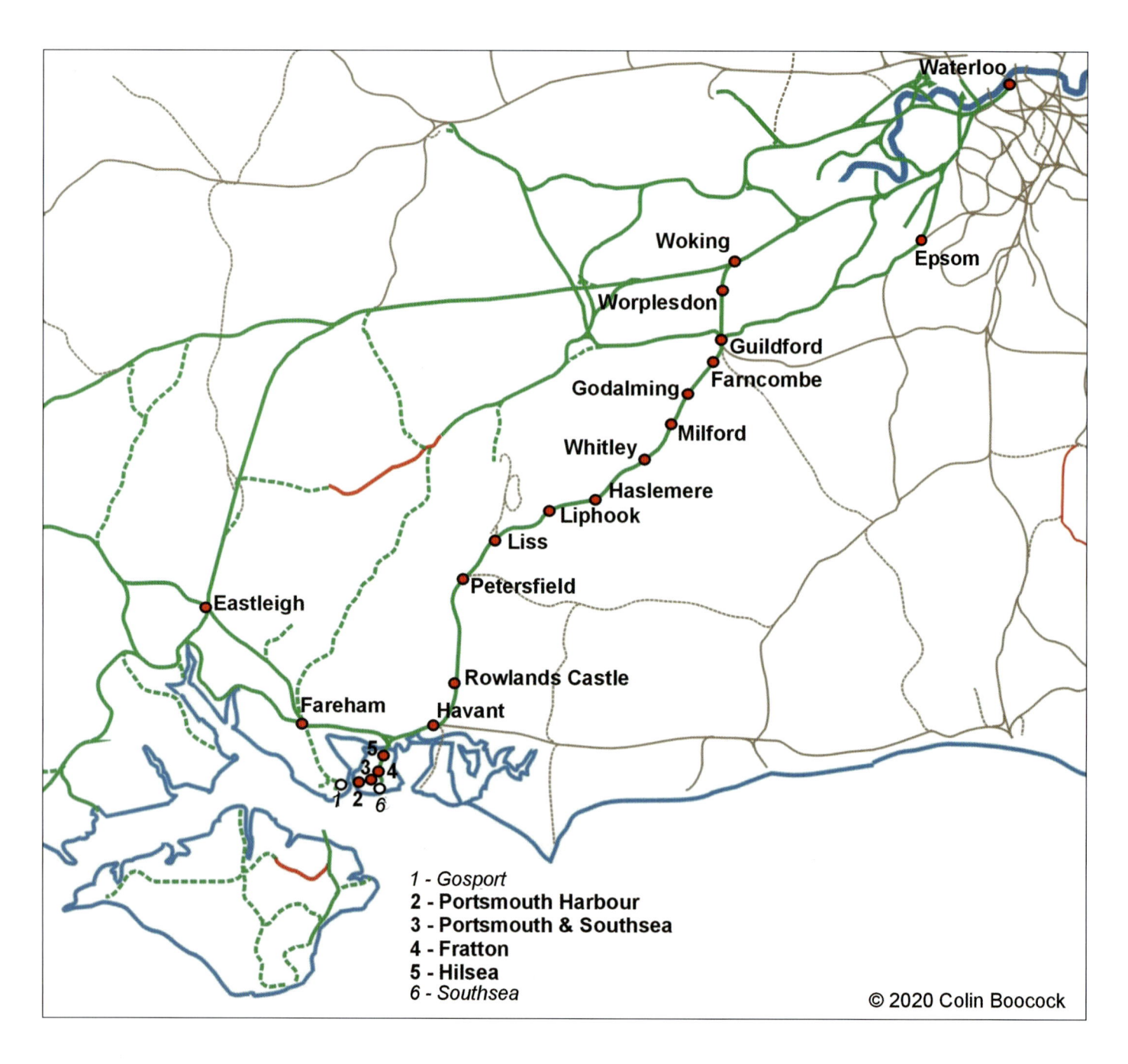

© 2020 Colin Boocock

Map 6 – Portsmouth direct.

guests at home, he would take them to the bottom of his garden at a specific time in the hour with complete confidence that they would see two Portsmouth EMUs passing each other there.

The design of the original electric trains was based on Richard Maunsell's standard locomotive-hauled stock but without automatic buck-eye couplings. The express units were four-car fixed sets classified 4COR (corridor) and 4RES (restaurant) and made up into eight- or twelve-car formations; one set in each train included a restaurant car. In each unit, the outer vehicles had one powered bogie at the driving end, giving a level of performance that quite outclassed the 4-4-0 steam locomotives of classes D15 and V that they displaced. BR replaced these SR units by new four-car sets from around 1965. These were based on the BR mark

1 carriage specification, with B.5 trailer bogies and mark 6 motor bogies for improved riding. The motor bogies were both under one vehicle, within the unit. While in some ways these 4CIG (corridor intermediate guard's van) and 4BIG (buffet) EMUs represented an improvement in passenger comfort, they were not a step change in running performance even though they were geared for 90 rather than 75 mph. The nature of the Guildford-Havant section precluded use of their higher maximum speed. Better acceleration performance had to wait until the present generation of Siemens-built classes 444 five-car and 450 four-car units, delivered early in the twenty-first century following railway privatisation and the establishment of Stagecoach Rail and its South West Trains franchise. These trains reflect the modern lifestyle that eschews restaurant and even buffet cars in favour of at-seat trolley service. This also helps the franchise commitment to provide more seats in a given length of train.

The original EMU build for local and stopping trains on the Portsmouth line was a fleet of 2BIL two-car non-gangwayed sets which generally ran in multiples of four to eight coaches. These were replaced in the late 1960s by the even then rather old-fashioned 4VEP units, which in turn were displaced by the Siemens class 450 four-car sets after privatisation.

Nowadays, the Portsmouth Direct line has a basic service of four trains an hour of which two are expresses. The current inclusion of more stops than the Southern Railway expresses served has kept the overall London-Portsmouth Harbour journey times roughly the same as the pre-war times, little over ninety minutes for the seventy-five miles.

If we join a Portsmouth fast service at Woking today, we can enjoy for the next fifty minutes or so what seems a rather leisurely journey through pleasant countryside and deciduous woodlands. It is firstly a short hop to Guildford, the largest town on this stretch of railway with its 1960s red brick cathedral. Its station of seven platforms is sandwiched between two junctions to its north and a tunnel at the south end. These junctions bring in the route from Waterloo via Epsom on the left, and the non-electrified line from Reading on the right. Nowadays, the latter is the domain of First Great Western's service of class 165 DMUs from Reading to Gatwick Airport. These trains turn left off the Direct line at Shalford soon after Guildford tunnel and head along the former SE&CR's Redhill and Tonbridge line, reversing at Redhill and then heading south along the LB&SCR's Brighton main line as far as Gatwick.

Guildford used to be served by a steam locomotive depot in a tight space on its west side. The covered part of this depot included a semi-roundhouse with the stabling tracks linked to the outside world by a turntable. A small shunting locomotive was used to move engines that were out of steam on and off the turntable. BR inherited an aged Adams B4 0-4-0T for this duty, and later replaced it with a USA 0-6-0T that was displaced from Southampton Docks. The depot site now hosts a multi-storey car park.

After the tunnel and the junction at Shalford, the Direct line undulates with an average uphill trend until Godalming and Milford, beyond which our train faces four miles at 1 in 80 to its summit at the well-heeled town of Haslemere. Then it's downhill, not quite as steeply but with curves that prevent unbounded fast running down to Liss. My first memory of Liss was back around 1949. Our family was travelling from the Isle of Wight towards London and I recall seeing former LB&SCR 4-4-2Ts, almost certainly of class I2, standing in a siding with WD

On the last day of steam working on the Southern Region, 9 July 1967, BR class 5 4-6-0 73029 passes Guildford with empty Bulleid carriage stock from Fratton to Clapham Junction. From the next day the SR would only use air-braked and electrically heated coaching stock for internal locomotive-hauled services. The locomotive depot in the background is already empty except for the depot shunter, USA 0-6-0T 30072 which is being prepared for its final departure light to Salisbury depot for storage. (*Keith Lawrence/Platform14/Anistr.com*)

markings and numbers and with sacking over their chimneys. I didn't know at the time that there used to be two stations here, the second one being the southern end of the former Longmoor Military Railway. That railway linked with BR at both ends, the northern end having a connection with the Botley to Bentley branch line just south-west of Eastleigh on the Fareham line. It last saw stock movements in 1971, two years after its formal closure.

Our train now has some more climbing to do until a secondary summit between Petersfield and Rowland's Castle, by which time we are coasting steadily downhill, reaching this railway's 'floor' as we enter the flat junction with the south coast route from Brighton and Hove that trails in on the left. What we cannot see is the former single-track ex-LB&SCR branch line that used to leave from an east-facing bay platform at Havant station and which turned south to head for Hayling Island. BR was unable to justify spending a large amount of cash to repair the bridge across a neck of Langstone harbour, and so closed the line in 1964.

A few miles further and we turn off to the left to head south across the short bridge that takes the railway onto Portsea Island. The junction is a triangle that allows trains from Portsmouth to head north-west and reach Fareham and Southampton, and it enables trains from Cardiff and Bristol to reach Portsmouth and Brighton.

We pass the site of the former gas works at Hilsea and then stop at the curved platform in Fratton station. The former steam locomotive depot is no longer here though there are servicing facilities for EMUs. Neither, of course, is the Southsea branch line here any more. Our train moves off and traverses the Portsmouth city section of this railway.

Portsmouth & Southsea station is interesting. Our train diverges here from the original route by climbing a little to the left to reach the two newer platforms that were added when the extension to the Harbour was being built. The original terminus platforms are lower down on our right and are still used for terminating trains. BR modernised the high level station in the 1980s and gave its island platform a semi-circular-section overall roof.

The rest of the line remains double track and snakes between classic buildings to reach the Harbour station. Most of this station is mounted on piers with seawater underneath. War damage still affects operating here as not all the original platforms are freely available to all trains even after remedial work. There are two passenger exits from this station. Passengers walking towards and passing the buffer stops are close to the embarkation point for the catamaran ferries to Ryde on the Isle of Wight. Passengers who cross by the footbridge to the main exit leave on the west side of the station and face the historic part of the docks with *HMS Victory* and *HMS Warrior* both within a short walk.

A Portsmouth Harbour-bound express service of 4COR-type stock passes behind Portsmouth College on 15 October 1960 just after leaving Portsmouth & Southsea high level station.

56 • SEVENTY YEARS OF THE SOUTH WESTERN

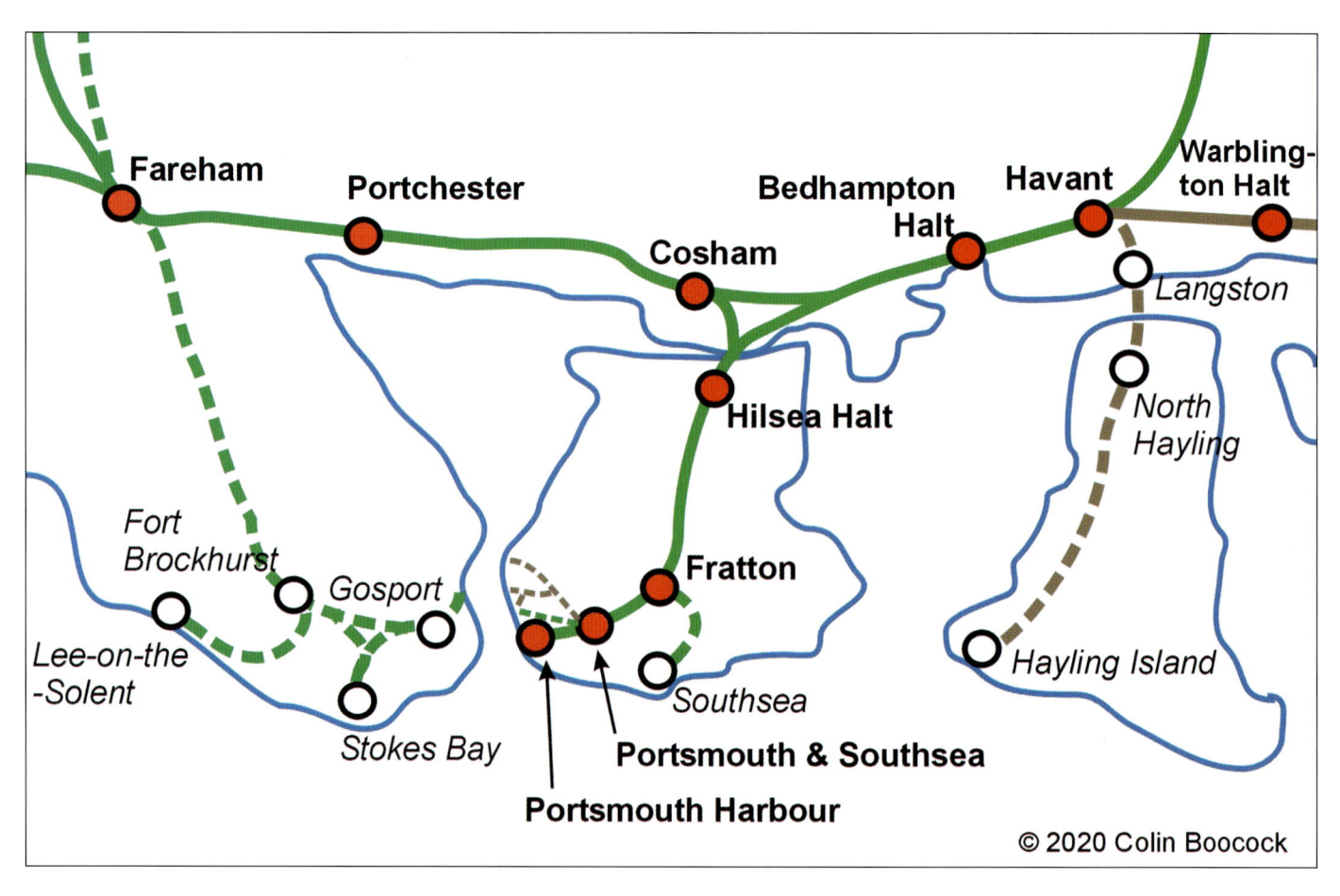

Map 7 – Portsmouth.

BR 4 2-6-0 No 76059 arrives at Portsmouth & Southsea terminus with an inter-Regional service from Bristol on 2 July 1959. The tracks on the far right lead to the high level platforms and the Harbour.

DIRECT TO PORTSMOUTH • 57

At Portsmouth & Southsea terminus on 19 May 1958, 75070 heads a Southampton and Bristol train, while a Hampshire DEMU awaits departure with an Andover Junction via Eastleigh service. Above and behind the tender of 75070 can be seen the old awnings covering the high level platforms on the Harbour branch.

At the high level platforms at Portsmouth & Southsea, 4VEP unit 3442 calls with a semi-fast service from Portsmouth Harbour to Waterloo. By 1989, this part of Portsmouth & Southsea station had been modernised with new platform awnings and passenger facilities.

This journey from London has taken us 93 minutes at an average speed of 48mph. The curvaceous nature of the Portsmouth Direct line once led me to read a paper to a railway conference in London that was discussing train designs for higher speeds. I proposed a tilting EMU that would enable timings between Waterloo and Portsmouth Harbour to be reduced by about ten minutes overall, most of the time saving being between Woking and Havant. Using the market elasticity figure that BR had measured in other areas when journey times were reduced, I assessed an increase in farebox takings of around 10 per cent (elasticity of 1.0). I also showed how the shorter journey times would enable the railway to reduce the number of trains needed to work the full timetable. With privatisation just then happening, this was probably one development too far for franchisees to grasp!

Bo-Bo diesel 33021 awaits departure from Portsmouth Harbour with the 11.10 to Bristol Temple Meads on 20 February 1982. Most of the platforms here are supported over the water on interconnected piers. In the background is the access bridge to the landing stage for Isle of Wight ferries. *(Colin J. Marsden)*

Almost brand new Siemens EMU 444018 leads an express from Waterloo arriving at Portsmouth Harbour on 15 June 2004.

CHAPTER 5

AN AMAZING TERMINUS
'HE MET HIS WATERLOO'

Named after a nearby road when it was first opened, the first Waterloo station was the L&SR's attempt to make amends from initially having to terminate at Nine Elms which was just not close enough to central London for the convenience of its passengers. In its turn, the street called Waterloo Road had no doubt been named a short time after the British and Prussian armies in 1815 had successfully defeated Napoleon Bonaparte's French troops at the location of that name, nowadays a small town in southern Belgium.

London's Waterloo station is a short distance south of the River Thames, within walking distance of London's theatre district across Waterloo Bridge. Today the station is very well connected with the rest of the capital by London Underground and by the other suburban railways that the London & South Western Railway and South Eastern Railway built, mainly in the nineteenth century.

The L&SWR had several attempts at enlarging Waterloo, the station reaching its twenty-one platforms size after the First World War, the platform layout that British Railways inherited in 1948. Under BR in the early 1990s, a five-platformed annexe to the station was completed for Eurostar trains, on time and within budget; this was virtually ready for traffic in 1993, about a year before the Channel Tunnel itself was ready, and the trains intended to go through it. Subsuming the former platforms 20 and 21, the Waterloo International project brought the platform total at the terminus up to twenty-four. For the Eurostar passengers

Waterloo is London's busiest terminus station with 24 platforms. On the morning of 17 August 2007, the station throat is busy with class 450 EMUs on semi-fast trains and 455 units working inner-suburban services. This view shows the pristine condition of the train shed roof and awnings following extensive refurbishing.

60 • SEVENTY YEARS OF THE SOUTH WESTERN

Waterloo (East)

W&CL

Jubilee Line

Platform 24

Waterloo (terminus)

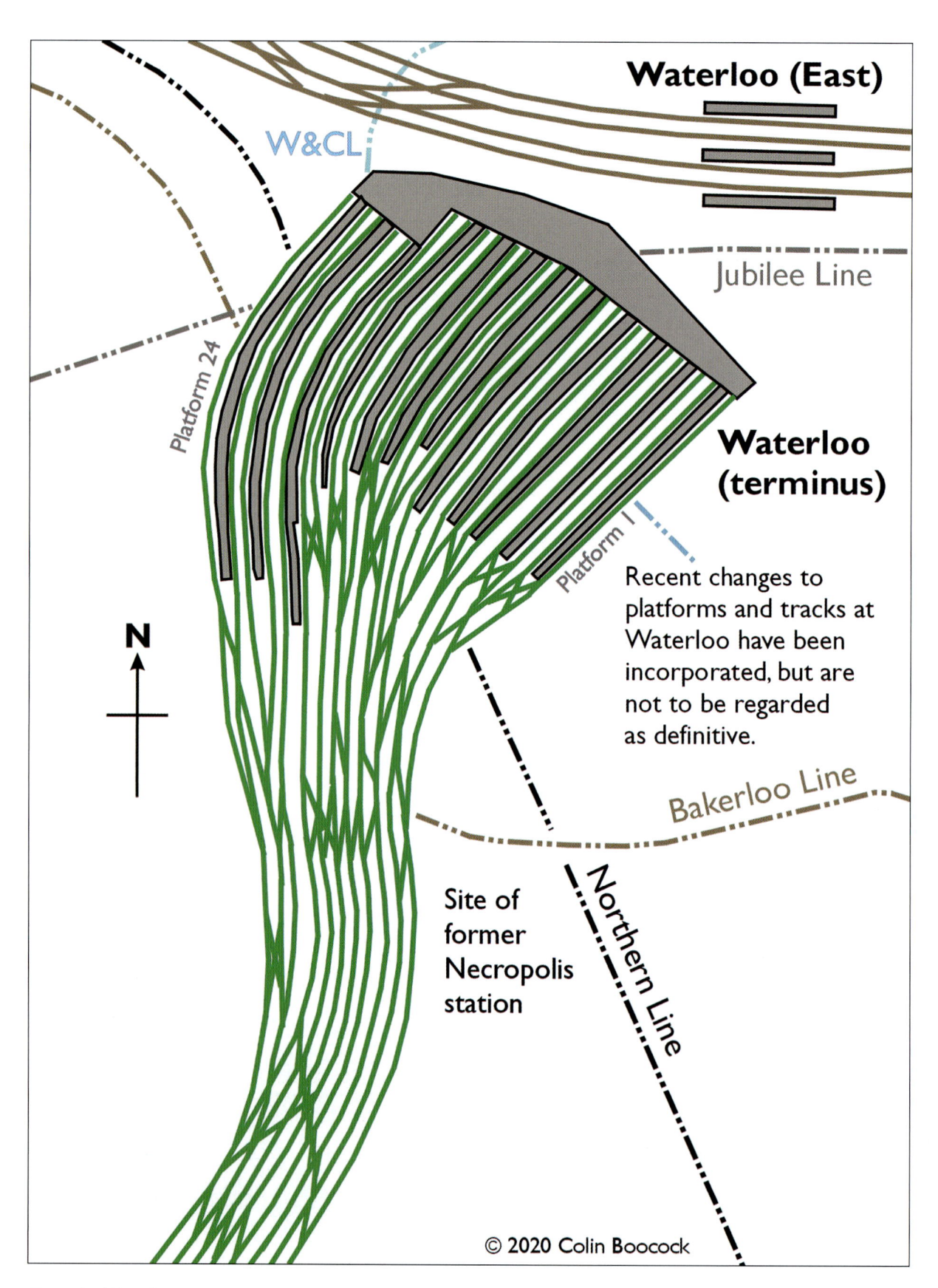

Platform 1

Recent changes to platforms and tracks at Waterloo have been incorporated, but are not to be regarded as definitive.

N

Bakerloo Line

Site of former Necropolis station

Northern Line

© 2020 Colin Boocock

Figure 1 – Waterloo

there were lower-level areas for security checks and waiting.

Because of its early piecemeal development, the twenty-one platforms at Waterloo that BR inherited were of varying lengths. The longest were the main line ones in the middle of the main terminus, capable of handling trains of up to twelve coaches, or ten modern ones of twenty-three metres length. Nonetheless, in steam days it was common to see a long train such as the Atlantic Coast Express or the Royal Wessex standing ready to depart with its train engine beyond the starting signal; there simply was not enough additional length to accommodate the tank engine at the buffer stops that had brought the train in from Clapham sidings and the train engine at the other end as well as extra coaches that were needed on these services.

Suburban platforms were able to accommodate electric multiple unit trains of eight coaches that were each up to twenty metres long. This was fine until the unexpected growth of rail travel that has occurred in the twenty-first century. Current policy is to expand all these trains to ten vehicles throughout the day. Lengthening of all the suburban platforms has been necessary to accommodate these longer trains, a difficult project that was achieved in 2018. Eurostar trains moved their London terminus to St Pancras in 2007 following completion of the high speed railway that we now call HS1. The five long platforms of the former Waterloo International have been rebuilt to accommodate up to twelve-car suburban trains from the routes known as the 'Windsor lines'. So Waterloo now has longer suburban platforms throughout, plus a net three new ones, all of which creates a useful increase in capacity.

Waterloo station once had a single track railway connection that crossed what is now its main concourse to join the SER's main line out of Charing Cross to Dover and Ramsgate. The nearby former SER's Waterloo station has four platforms indicated as capital letters A to D, thus avoiding any possible confusion with platforms 1 to 4 at the terminal station. This through station is now known as Waterloo East and is linked by a modern pedestrian bridge to the new mezzanine level along the terminus station's concourse.

My early recollections of Waterloo station date back to the 1940s when our family lived in Surrey. We would travel in from Weybridge on SR green EMUs, often with carriages of L&SWR type extended by one wider Bulleid coach. There were two prevailing sounds that greeted arriving passengers; at busy times strong martial music was pumped out of the loudspeakers, apparently to hurry people along; and there was the open hiss of Bulleid Pacifics' vacuum ejectors as locomotives that had recently arrived from distant parts awaited their turn to back out of the station. The concourse was always busy, so it seemed. Passengers would stand in a group watching for their trains to appear on the departure indicator. This was a tall and wide timber structure with rotatable green slats that bore the names of calling points in yellow capitals. Railwaymen with long poles with end hooks would deftly swing them up and the slats would turn to reveal the stations, time and platform of the next train to wherever, all displayed in an easy-to-read column. This magnificent feature gave way during BR's later modernisation phase to two electrically operated boards, and later still to the electronic displays we can now see. More displays at the platform ends were in the form of timber arrows which showed where the train standing in that platform was going. These are now modern illuminated displays.

I remember as a young man heading up a dark stairway behind a door off the concourse to eat in the Surrey Rooms restaurant. This was a bit up-market but very enjoyable; white-jacketed waiters would serve customers from an extensive menu. My memory is of glossy wood panelling around the walls, and wide windows overlooking the platforms. Looking down from a window one could see the accumulated dirt and dust that was on the roof of the large W.H. Smith's bookshop in the middle of the concourse. Otherwise, Waterloo always gave the impression of being a clean station even if the overall roof glazing was stained after decades of steam locomotive exhaust drift. At a higher level at the south-east end of the concourse was the cinema which specialised in news films.

Today, after the modernisation that took place earlier this century, the concourse is very much brighter. It has clean cream tiles on its floor, bright clear glazing in the extensive roof and a new mezzanine level that accesses several food outlets that have replaced the long-lost Surrey Rooms and the cinema; neither of these is perhaps seriously missed in this faster-moving modern world. At the north-west end of the concourse is a wide ramp that leads up to the platform ends of the Windsor lines, platforms 20 to 24. The buffer stops here were moved back to make room for a local sub-concourse serving those platforms. The platforms had been shortened at their outer ends as well to accommodate additional track switches to increase the number of possible train moves from the six or so per hour in Eurostar days to the twenty or more needed now.

Approaching Waterloo from the outside, one's impression depends on which entrance one uses. By far the most impressive is the monumental archway entrance set in the northern corner of the buildings that flank the end of the station. Built of white Portland stone, it is known as the Victory Arch and was erected as a memorial to the L&SWR employees who lost their lives in the First World War. A little further south, there is also a more modern-looking pedestrian entrance on Waterloo Road that leads firstly into the Underground and then via escalators up to the Waterloo concourse. The vehicular entrance is from the south-east side up a ramp and to the side of the main building where taxis deposit passengers just short

The 'Victory Arch' street entrance to Waterloo station acts as the L&SWR's first world war memorial. The inscription round the edge of the windows states: *Dedicated to the memory of employees of the company who fell in the war*. The outer ring of stone wreaths shows the battlegrounds in which they died: (from left to right) *Belgium, Italy, Dardanelles, France, Mesopotamia, Egypt* and *North Sea*.

of a relatively insignificant gateway in the concourse end wall. Taxis then creep round to the front of the building to the fare pick-up point. There is also a pedestrian access bridge that leads into the north-west end of the concourse from the South Bank.

Two other early features of the terminus station area deserve mention. The L&SWR opened its own underground railway in 1898, the Waterloo & City line. It started at a platform roughly underneath the station concourse, accessed by steps and tunnels. Its two platform tracks were extended backwards away from its running line tunnels to a small depot at which the trains were serviced and cleaned. For access to the outside world, carriages had to reach daylight via the Armstrong Lift that connected with sidings along the north-western wall of the station. This unusual feature was buried in 1992 under the works for the Eurostar station. London Underground Limited (LUL) now operates the W&C Line. On the rare occasions that a carriage needs attention that cannot be given at the depot, it has to be craned out through a shaft on the south-east side of the station building and taken away by road.

An earlier activity in that part of the station grounds was connected with the funeral industry. When London's

Waterloo's main concourse is light and airy in spite of its large area. In the twenty-first century it has been modernised with a clearer floor area, a mezzanine floor (right) housing food outlets and the access to Waterloo East, and modern passenger information boards. The picture shows the off-peak scene on 1 July 2019.

Decked out in the Stagecoach holding company's colours initially adopted by South West Trains in the late 1990s, EMUs of class 455 stock await departure from the inner suburban platforms at the south-east side of Waterloo in 2003. The nearest train is labelled for the Shepperton branch.

cemeteries became seriously short of burial space as the city expanded, a new necropolis was opened in 1854 near Brookwood alongside the Southampton main line. Trains of occupied coffins were loaded at an outside platform at Waterloo and hauled west to Brookwood cemetery, where a purpose-built long siding received each train for unloading. This was the only route out of Waterloo which had no return traffic (other than empty rail vehicles). Most old pictures of these trains show they were worked by Drummond M7 0-4-4Ts. The service ceased in 1941 as a result of enemy bombers destroying the necropolis platforms at Waterloo; the coffin trains were never resumed.

Waterloo station ranks top among Britain's busiest railway stations, whether measured by the number of train movements or by the passenger count.

Modern train services into and out from Waterloo are largely formed by electric multiple units grouped into distinctive main line, outer suburban and inner suburban types. By the time this book is in print we can expect to see brand new trains of ten-car Bombardier-built class 701 EMUs working the key inner suburban routes, providing some capacity expansion for hard-pressed commuters. All these routes operate as regular-interval services at mainly half-hourly intervals, as is described in more detail in a later chapter.

AN AMAZING TERMINUS • 65

A Bournemouth express service sits at Waterloo on 17 June 1998 formed of class 442 EMU 2416, soon after repainting in the new Stagecoach livery designed by Ray Stenning of First Impressions. Alongside on the right is a class 159 DMU arrived from the Exeter line.

New platform end indicators provide much more useful information as modern technology increases the ability to harness and present masses of data in passenger information systems. On 17 May 2011, the stopping pattern of the 16.30 to Portsmouth Harbour is clearly displayed to boarding passengers.

The diesel exception to all this is the longer-distance route to Salisbury and Exeter. Because everything west of Worting Junction on the Salisbury route has not been electrified, South Western Railway continues to use its class 159 and a few 158 diesel multiple units. These DMUs run out of Waterloo normally as six- or nine-car formations.

The view of Waterloo station from high up on the London Eye on 8 August 2009 shows the main concourse to the left, the platform awnings in the centre, and the curved shape of the former International section in the foreground. Two 444s and a 455 are visible on the right. In the top left corner are the platforms of Waterloo East.

A completely new ramp leading to a new concourse for the Windsor lines' platforms 20 to 24 was opened in 2019. This covered over the former Eurostar reception area and has added usefully to the circulating space at the north corner of the main concourse.

CHAPTER 6

CLAPHAM JUNCTION
ORDER OUT OF CHAOS

Clapham Junction is Britain's busiest through station. It sits astride two important main lines and is the terminus for a London orbital service as well. The main lines are the one from Waterloo to Portsmouth, Weymouth and Exeter, which was formerly part of the L&SWR system; and that from Victoria terminus to Brighton and the seaside resorts along the coast either side of it, one-time of the LB&SCR. Each of these two main line groups has platforms dedicated to main line and to suburban routes. Connections by foot between these four main traffic flows generate the huge amount of passenger interchange traffic here. The wide footbridge that links all these platforms also connects across the gap occupied by the SW's carriage sidings to link the main lines to the platforms of the 'Windsor lines' that serve not just Windsor but also numerous routes and branches as far west as Reading.

Years ago, there used to be an occasional local service that left this station and pottered north up the

West London line towards Kensington Olympia. For a century it was a steam tank engine hauling three or four old carriages. In the mid-1960s, this train was one of the first on BR's Southern Region to employ a modern form of diesel locomotive-worked push-pull system, in this case using converted ex-Portsmouth express carriages. The train was always affectionately known as the 'Kenny Belle'. The modern railway has transformed this service completely. Now frequent five-car EMUs start and finish in two short platforms serving either the South London line via Peckham Rye, then curving north on new track to join the East London line to Dalston Junction and terminating at Highbury & Islington; or the other leg of this orbital route that also starts at Clapham and heads along the West London line to Kensington Olympia and on to Willesden Junction High Level, then eastwards on the North London line to Stratford (east London), connecting with the aforementioned service at Highbury & Islington on the way. All this is now part of Transport for London's highly successful London Overground network, currently operated by Arriva.

If one stands on a platform at the 'sharp end' of Clapham Junction station looking east (i.e., towards central London), one can be forgiven for thinking that the very wide expanse of tracks ahead is so complicated that it would be wonderful if any railway could run a reliable train service through it all. In fact, it's not complicated at all. Basically, towards the right there are the two pairs of tracks from Victoria that run alongside the SWR tracks and serve four platforms. There is also on the extreme right a pair

Looking towards Waterloo, this 1967 view of the approach tracks to Clapham Junction station illustrates the multiple tracks involved, but also their relative lack of complexity. The view is from a platform end between the South Western's Down main line (left) and Up suburban line (immediate right). The four tracks to the far right are those of the Southern Region Central Division (nowadays the Southern Railway franchise). To the extreme left under the overhead signalbox are the Windsor lines tracks and those leading to the carriage sidings and depot. The two 4VEP units are on a Waterloo to Basingstoke service.

In 1965, the structure supporting the large signalbox over the Windsor lines collapsed at its north end. The cause is understood to have been the additional weight of the heavy metalwork laid on its roof during the last war to provide protection from enemy action. Initially the cabin was temporarily supported with the help of the Hither Green breakdown crane, visible in this May 1965 picture. The structure was soon considerably lightened and the supports strengthened to enable the signalbox to continue in service for another two or more decades. BR 4 2-6-4T 80095 brings a train of empty coaching stock from Waterloo into the carriage sidings for servicing. (*Derek Martin collection*)

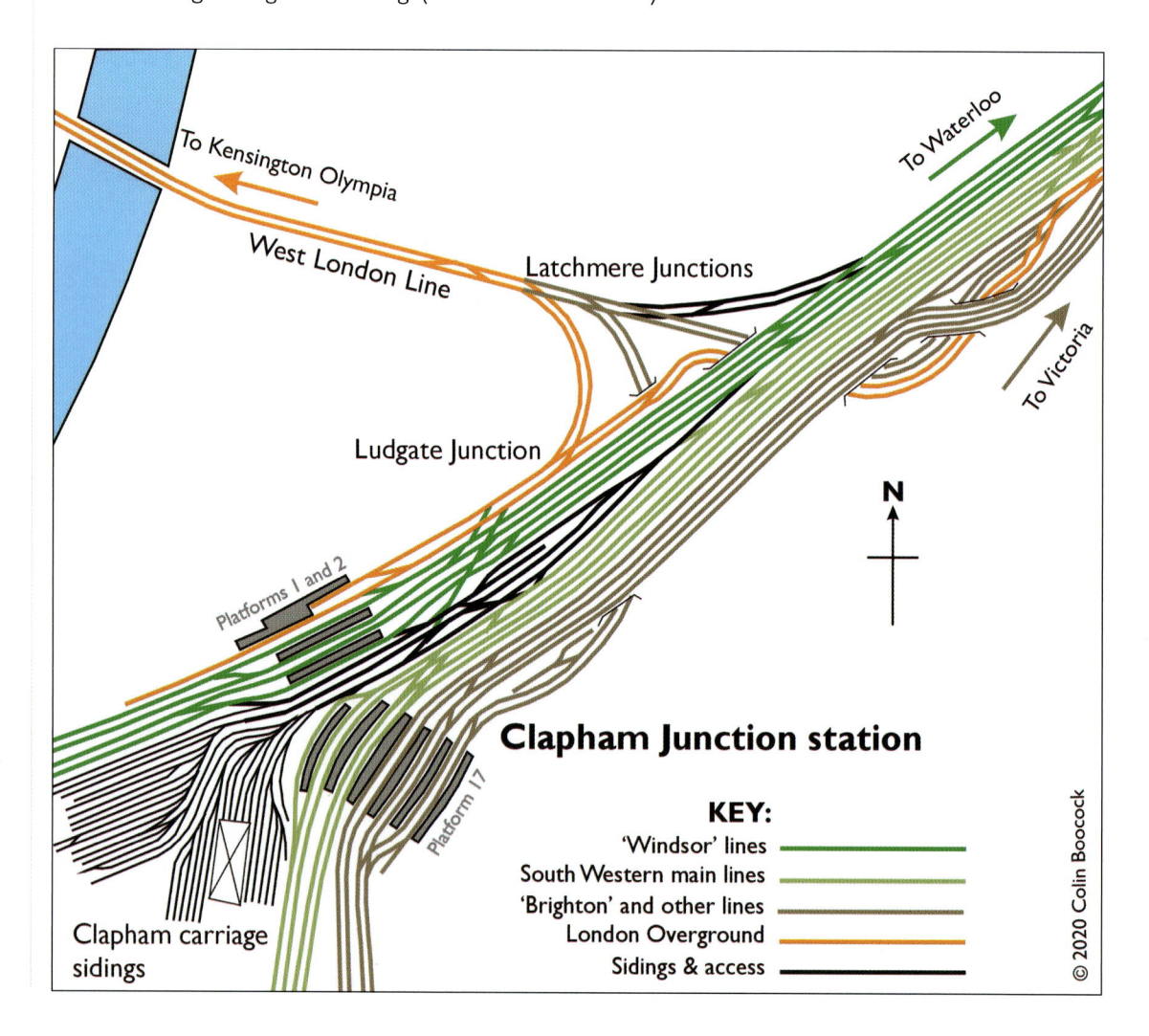

Figure 2 – Clapham Junction.

of tracks that enable freight trains to pass through without getting in the way of other services, at least until they have passed through the station.

As one looks eastwards, to the left of the 'Southern Railway' (as it likes to call itself today) tracks are the main line and suburban pairs of tracks that the South Western Railway uses from Waterloo. The Up main line here throws off a loop line to feed an additional platform before combining again beyond the station. While there are links between these track groups, the normal train services actually keep rigidly to their own tracks. Passenger trains do not cross from the Southern to the South Western nor vice versa. Nor do they normally cross between adjacent suburban and main line tracks.

Again, still looking eastwards, even further left are tracks that bring empty stock trains into the carriage sidings for stabling between peaks and for servicing. We can see the carriage washing plant out there. Beyond that are the 'Windsor Line' tracks, operated separately from the other SWR lines all the way from Waterloo, and their trains stay separate from those running on the tracks alongside.

So actually, it's not complicated at all. The key to smooth train operation here is the separation of the flows of trains to their own track pairs with just minor deviations to use the loop platform when necessary. It is the passengers who have to switch trains and tracks to continue their journeys. To provide trains that would enable through journeys for all the thousands of individual journey choices wanted by these people would be highly complex and would not enable such excellent service frequencies that are available today by simply changing trains at Clapham Junction.

A modern platform view shows 444019 arriving with a Waterloo to Bournemouth semi-fast service. The long footbridge connects all platforms, the Windsor lines being to the left at which a class 458 train is calling.

72 • SEVENTY YEARS OF THE SOUTH WESTERN

66783 in Biffa livery comes off the line after threading the underpass that has brought its train of empty stone hoppers from North Kent, and heads towards the route that will take it eventually to the Somerset quarries. The trailing junction in front of the locomotive is that from the West London line via Kensington. (*Hassard Stacpoole*)

The south-east side of Clapham Junction station includes the street entrance and booking office (extreme right). 73901 and 73963 top-and-tail a Network Rail test train en route from Tonbridge West yard to London Bridge on 23 June 2020. The train is on the Down suburban line of the 'Brighton' group of tracks through the station. The far right pair of tracks is that from the West London Line that has burrowed under virtually all the other tracks on the north-east end of the station to get there. (*Hassard Stacpoole*)

There are in fact six platforms on the former LB&SCR side (the Victoria group). The highest-numbered pair (16 and 17) are linked to the West London line via an underpass under all the approach tracks some distance east of the station; these two platforms are passed mainly by freight trains. They are also where the hourly Southern trains from East Croydon to Milton Keynes deign to stop. The former L&SWR lines have five platforms south of the carriage sidings. The 'Windsor lines' use four platforms north of the sidings, and there is one further platform occupied by the Overground services; this has in effect a bay section cut into it at the east end, so it is split in accordance with the destinations of the services, these platform faces being numbered 1 and 2.

Thus, there are seventeen platforms altogether. Not only are these all linked by the footbridge near the west end of the station; there is also a useful subway at the east end, making transfers between groups of platforms shorter in terms of walking distance because this is where the tracks are converging.

Most trains stop at Clapham Junction. Only a few expresses on the SWR tracks pass through, restricted to 40mph by track curvature; these trains are mainly bound for the Portsmouth, Bournemouth and Weymouth lines. On the Victoria tracks, the Gatwick Express trains and some other expresses do not stop. Otherwise, the station is daily host to hundreds of trains that call to afford the passenger connections for which Clapham Junction is renowned.

In terms of the number of trains using Clapham Junction station, between 120 off-peak and nearly 200 peak hour trains call there each hour during the working day, making it the busiest station in Europe. Around 80,000 passengers a day alight from or board trains at the station, the majority not joining or leaving the railway there but making interchange between trains. This makes it the UK's busiest interchange station by far.

On the Down South Western main line, a new class 701 EMU passes on a trial run to Eastleigh on 25 August 2020. (*Hassard Stacpoole*)

74 • SEVENTY YEARS OF THE SOUTH WESTERN

The carriage sidings at Clapham Junction are located between the South Western main line tracks and those of the 'Windsor lines'. This view on 25 April 1983 shows 4CIG (class 421) and 4VEP (423) units stabled in the sheds.

Morning rush hour at the South Western's side of Clapham Junction station shows the intensity of operations there in modern times. While a class 158/159 DMU formation to Salisbury calls at the Down main platform, no less than six outer-suburban (blue) trains are visible, all formed of pairs of class 450 or 458 units, and there are also two inner-suburban (red) class 455 trains. A 377 on a Southern Railway service creeps round past the former Brighton line signalbox, too. With ten trains visible, it is, after all, Britain's busiest junction station! (*Hassard Stacpoole*)

CHAPTER 7

SUBURBAN SOUTH
FLYOVERS AND FLYUNDERS

Because of its apparent complexity, I have divided the description of the South Western suburban network into two chapters. This chapter covers the lines that run largely south of the River Thames. Chapter 8 will deal with the so-called 'Windsor lines' and those that link to them.

Heading west from Waterloo, Raynes Park is the diverging point for the first of the former L&SWR branch lines. Here is a burrowing junction, the constructing of which was the reason why the station's platforms are staggered. The Up platforms are the faces of an island on which the south face is by the main line's Up suburban track and the north face catches the last part of the incline of the Chessington line as it climbs out from the underpass. On the south side of the station, the Down island platform is laid further west and accommodates on its almost separate south face the Chessington branch track as it drops down to head south-west. This branch line soon splits into two routes, the Chessington line being the right-hand fork with four stations before reaching its terminus at Chessington South.

My first recollections of Chessington were when my parents took me to the zoo there during the war. During that period of extreme petrol rationing, the zoo's steam-outline miniature railway train was running by dint of substituting coal gas for its normal fuel. This was contained in a flexible bag on the roof of the leading carriage. 'Health & safety' wasn't an issue in those hazardous days! Today, the zoo is marketed as a theme park.

The first station out of Waterloo is Vauxhall where the suburban north and south lines run parallel, with the SW main line tracks between them. 456017 leads two class 455 units on a stopping service heading towards Woking on 4 July 2018.

76 • Seventy Years of the South Western

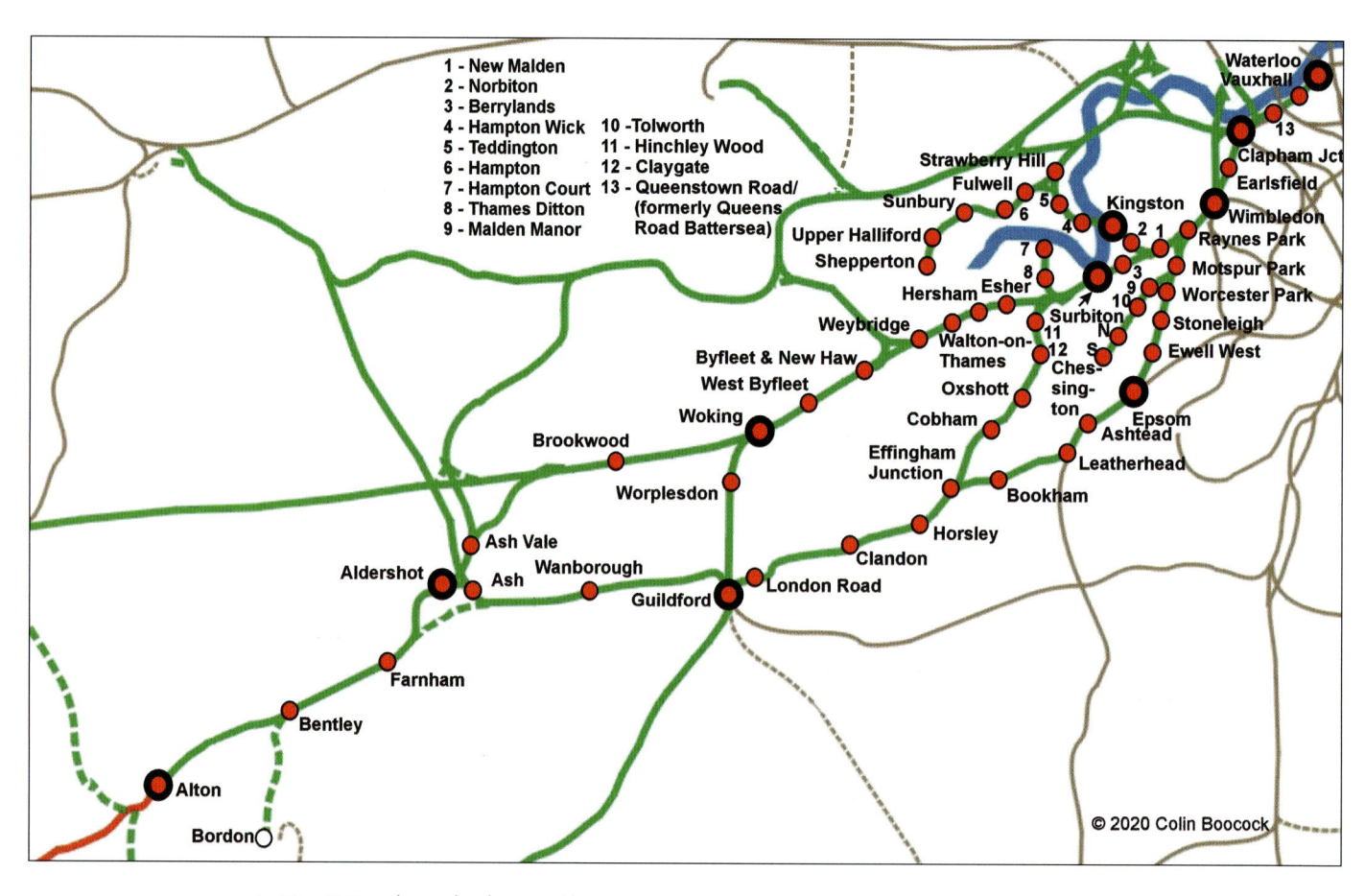

Map 8: London suburban south.

The EMU maintenance depot at Wimbledon is located on the north side of the tracks and was photographed from a train on the Up suburban line flyover where it crosses the Up and Down main lines. In the sidings alongside the depot on 10 April 1983 are units of classes 415, 508 and 455.

SUBURBAN SOUTH • 77

Class 455 EMU 5718 arrives at Raynes Park in 1988 while working an Up inner suburban service. The platforms here are staggered to make room for the dive-under track that brings the Chessington branch underneath the main lines. The Up Chessington line uses the far side of the island platform, the awnings of which can be seen beyond and above the train. The Down branch track peels off just between the signalbox (extreme right) and the Down platform end and has its own almost separate platform.

At the junction a mile or so south of Raynes Park, the left-hand route is the more major one, sometimes known as the Mole Valley line. It heads south-south-west to join at Epsom the former LB&SCR line from Sutton as far as Leatherhead, where the line splits again as the Brighton's line to Dorking heads off south, the SWR trains moving on west heading for Guildford. Not quite half-way along this section is Effingham Junction where another South Western line comes in on the right, this having left the main line at Hampton Court Junction and providing yet another route by which suburban trains can travel towards Guildford. When engineering works affect the Portsmouth Direct line, main line trains are sometimes diverted along this route. These outer suburban lines are all double track.

Back on the main line, where the suburban tracks are the outer ones of four lines, there is a grade-separated junction at New Malden where the Kingston line turns off to the right. A few miles after Kingston, this line reaches a triangular junction at Strawberry Hill, but the triangle is before the station of

Unit 5848 trundles along the Down Chessington branch track near Tolworth on 19 April 1985. (Colin J. Marsden)

that name; this is where the Shepperton branch peels off westwards. The east side of the triangle takes trains northwards to Twickenham, facing London now, and becoming part of the lines that are the subject of the next chapter. Within the triangle at Strawberry Hill is a depot area. This once held facilities for an allocation of steam locomotives, but the Southern Railway made use of the site for a depot for electric multiple units. It was a convenient base for trials and experiments which could be tested on the Shepperton branch without impacting on the train service. Strawberry Hill depot has been used not only for stabling and servicing but also for undertaking commissioning and modification work to SWR EMUs.

Turning off the main line northwards at Hampton Court Junction is the short branch line that gave the junction its name. The terminus station is by the south bank of the River Thames. Visitors to the Palace need to walk from the station across Hampton Court Bridge but they are for the most part in sight of the great attraction itself. The branch has only one intermediate station, at Thames Ditton.

Further west along the main line we come to Weybridge, a small town named from its position on the River Wey, a tributary to the Thames. Like all the suburban stations west of Wimbledon,

SUBURBAN SOUTH • 79

The rainswept and rationalised terminus station at Hampton Court is host to class 455 unit 5849 on 22 May 1984 as it awaits departure on its return trip to Waterloo. (*Colin J. Marsden*)

A Shepperton to Waterloo service formed of two 4EPB units (class 415) led by 5110 approaches Wimbledon station on 2 June 1983. These were built in early BR days with Bulleid-style lightweight bodies on second-hand carriage underframes and bogies with new traction equipment, but unlike the 4SUBs before them they had electro-pneumatic brakes, hence the EPB designation.

At Effingham Junction on 3 June 1985, 4VEP unit 7750 (right) arrives on the 08.50 Guildford to Waterloo via Oxshott and overtakes 5874 waiting to enter the station to take up the 09.14 working to Waterloo via Epsom. (*Colin J. Marsden*)

the station has its platforms alongside the outer two tracks. While a few suburban stations on the main line still show signs of there having been a central island platform for main line trains, none is in use today. Weybridge indeed, like most of the others, had no platforms for the main line tracks. The station has however a west-facing bay platform on its north side. From here, trains for London head north and join the Reading line at Virginia Water, thus becoming of interest to Chapter 8 in this book. There is a triangular junction at Weybridge, and the west curve enables trains from the Virginia Water direction to head along the main line towards Woking. This is sometimes used as a diversion route for main line trains when engineering possessions occupy the main line somewhere east of Weybridge.

The deep cutting east of Weybridge is where I first saw steam trains at around the age of four. My parents used to park me by the fence overlooking the four tracks there, and I watched malachite green and war-time black Maunsell 4-6-0s passing through on expresses at or near the war-time railway speed limit of 60mph, which to me in my very young naïvety looked very fast because nothing else I had seen on land at that time ever moved so swiftly! I also noticed that the sleepers under the main line tracks rose and fell significantly as the trains passed over them, such was the limited maintenance the civil engineer could afford to give them during war-time conditions.

After Brookwood, another flyover junction leads the Alton branch away to the south-west. Proceeding along that route, the line is shortly joined from the north by the single line branch from Ascot on the SWR's Reading line. Our train soon crosses over the former SE&CR's Reading to Guildford line and arrives at Aldershot, home to much military activity being an army garrison town. Beyond Aldershot, the line heads mainly south-west to reach Alton. Here ends the Southern Railway's electrification that was completed around the same time as that to Portsmouth via Havant, but there is a railway beyond here. Nowadays it is the heritage railway known as the Mid-Hants Railway. It is dubbed locally the 'Watercress

Line' because of what is grown in the area, but in earlier times it was known by railway people as 'over the Alps' due to its steep gradients; the former railway carried on beyond its present southern terminus at Alresford to connect with the main line north of Winchester. It was used on some weekends as a diversionary route when there was engineering work on the main line via Basingstoke and is one of the interesting by-ways described in Chapter 17 of this book.

If we had alighted at Aldershot, we would have had the opportunity to take a local EMU to Guildford. Heading east out of Aldershot, this would then take a right junction and a short curve south to a junction at Ash Vale on the Reading to Guildford line; the short section from Ash Vale to Guildford was part of the L&SWR, though the rest, from near Reading to Redhill and beyond, was built by the South Eastern Railway. If you think all this is complicated, as do I, please study the maps!

An example of the new order for South Western Railway which is replacing all its older inner-suburban EMUs with one standard type is this Bombardier 'Aventra' class 701. A ten-car version of this class was passing Clapham Junction in summer 2020 on a trial run to Eastleigh. (*Hassard Stacpoole*)

As part of its pre-war modernisation of suburban services, the Southern Railway rebuilt several stations in the art-deco style. This is the exterior of Surbiton as seen on 20 January 2016.

CHAPTER 8

SUBURBAN NORTH
A USEFUL DIVERSION

The so-called 'Windsor lines' go to many more places than Windsor. For example, my early reminiscences of the South Western's Reading line were occasional visits to a relative who lived at Mortimer. Until 1945, we lived at Addlestone, a station on the Weybridge to Virginia Water line. Addlestone's minor claim to fame was the presence of Weymann's factory there, and also it was not far from Runnymede where Magna Carta was sealed by King John on 15 June 1215. The Weymann works in peacetime made buses, but one can assume it switched to armaments during the war, and my parents were certain it would be a target for enemy bombers during that period. Addlestone station was typical of the L&SWR's suburban and wayside stations with two platforms, brick buildings and long awnings, with a brick signalbox at the south end in which was a large wooden wheel that the signalman rotated every time the heavy timber level crossing gates needed to be opened or closed across the main road. I recall the steel stops that

For two decades the class 458 EMUs were the mainstay of the Waterloo to Windsor services, like No 458502 seen at Waterloo on 31 March 2015. Even though this scene was little over five years ago, it is already becoming history as the Windsor lines trains now mainly leave from platforms 20 to 24, the former international station, and the 458s have been replaced by Bombardier 701s.

SUBURBAN NORTH • 83

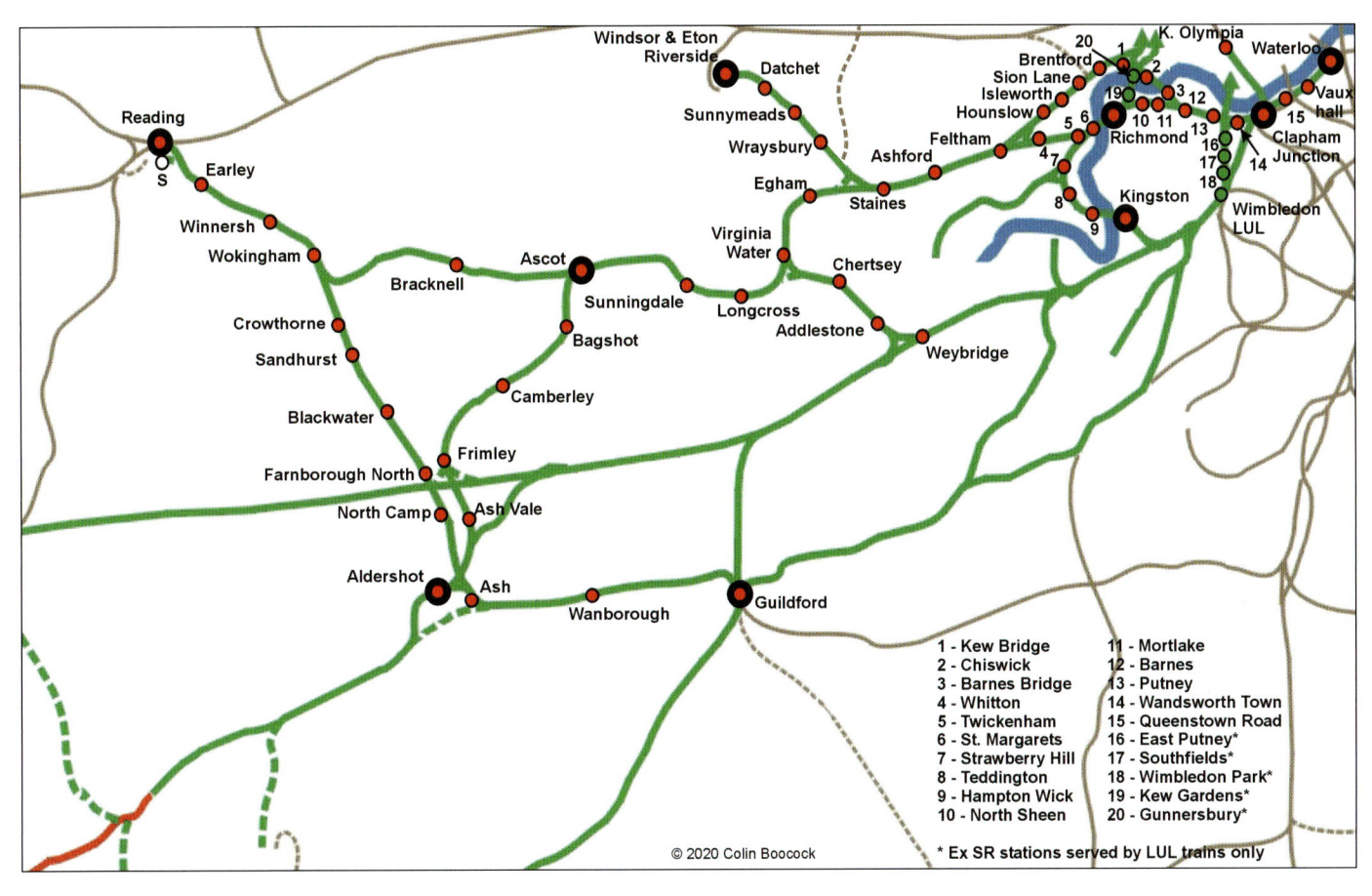

Map 9 – London suburban north.

These Bulleid 4SUBs, later class 405, were the most modern suburban EMUs that BR Southern Region inherited in 1948. Two of these reliable if basic workhorses call at Vauxhall on an inward working from the Hounslow direction on 6 May 1981. Like all SR-built EMUs, they were fitted with the standard automatic air brake.

For many years of BR's life the Reading to Guildford line services were steam-hauled, mostly beginning their journeys at Reading South. On 15 August 1951, U class 2-6-0 31797 was receiving crew attention.

emerged from the road against which the gates would stop with a clatter.

On one of our family journeys, we were changing trains at Virginia Water to catch a train to Reading South. I recall a long freight approaching from the Feltham direction headed by a Bulleid Q1 0-6-0. The engine was somewhat off-beat, and I dubbed the type 'hiccough engines' in consequence. The train would have taken the line through Chertsey and Addlestone and turned west before Weybridge so as to gain the main line to the south-west, possibly bound for Southampton Docks or Portsmouth.

Another EMU would soon come along to take us to Reading. One of the calling points was the station at Ascot which was and is an oddity. The Up line runs between two platform faces, both of which for the most part have carried the platform number 1. With slam door stock, passengers could alight or join on either side, but with modern power doors only the north side is now used, which has direct access to the booking hall. The other side of the island is platform 2, used by Down Reading trains. On the south side of that is a Down loop which is the starting point for trains heading for Guildford via Camberley, and alongside this track on the south side is platform 3. The Guildford line becomes single track just south of Ascot.

In early BR days, the approach to Reading included sight of the Southern's locomotive shed before we arrived at Reading South station, a terminus typical of L&SWR suburban architecture. That station is no more, because the early British Railways rationalisations diverted all trains from the SR up into Reading General station on the former GWR main line from Paddington to the west. Much more recently, an additional platform has been added to the former platform 4 terminal group to allow for trains being extended to ten cars, and still to have room for the regular GWR DMUs that run through to Gatwick Airport. At the demise of the SR station, the General station became just plain Reading.

In earlier SR years, but after electrification, the locomotive shed at Reading South was kept open for steam locomotives arriving from the former SE&CR route from Tonbridge and Redhill. As the Southern Railway matured after the war, old pre-grouping 4-4-0s, apart from Drummond T9s which seemed to go on for ever, were replaced by Woolwich Moguls of classes N and U or U1. Freights had 0-6-0s of Wainwright, Maunsell or Bulleid origin, or the heavier trains from Feltham arrived behind Maunsell S15 4-6-0s. After Reading's rationalisation, dieselisation of SR secondary routes was proceeding apace. BRCW Type 3s appeared, later known as class 33s or 'Cromptons', and later still came the rather odd 'tadpole' diesel electric units. These were made up of a motor coach and standard class trailer from semi-redundant Hastings DEMUs displaced by closure of the Bexhill branch. These coaches were of main line interior layout but had been built with flat sides for passage through the tight tunnels on the Hastings main line. For a driving trailer, each unit acquired an inner-suburban type full-width driving coach from 2EPB stock. As three-car DEMUs the trains were unremarkable, but their appearance with two narrow coaches and one wide one earned them their nickname.

The old SR EMUs on the Waterloo to Reading line, which included some of the 4COR type also seen on the Portsmouth lines, were upgraded to corridor 4CIGs and 4VEPs in the late 1960s and early 1970s. When in the first years of the twenty-first century it became fashionable,

After the closure and demolition of Reading South, all Southern Region services terminated at Reading's WR station, the former General, which had its platform 4 area electrified to accommodate the change. In the mid-1970s, a foggy day veils this view of a train of 4CEP units (class 421) having arrived from Waterloo while a WR HST runs through on the Up fast line bound for Paddington.

indeed sensible, to replace slam-door stock such as these with trains with power-operated doors, their replacements were air-conditioned Siemens-built class 450 units with swing plug doors. Many of these units used on the 'Windsor lines' were internally configured as high-density sets with no first class. All were built as four-car units in Siemens's factory at Krefeld in Germany.

A main line journey in 2020 served to remind me of the characteristics of these lines. My wife and I were heading west on a class 159 DMU from Waterloo to Exeter on a Saturday morning when Network Rail was doing 'railway improvement work' on the main lines somewhere between Wimbledon and Weybridge. On this day, all trains on the Portsmouth, Bournemouth and Exeter routes were being diverted, so we were treated to an extra half hour's railway entertainment by travelling non-stop but rather slowly via the north side of Clapham Junction, Richmond, Twickenham, Staines, Virginia Water and Addlestone. We re-joined the four-track main line at the burrowing junction just before Byfleet & New Haw (formerly West Weybridge).

Until after passing Staines, this route is intensely suburban in nature. From Clapham Junction it is four tracks as far as Barnes, but before then we pass through Putney, where there is a junction with the London Underground District line from Edgware Road to Wimbledon. This shared branch has been used in the past as a shorter diversion route, enabling main line trains to re-join their normal route just east of Wimbledon station. But our diverted train is heading further into outer suburbia before reaching normality again. Putney is well known for Putney Bridge on the Thames, site of the annual boat race between rowing eights from Oxford and Cambridge Universities. We are soon passing through Barnes station. Back in my early memory is reading about the horror of the train crash there between two timber-bodied Southern Railway EMUs which resulted in a fire that caused many deaths.

Map 10 – Inner suburan north.

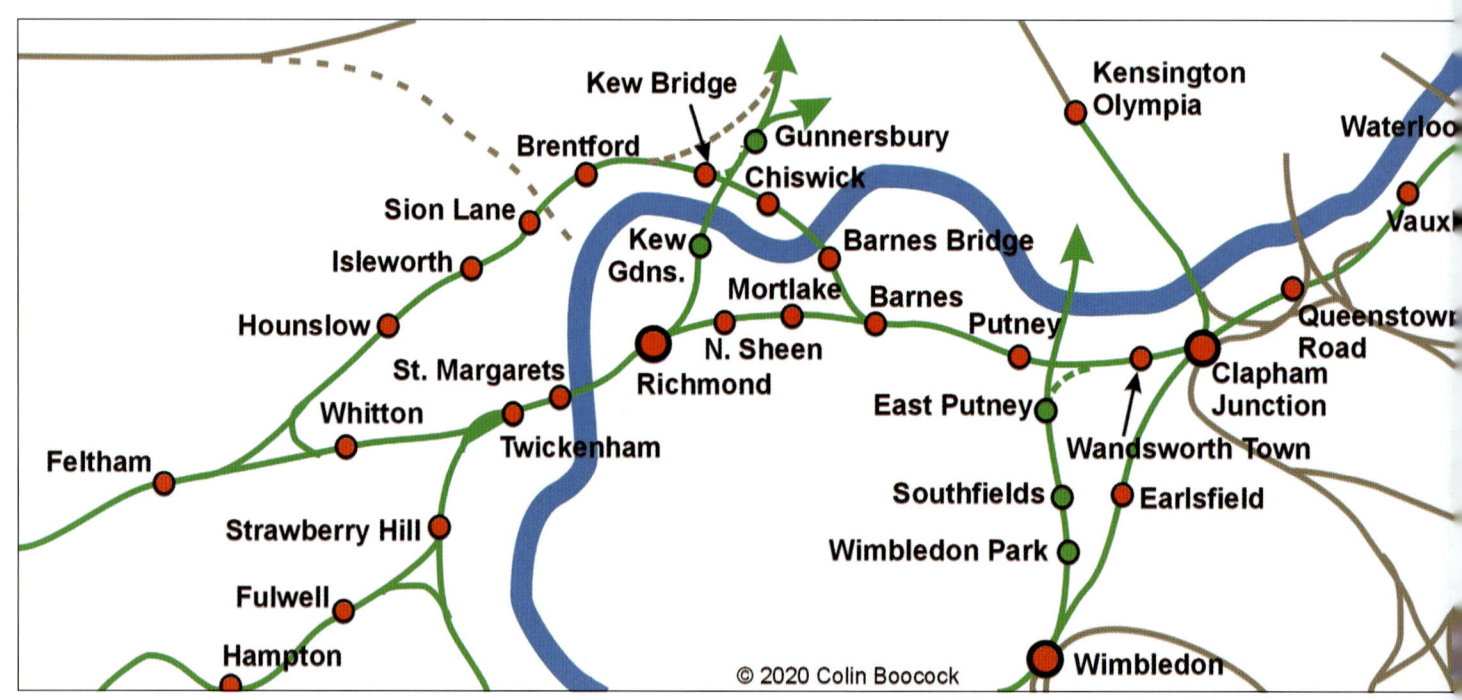

Barnes is where the four tracks peel off into two diverging routes. Until that point, the northernmost pair of tracks is for trains for the north part of the Hounslow loop. The southern pair leads towards Twickenham, Staines, Windsor, Reading and Weybridge. Our diverted train is slowly making its way along the Twickenham line, but first we run through Mortlake, North Sheen and then Richmond where again we see LUL District Line trains in the terminal platforms as well as London Overground units; these have come in on our right off the line through Kew. Soon after Richmond, we cross the Thames with a good view of the many houseboats lining the banks here.

Through St Margarets (no apostrophe – how many Margarets were there that gained sainthood?) we soon approach Twickenham and then another grade separated junction from which the line to Strawberry Hill and Kingston peels off to the south. Trains for this line from Waterloo are shown as heading for Kingston, but, in reality, they just go on from there, back up the main line to Waterloo; hence their nickname as 'Kingston roundabout' trains. More houses pass by, and playing fields and gardens, as we head through Whitton. Then a pair of tracks peels off right and heads back to London via Hounslow, the aforementioned Hounslow loop.

We continue westwards, past the third side of the triangular junction, and reach Feltham, one-time site of a large marshalling yard with its wagon distribution hump shunted by one or more of the four massive Urie 4-8-0Ts of class G16, all long since gone. We can speed up now as the relatively straight railway passes through open country, dotted with ponds and reservoirs. Next station is Ashford, sensibly tagged

Despite widespread electrification of the suburban lines, freight in the area was still in the hands of steam traction well into the 1960s before diesels fully took over. This scene at Feltham depot on 26 September 1964 shows, from right to left, Maunsell S15 4-6-0 30839, one of the long-distant freight haulers; Bulleid Q1 'austerity' 0-6-0 33020 for lighter goods trains; and W class 2-6-4T 31912 which had replaced one of the old Urie H16s on cross-London freight workings. (*Alan Trickett*)

Unit 5705 leads a Hounslow loop service approaching Vauxhall on 15 September 2005. These class 455 units are among the classes being replaced by 701s.

'(Middlesex)' to delineate it from the one in Kent[7]. Then we slow through suburban Staines which is followed immediately by a sharp left junction that turns us away from the line that heads straight on towards Windsor and its Riverside station.

We cross the Thames again and make good progress through the suburb of Egham; then we speed through open countryside, and eventually reach Virginia Water. Then for a few miles we head south-east along the line through Chertsey and Addlestone that takes electric trains that terminate in the bay platform in Weybridge. But before we reach Weybridge, as a main line train on diversion we must take the west side of the triangular junction there to reach the South Western main line by means of a burrowing junction from which we emerge on the south side of the main line just before Byfleet & New Haw.

Earlier in our diverted journey, we had forked left at the junction immediately after Barnes. Had we been travelling in a suburban train booked to run along the north side of the Hounslow loop, we would have forked right there, which would have taken us quickly to Barnes Bridge station and then across the bridge of that name over the Thames. At this point the river forms a loop around most of Chiswick, where we call briefly, before continuing through a quite-well-heeled suburban area that leads us to Kew Bridge station, a little way after our line has passed under the LUL route to Richmond. At this point, we are north of the river whereas the well-known Kew Gardens are on the south side. There is a triangular junction here on the right, where a link comes in that enables freight trains from the Willesden area to reach the South Western tracks past Feltham.

After Brentford, Syon Lane and Isleworth, we arrive at Hounslow, not the terminus of our train which is destined to return to Waterloo via the east side of the triangular junction to follow the eastbound route through Richmond, re-joining its tracks at Barnes before

---

7. Technically, the administrative county of Middlesex no longer exists having been largely absorbed since 1965 into Greater London.

heading back into London. Other trains on this route take the west side of the triangle to call at Feltham, Ashford and Staines.

Staines is where trains bound for Windsor head straight on, and then north-east to call at Wraysbury, Sunnymeads and Datchet before the curves that lead into the terminus at Windsor & Eton Riverside. Here we are in sight of the castle, and only a few minutes' walk uphill to the smaller former GWR station at the southern end of the short single-line branch line from Slough. That station has become more of a museum dedicated to Queen Victoria and her early travels by railway.

For the route to Windsor & Eton Riverside in particular, South West Trains leased some new Alstom class 458 four-car outer-suburban sets. These 458s had flat, raked-back cab fronts. The intelligent work initiated by the leasing company Porterbrook in the early 2010s that reformed and modified these sets using extra vehicles from the displaced Gatwick class 460s enabled additional 458s to be created and for these and all existing 458s to be stretched to five cars each and suitably refurbished; these normally now run as ten-car trains. South Western Railway has targeted these units for replacement by their new universal suburban ten-car class 701 units from Bombardier. The aim is to use these latest electric units to replace all existing SWR inner suburban EMUs, namely BR-built classes 455/456 (including many that have new, modern traction packages), the refurbished Alstom 458s and the new Siemens 707s that were introduced in 2017. There will be sixty ten-car and thirty five-car class 701 units, and these will operate all the services described in Chapters 7 and 8 in this book other than those covered by Siemens class 450s. The concept is for SWR to have a homogeneous fleet for its inner suburban

On 4 July 2018, a pair of 458s has arrived from Waterloo at Windsor & Eton Riverside station. There is a proposal to build a tunnelled railway to link this line with the branch line from Slough, but local opposition is high.

Staines is the junction where the Windsor line turns off the line serving Reading and Weybridge. A service from Weybridge to Waterloo via Virginia Water arrives at Staines formed of unit 707017 on 4 July 2018. These units have been transferred to SouthEastern.

services, with delivery well under way by the time this book appears in print.

Twenty-eight sets of the displaced 458s are being reformed to four-car units, reset for a top speed of 100mph and refitted with less dense seating so that they can be used to improve passenger experience on the Portsmouth Direct line.

Missing from this narrative so far has been the Shepperton branch, a double-track line that heads west from the triangle at Strawberry Hill. This line has only four intermediate stations, though it is double-track like almost all the inner suburban routes I have described in this chapter. Its terminus station at Shepperton for a couple of decades in the 1980s and 1990s hosted on a parallel siding a twelve-wheeled Pullman car (now on the Bluebell Railway). This was opposite the offices of the railway book publisher Ian Allan Ltd and was used for meetings and occasional entertaining. That need and the facility have more recently disappeared.

CHAPTER 9

RAILWAY HUB – SOUTHAMPTON
FROM WAGONLOADS TO CONTAINERS, OCEAN LINERS TO CRUISE SHIPS

The directors of the London & South Western Railway made a shrewd purchase when the railway bought the docks at Southampton in 1892. The docks were clearly an expanding facility with connections world-wide and would be a source of rapidly growing freight traffic for the railway. Over the next decade or so, the L&SWR set up a flow of heavy freight trains to Feltham near London, and they built a large hump marshalling yard there so that wagons could be sorted into trains heading to all parts of the country. Other freights left Southampton for Nine Elms yard with cargos for London and the Home Counties.

In 1934, because the docks were struggling to manage the seemingly endless increases in traffic, the Southern Railway opened the so-called New Docks a little north-west of the city centre. This was actually just one straight quay, almost one-and-a-half miles long, built on the edge of about 400 acres of newly

Almost brand new BR 4 4-6-0 75074 slowly crosses Canute Road as it eases a fully-fitted train of vans away from the Eastern Docks on 12 June 1956. Road traffic is held back by two railwaymen with red flags. The man on the left carries the highly polished brass bell that augmented the impact of the flags.

reclaimed land. Beyond that was a huge dry dock that was big enough to handle work on the world's largest ocean-going liners, including the Cunard ships *Queen Mary* and *Queen Elizabeth*. This dock could be seen clearly by passengers in passing trains near Millbrook station. Much more recently an area even further west of the long quay has been developed as a container port. This sits opposite the much smaller original Freightliner yard just west of Millbrook. Both container areas are in constant use.

As the twentieth century came into its latter years, freight handling started changing out of all recognition, as small wagonloads and block trains of perishables such as bananas gave way to the world's largest container ships unloading ISO containers for onward movement by rail and road. Today there is a regular flow of heavy container trains from Millbrook up the main line to Basingstoke and then north through Reading, Didcot and Oxford to the West Midlands and beyond. If the main line is struggling for capacity, some of these trains can be routed through Romsey, turning right before reaching Salisbury so that they take the Laverstock curve

The Western Docks were built by the Southern Railway on a wide strip of land reclaimed from the estuary. They are capable of handling some of the biggest cargo, container and cruise ships. Until the advent of the frequent electric train service on the Bournemouth line from 1967, passenger boat trains could gain access to these docks via a sharp curve just west of Millbrook. Nowadays the main traffic is container trains, but on 19 June 1993 an enthusiasts' special was brought into the Western Docks with 47463 at one end and 37375 at the other. (*Patrick Fitz-Gerald*)

(reopened in the 1980s) and join the West of England main line to reach Basingstoke that way. Freightliner Limited has a locomotive and crew depot at Millbrook, and sends any wagons needing heavier attention to the works at Eastleigh where its own staff can overhaul the wagons.

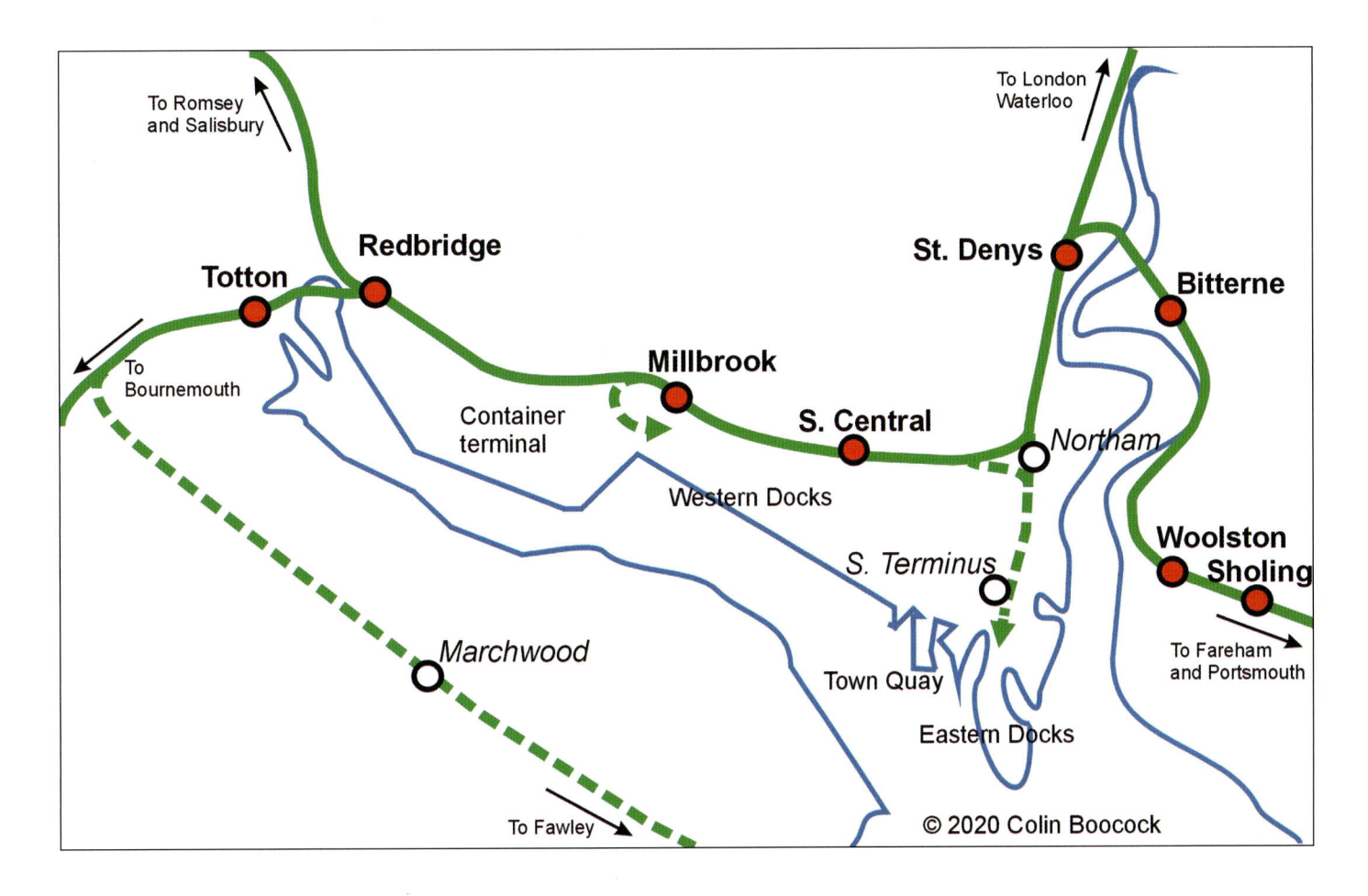

On the passenger side, there has been a similar revolution in the handling of travellers through Southampton Docks. For many decades we were used to frequent departures of Cunard and other liners bound for New York, a popular destination. I knew one or two people who travelled on the *Queen Mary*, for example, just to sample the luxury before hopping off when it called to pick up trans-Atlantic passengers at Le Havre in northern France!

Every Thursday at 4pm, a Union Castle Line ship would leave the New Docks bound for Cape Town and Durban. These were visually distinctive ships in that their hulls were painted a light purple/mauve colour. Each ship was named after a castle somewhere in their range of travels (e.g. *Cape Town Castle*). The service ceased in 1977.

Many other lines had ships departing from Southampton. These shipping lines were honoured when the Southern Railway named its fleet of 'Merchant Navy' class express steam locomotives after them. Also, the more important ocean liner departures were fed by boat trains from London Waterloo. These were usually given the name of the line, such as the Cunarder train that ran whenever either of the 'Queen' ships was due to depart for the USA. These trains sometimes included a de-branded Pullman car for catering and were hauled by 'Lord Nelson' 4-6-0s or Bulleid Pacifics, usually of the 'light' variety. Cunard boat

Map 11 – Southampton

Between the wars, the Southern Railway built the well-known Ocean Terminal in the Eastern Docks at Southampton. This scene shows the liner *RMS Queen Elizabeth* and 30850 *Lord Nelson* which is just pulling away with the London-bound Cunarder boat train formed mainly of Pullman cars. Some quality motor cars are waiting to collect travellers from the liner. (*Dave Peel collection*)

trains were able to platform at the side of the big, SR-built Ocean Terminal building in the Old Docks.

Nowadays, because people normally travel by air for long-haul journeys, the emphasis at Southampton is on accommodating cruise liners, the ocean-going passenger liners being largely a thing of the past now. This is an area of commerce where the Southern Railway's foresight has paid off handsomely. The long straight quay that forms what are now called the Western Docks can service an almost limitless size of cruise ship, which is just as well in view of the enormous size of many of them. Similarly, it enables Southampton to handle the biggest container ships. This part of the world has changed.

Within the Docks, the railway still has a presence. In the 1950s, when a friend and I learned that the best way of getting a sight of the 'foreign' looking USA tank locomotives was to walk straight past the security people at the docks gates looking as if we had every right to be doing that, we did just that. The Old Docks, that became the Eastern Docks under BR's ownership, had myriad railways and sidings that fed every dockside and every freight-handling building and warehouse. By the late 1950s, fourteen 0-6-0Ts were actually not enough for the docks workings. Some former London Brighton & South Coast Railway 0-6-0Ts of classes E1 and E2 were also allocated to the small engine shed there. There were sharp curves within the dock areas round which these engines may have had to give way to the shorter-wheelbase USA 0-6-0Ts, but they were quite at home pulling goods trains between the Eastern and Western Docks. This necessitated their passage along the aptly named Canute Road, passing the very sharply-curved connections into the Town Quay on the way to reach the southernmost gate accessing the Western Docks. To control the fleet of shunting locomotives, Southampton Docks had a railway control centre which used radio to contact the driver on each locomotive as required; each was fitted with an aerial for radio reception. Thus it was rare to find a locomotive just sitting there doing nothing, apart from the ex-LB&SCR locomotives whose need for action appeared to be more intermittent. The steam fleet was replaced from 1962 by fourteen Ruston Hornsby diesel electric 0-6-0s of class 07.

To reach the outside world, longer-distance trains leaving the Old Docks used a gate opposite Southampton Terminus station to cross Canute Road and reach the main line via the triangular junction at Northam. BR soon found that virtually all traffic headed north from there, needing the western side of the triangle very rarely if at all. That side was closed and the track lifted. Both Southampton Terminus and Northam stations had been closed in the mid-1960s as all trains were diverted to use Southampton Central.

It hasn't been just ocean liners and cruise ships that brought passengers into the docks, however. In my youthful days working at Eastleigh, we would use the Southampton to Le Havre or St Malo ferry services to reach France. These were mainly overnight crossings in British Railways ships like the TS *Normannia* (about 5,000 tons displacement), enabling

In the 'Old Docks' in 1955 are two of the fourteen USA 0-6-0Ts that the Southern Railway purchased after the second world war. 30068 (right) is moving a mixed rake of wagons, while its colleague on the left carries duty No 2 as it moves away to engage in yet another shunt. The locomotive crews were centrally controlled by radio to boost their utilisation.

From 1962 BR replaced the USA 0-6-0Ts with the same number of Ruston Paxman diesel hydraulic shunters, three of which are displaying duty numbers 1, 2 and 3 in this late November 1968 view. 'Southern stock green' D2985 is on the left on the same track as rail-blue 2993. (*John H.Bird/Anistr.com*)

us to leave work on a Friday afternoon, wake up next morning in a port on the coast of Normandy, and then to reach Paris or Brittany by train well before lunchtime on the Saturday.

We must not ignore the Isle of Wight ferries either. From Southampton's Town Quay there are still ferries run by Red Funnel Line that head off for Cowes. The Town Quay no longer handles goods traffic, but until the late 1960s it did, and it needed a locomotive with a very short wheelbase to get round its sharp curves. Eastleigh depot supplied a class C14 0-4-0T for this. Occasionally, the operators purloined the departmental one that was supposed to be the Redbridge sleeper depot shunter, No 77S. The rails into the Town Quay stopped being used in 1970 and were lifted many years later. In the absence of anything smaller at Eastleigh depot, I have to assume that the last few years of operation used one of the class 03 or 04 0-6-0 diesels.

For day-to-day passenger traffic, the two main stations in the city were Southampton Terminus and Southampton Central. The Terminus station was the first, opened in 1840 at the southern end of the London & Southampton Railway's main line, just alongside the railway that headed across the nearby Canute Road and into the docks. Initially named just Southampton, the station was renamed in 1858 as Southampton Docks, then again in 1896 as Southampton Town & Docks, then in 1912 as Southampton Town for Docks, and lastly in 1923 as Southampton Terminus (for Docks). It had a substantially built main building in typical style followed by other later stations on the L&SWR,

Southampton Terminus was blessed with six platforms. In this view on 1 May 1956, three Drummond T9s are present. In the centre is 30732 on a stopping service to Bournemouth via the 'Old Road', on the right is a train for Portsmouth & Southsea, and in the foreground is 30310 awaiting a later turn. The tracks in the left background lead to the Eastern Docks. Unusually, both Cunard 'Queen' liners are present, *Queen Mary* on the left and *Queen Elizabeth* on the right.

and which survives intact today as a casino. The station's six platforms, all seemingly curved to fit the restraints of the site, served local trains destined for Portsmouth, Alton, Bournemouth and Salisbury. Before 1895 when Central station opened (as Southampton West), services would have included some express trains to and from London Waterloo.

These local services were steam hauled through most of the Terminus station's life. L&SWR locomotive classes were prominent right through into the early 1960s, together with other SR secondary train types such as the Woolwich Moguls (the Maunsell N and U classes in particular). BR standard types such as class 3 2-6-2Ts and 4 4-6-0s and 2-6-0s became common from 1953 onwards. Dieselisation of the Hampshire area local services took place from 1957.

British Railways closed the Terminus in 1966, surviving local services being diverted to Central station. Over the decades, the commercial centre of Southampton had spread mainly north-westwards, and Central station was just

Southampton as a railway centre was always interesting to behold. Under the magnificent signal gantry at Southampton Central's west end on 10 April 1956 are 34039 *Boscastle* leaving with the daily Brighton to Plymouth through train, 30850 *Lord Nelson* with the 11.30am from Waterloo to Bournemouth, and 30851 *Sir Francis Drake* in the bay waiting to take over a stopping service for Bournemouth.

as convenient for most passengers, if not more so due to the better road access around it.

There once was a station on the western edge of old Southampton called Blechynden that the L&SR opened in 1847. This was replaced by a new station called Southampton West in 1895, doing justice to the main line which now served Bournemouth via the direct route from Brockenhurst through New Milton and Christchurch. When built, Southampton West was right alongside the edge of Southampton Water, but this changed dramatically when land was reclaimed south of the railway to form the foundation for the New Docks. By the early-1930s, railway passenger traffic was increasing such that the SR decided to expand the station to four through platforms and the railway renamed it Southampton Central in 1935. The extra platforms were added on the south side and there is also a west-facing bay platform. A new road approach gave better access to the city centre and the new buildings were of 'modern' Art Deco style in line with the Southern Railway's current thinking. During the war, these new buildings were significantly damaged by enemy action.

When British Railways was formed in 1948, the motive power for main line passenger trains through Southampton were Maunsell 4-6-0s of the 'King Arthur' and 'Lord Nelson' classes, with Bulleid Pacifics gaining ground rapidly on the heaviest of the fast trains, the two-hourly London to Bournemouth and Weymouth expresses which included the all-Pullman train the Bournemouth Belle. Diesel locomotives graced the main line from 1951 to 1955, the three Bulleid 1Co-Co1s being joined in 1953 by the LM 'twins' 10000 and 10001. All five diesels went off to the LM Region early in 1955, never to return. BR class 5 4-6-0s replaced 'King Arthurs' on some of the Bournemouth to London semi-fast trains.

Hampshire diesel units first appeared at Southampton Central when the Salisbury to Portsmouth route was upgraded from 1959. Soon, the Western Region began sending its own diesel mechanical units on some of the Cardiff and Bristol to Portsmouth trains. These latter later included the so-called Inter-City four-car express diesel units that became class 123.

The daily longer-distance cross-country trains from Bournemouth went ultimately to York and Newcastle and to Birkenhead. From 1962 the Pines Express was rerouted off the Somerset & Dorset to run via Basingstoke and Oxford to reach Birmingham New Street and Manchester. BR subsequently greatly increased the offering of long-distance trains. These became regular sights with mark 2 coaches being headed by blue diesels of both hydraulic (Hymek) and electric (33 and 47) varieties.

Third rail electrification came in 1966-1967 with the frequent and faster services of multiple units already described. Today, cross-country trains are hourly rather than daily to Manchester and two-hourly to Newcastle and sometimes beyond; these are Voyager units from CrossCountry. The Cardiff-Bristol-Portsmouth and Brighton trains have for many years been formed by Great Western Railway DMUs of classes 155, 156 and 158, but 165s are being introduced to these services at the time of writing.

BR's input to Central station's architectural desecration was the replacement of the iconic brick-built Up side building and its well-liked clock tower with a long, high, oblong of modernity which was done early in the 1960s; it's now called Overline House. Happily, the splendid Art Deco buildings on the Down side have recently been refurbished to a good standard. Also, resignalling has necessitated the removal of the fine gantry of semaphore signals that graced the western departure end of the station, replaced by multiple aspect signals.

When the Terminus closed, Central station became just Southampton. Between Eastleigh and Swaythling stations, alongside what I knew as

Carrying an incorrect disc headcode on 2 November 1954, 34046 *Braunton* arrives at Southampton Central with the Brighton to Plymouth train. In the background is the western mouth of Southampton tunnel. Just beyond the large building on the right can be seen faintly the railway line that crossed the road at the foot of the hill into Southampton power station. The tall tower in the left background is the Guildhall.

For a busy station, Southampton Central has only four through platforms and one west-facing bay. This 1968 view, soon after electrification, shows the office block known as Overline House that replaced the L&SWR buildings and clock tower. From right to left, a TC+REP+TC formation calls with a semi-fast from Bournemouth to Waterloo, a 'Hampshire' DEMU awaits departure with a Salisbury to Portsmouth train, 4VEP 7701 is on a Waterloo to Bournemouth stopping service and another 'Hampshire' unit heads towards Salisbury.

Eastleigh Airport when I was young, BR built a new two-platform station to serve the airport, by then called Southampton Airport; this new station opened in 1966. Twenty years later, local people were warming to the idea of 'park-and-ride', so the station gained more extensive car parking; it was renamed Southampton Parkway in 1986 and began to take over from Eastleigh station the calls made by semi-fast trains. Yet more expansion of car parking and station facilities has been on-going since then, 'ever upward' as they say, and in 1994 it became Southampton Airport Parkway; this name appears now to be settled as both the airport and 'park-and-ride' are big drawers of passengers to the station. Virtually all trains now call there, and it is indeed a very busy place for a two-platform station. Also in 1994, the name Southampton Central reappeared at the station in the city and reconfirmed what most people still called it anyway. This was an eminently sensible decision because many visitors to the city get confused when their train stops first at a station with Southampton in its name, but that is actually at the airport which is nowhere near the city centre.

Northam station was on the branch to Southampton Terminus, the end stub of the original London & Southampton Railway's main line. Leaving Northam on 12 June 1956 is Collett 0-6-0 3212 with a train from the Didcot, Newbury & Southampton route. The road girder bridge in the background is over the line from Northam Junction to Southampton Central, and the tracks on the left are the third side of the triangle; these latter tracks together with Northam station were lifted and demolished in the 1960s and enabled the main line curve to be eased with a higher speed limit. The tracks on the right lead freight trains towards the Eastern Docks. The wagons stabled there were for Northam gas works.

WR 2-6-0 5330 arrives at Northam station with a train from Didcot to Southampton Terminus on 5 June 1956. Behind the train and to the left are the sharply curved tracks of the main line to Central station.

St Denys station is the junction where Southampton to Portsmouth trains diverge from the London main line. In 1968, a class 33 diesel electric comes off the line from Fareham and Portsmouth with a civil engineer's spoil train.

A new station was built in 1966 to serve the local airport, the old Eastleigh Airport having been upgraded with a paved runway to become Southampton Airport. Since then, the station's passenger facilities have been repeatedly upgraded and enhanced as passenger numbers have grown substantially. Electro-diesel Bo-Bo E6104 passes southbound through Southampton Airport station (now Southampton Airport Parkway) in 1968 with the daily Waterloo to Weymouth Channel Islands boat train.

CHAPTER 10

RAILWAY HUB – EASTLEIGH

'…THE MOST COMPLETE AND UP-TO-DATE WORKS OWNED BY ANY RAILWAY COMPANY….'

In the late nineteenth century, Eastleigh was a hamlet on the west side of the London & Southampton Railway just opposite the village of Bishopstoke which stood on the east side of the railway on the road to Bishop's Waltham. Bishopstoke station was a railway cross-roads; the line from Salisbury and

30857 *Lord Howe* rolls through Eastleigh with the 11.30am Waterloo to Bournemouth semi-fast service on 8 September 1959. The first six coaches which include the kitchen, restaurant and buffet, are one of the eleven comfortable carriage sets provided by O.V.S. Bulleid for the Bournemouth line from 1947. The station is in the background and the bricked slope on the left flanks the ramp up to Campbell Road bridge that gave access to the locomotive works. Two parallel tracks on the right led to and from the steam and diesel traction depots.

Andover via Romsey joined the main line here before heading off to Fareham, Gosport and Portsmouth. In 1891, the L&SWR opened its new carriage works alongside the Bishopstoke Road and adjoining the down goods yard. This works was to replace the cramped one in London at Nine Elms. The facilities were housed mainly in seven large square brick buildings, linked by railway tracks and traversers, each building having its own purpose in the string of activities involved in carriage construction and overhaul.

Bringing so many men and their families down from Nine Elms necessitated construction of housing. There was space around Eastleigh, and the hamlet quickly grew into a small town, very much a railway town with streets of tightly packed red brick terraced houses among which people very quickly formed a community of railway-minded folk. In 1909 and a little south of what was by now called Eastleigh station, in the vee of the junction where the Fareham line struck off to the south-east, the L&SWR's Chief Mechanical Engineer Dugald Drummond was proud to open what he described as 'the most complete and up-to-date works owned by any railway company'. This locomotive works site occupied over forty acres of formerly green field land. With this further influx of employees, some transferred from London and others recruited new, Eastleigh became a borough in its own right, the people elected councillors who in turn elected a mayor to preside. All this was a far

On 3 July 1956, Salisbury depot-based H15 30333 leaves the borough of Eastleigh with an evening freight via Chandler's Ford and Romsey heading towards Salisbury.

RAILWAY HUB – EASTLEIGH • 105

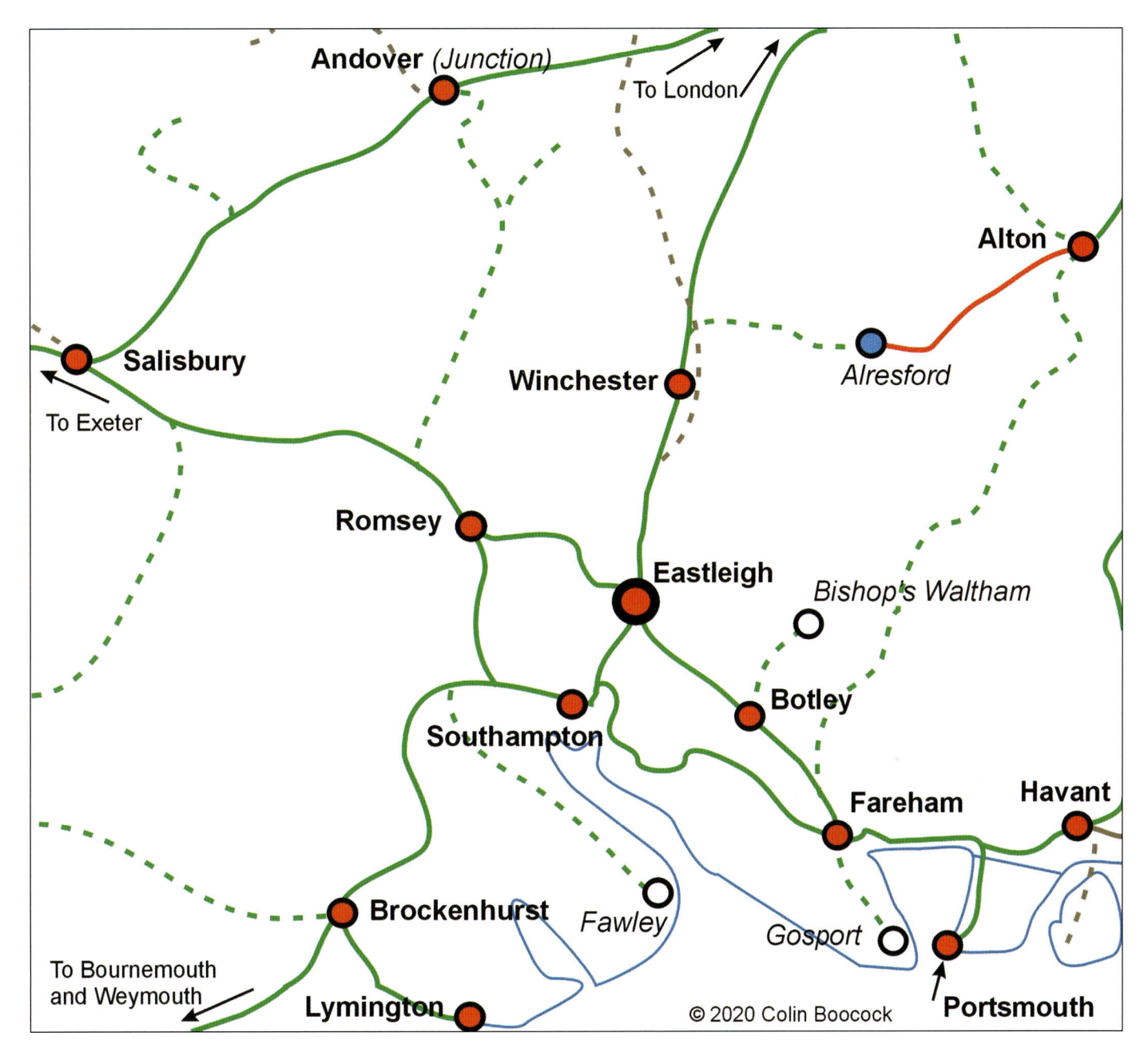

Local stations omitted for clarity.

cry from the quietness of a few decades earlier.

Alongside this activity, Eastleigh station grew until it had four long through platform tracks paired either side of two island platforms. Between all this infrastructure, the main lines passed through straight as a die, aloof from the mundanity of local trains, goods and parcels that kept the operating railway busy here. Even though there were junctions at each end of the station, both of which joined and crossed the main line tracks, high speed was permitted through the station. It was not unusual, even before electric trains took over, to watch a fast Bournemouth express or a Southampton boat train tearing through the station at eighty miles per hour, but well clear of the platforms themselves.

Map 12 – Eastleigh

This was in the Down direction. Up trains had perforce to start from Southampton which was just six miles away; their locomotives were facing sixteen miles of continuous climbing at 1 in 252, not perhaps a steep gradient as such, but a long and gruelling grind for engine and fireman alike. It was the joy of speeding down this long incline that gave the freedom for trains to flash through Eastleigh with apparently gay abandon. Anyone looking in the Up direction and watching an approaching express train would notice how the Bulleid Pacific at the front of a Down express train would roll from side to side as it hit the sharp angle of the Romsey line tracks crossing its own. This was all part of the spectacle. Nowadays, as all trains have to stop at Southampton Airport Parkway station, most Down trains are slowing down before they reach Eastleigh, so we don't see the high speeds there any more.

But back in the 1950s, a heavy freight train from Southampton Docks would approach northbound with the deep pulsating exhaust of the Maunsell or Urie 4-6-0 at the front echoing round the station; the noise would not subside until all sixty wagons had passed through. Southbound, these freights, particularly if they had been marshalled with brake-fitted wagons behind the locomotive, would rattle through at around forty or more miles per hour if faced with clear signals.

Every two hours, one of the Bournemouth semi-fasts would call at a main platform. Usually made up to eleven coaches, people would alight at Eastleigh, some for the town or for Bishopstoke, and others looking for local trains to take them onwards, say to Fareham or Romsey. Other main line stopping trains were irregularly timetabled in steam days, having been put into the table to meet a particular local traffic need.

Nowadays, the pattern is different. Eastleigh, like much of the South Western, has a regular interval service that repeats itself every hour throughout the working day. Unlike in steam days, the station is now ignored by CrossCountry trains and South Western Railway's expresses. Most local travellers prefer to drop off at Southampton Airport Parkway and drive back to Eastleigh. There is a service from London to Portsmouth, introduced in 1990 when conductor rails had been added to the lines converging on Fareham and Portsmouth; this service calls at Eastleigh and then turns off to stop at most stations

On the same line but in the opposite direction, Maunsell H15 30521 approaches the junction with the main line through Eastleigh on 14 June 1956 with a freight from Salisbury.

via Fareham to Portsmouth, a modern echo of the original L&SR way of getting to the Gosport/Portsmouth conurbation. There is also an hourly stopping service from London Waterloo to beyond Southampton that maintains a half-hourly interval with the Portsmouth service. In the Up direction, passengers can change at Winchester or Basingstoke to board faster trains to London that overtake the stopping trains en route.

The other modern innovation is the 'Romsey rocket', its nickname being an example of British sarcasm in view of its slow progress. This is a two-car SWR 158 DMU that starts from Romsey, calls at Chandler's Ford and Eastleigh, stops at all the Southampton stations and then loops back to Romsey via Redbridge and goes on to Salisbury, stopping everywhere on the way. Thus, Eastleigh is still connected, but not as directly as in the more distant past when the York to Bournemouth trains for example used to call there.

Beyond the locomotive works is the traction depot. For seventy years this was a steam depot with a large allocation, often of well over one hundred locomotives. My lodgings were in Southampton Road just opposite the depot. On a Sunday evening in particular, when the depot firelighters were getting steam locomotives lit up and readied for the Monday morning services, a pall of brown smoke would commonly darken the atmosphere here for several hours until the fire grates were hot and steam pressures rising.

Alongside this depot in the late 1950s, a diesel traction depot opened, initially to service and maintain the Hampshire DEMUs. Later this took on maintenance of the Sulzer/Crompton class 33 diesel fleet. This depot was a modern facility, managed by a leg of the SR's M&EE department based in London Bridge, and was deliberately quite separate from the steam depot which was part of the local operating railway with a reporting arm to the M&EE team at Brighton who oversaw the decline and elimination of steam. This thick 'Chinese wall' between the two managements was a neat method of ensuring that old steam people and practices didn't leak across to hinder

The signal gantry across the main line south of Eastleigh station carries the Down advanced starter (with the Stoneham/Swaythling distant below) and the Up outer home and distant signals routing trains into or through the three northbound passenger tracks at the station. On 12 July 1956, B4 0-4-0 dock tank 30087 was waddling down the main line to take up a duty in Southampton, possibly in the Docks or on the Town Quay.

progress with the new, modern diesel traction on the Southern. As a result of this philosophy, the Southern's and South Western's modern traction reliability has been second to none through most of my adult life.

Eastleigh station lost its Up loop line and platform around the time of electrification. The absence of trains going to Didcot, Alton and Andover facilitated this closure, which in turn made space for a better circulating area around the station entrance.

In more modern times, on 19 July 2005, Freightliner Ltd's 66620 approaches Eastleigh station with a train of road vehicles from Southampton Western Docks to the north. The two foreground tracks lead to and from the electric traction depot and sidings.

This April 1960 view of the inside of one of the four bays of Eastleigh Locomotive Works erecting shop shows steam locomotives of Bulleid, Maunsell and Riddles genres undergoing overhaul.

By 1967, a very great reduction had occurred in locomotive overhaul work right across BR after Dr Beeching's route rationalisations and as steam locomotives disappeared. The new plan saw the work of Eastleigh carriage works transferred to a thoroughly rebuilt facility within the locomotive works' walls and site. The carriage works had ceased building new stock around 1962 and had then concentrated on overhauling all the Southern Region's coaching stock. These overhauls were organised on a 'progressive' basis, that is carriages were moved from stage to stage through many of the seven buildings as work on them progressed, the heaviest overhauls visiting forty-four stages in all. A new carriage repair layout was laid down in the former locomotive works, and by the end of 1967 was achieving overhauls at the same rate as before but through only twenty-two stages for the same output. This productivity improvement enabled the number of coaches on the works premises to be reduced from 330 in 1966 to just over 110 in 1968, giving the SR over 200 more carriages for its operations. The buildings of the old carriage works are now the foundation of an active industrial estate.

Eastleigh works closed in 2006 because its lessee, the French train builder and maintainer Alstom, failed to get the contract for replacing the slam door stock used by the South West Trains franchise, the new stock instead being supplied by Siemens. Alstom auctioned off all the equipment it could, leaving the works buildings practically empty, other than the fifty-tons capacity overhead cranes in the erecting shop bays which it regarded as uneconomic to dismantle.

New life entered the Eastleigh Works story just a year later. Knights Rail Services leased part of the works, initially for renting out tracks for covered storage of rail vehicles that were off-lease, and

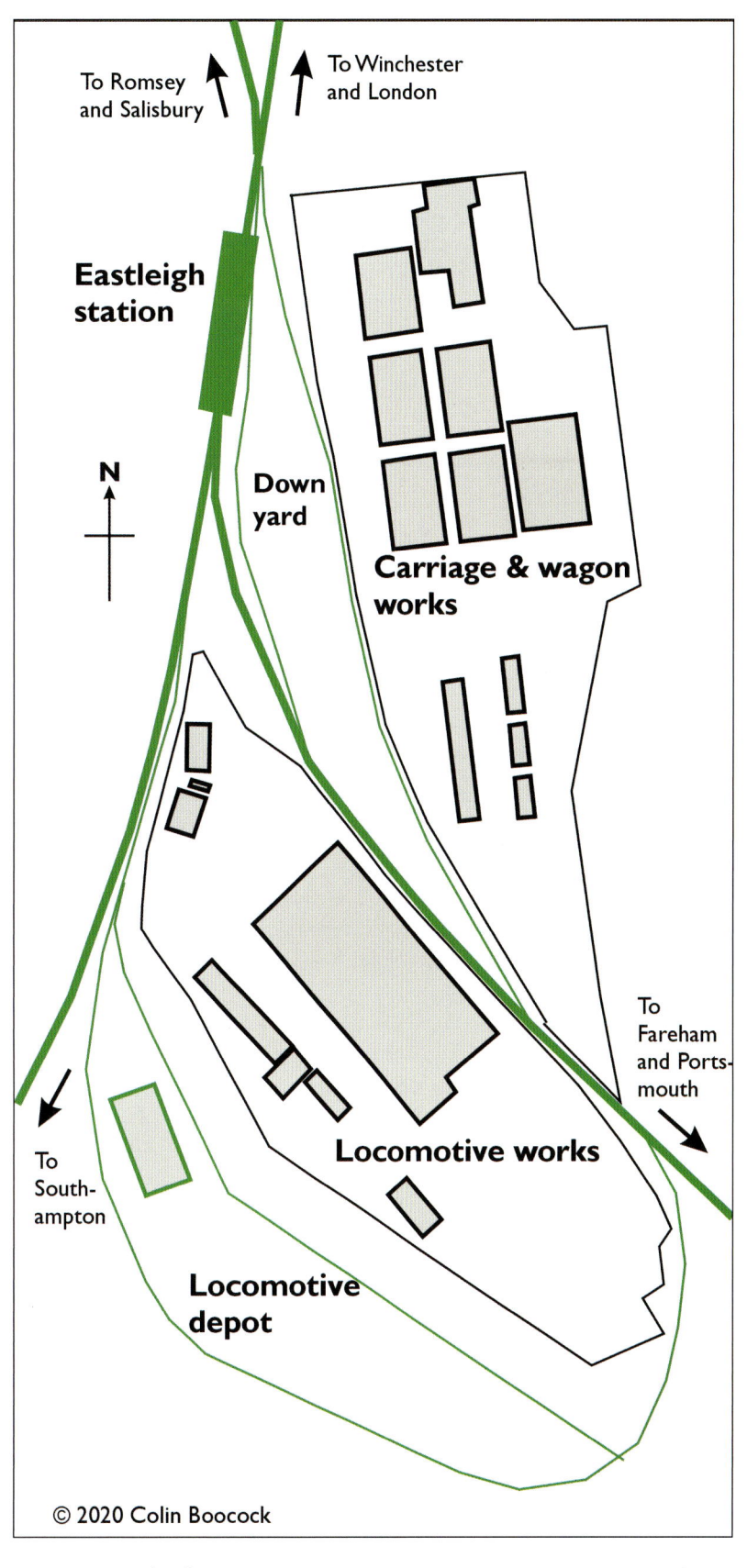

Figure 3 – Eastleigh pre-1967.

The southern throat of Eastleigh station on 19 July 2005 hosts a Waterloo to Portsmouth train formed of two Siemens class 444 EMUs turning off the main line and heading towards Fareham. A South West Trains class 170 DMU arrives on a Totton to Romsey stopping service. In the background is the Eastleigh Works complex that was being slowly abandoned by its lessor, Alstom. Thankfully, the works was taken over in 2007 by Knights Rail Services and has since become a useful centre for overhaul, refurbishment, repair and storage of trains of all kinds; it's now under the management of Arlington Fleet Group Ltd.

subsequently to allow other companies to use the premises to do work on locomotives, carriages or wagons using the rented tracks, access pits and overhead cranes. Knights Rail Services had had to re-equip the leased areas with everything needed, including electricity outlets, heating, lighting and all services, so this was quite an adventure. The adventure paid off however, and ironically Siemens has since decided to use Eastleigh Works for the overhaul and refurbishment of its own classes 444 and 450 EMUs. Arlington Fleet Group Ltd is the current principal occupier of the works now and has added to the railway activities there.

When I began working in Eastleigh Locomotive Works in 1954, it provided employment for around 2,500 people; the carriage works was similar. By the end of 1967, the combined works had less than 3,000 employees. Today, less than 300 people work there, but others are often drafted in with repair or overhaul work by firms happy to use the facility, often on a short-term basis.

Despite Eastleigh Works' railway-locked situation, its location just beyond the north end of the airport runway, and the dog-legged road bridge in Campbell Road which is the only way road vehicles can get to the site, the works is still functioning. The site is not suitable for residential development because of the frequent low overflying of aircraft, and its prospects as an industrial estate are severely limited by that awful road bridge which articulated lorries negotiate with extreme difficulty. As a railway works with direct access to a main line railway system, the prognosis is much more positive!

Knights Rail Services leased part of the redundant Eastleigh Works from 2007 to enable off-lease rolling stock to be stored and for overhauls and repairs to be undertaken by companies who could bring in their own manpower, or by Arlington Fleet Services staff on site. On 4 September 2008, Colas Rail's Co-Co 47739 was being overhauled by Wabtec in Eastleigh's erecting shop. The overhead cranes were in position to lift the locomotive back on its bogies.

CHAPTER 11

RAILWAY HUB – BOURNEMOUTH
FROM FISHING VILLAGE TO CONURBATION

About a year after our family had moved to Bournemouth in 1945, a friend invited me to his house after school. The rear garden backed on to the railway just east of Cleveland Road overbridge. What I saw that day influenced my life for ever! Shortly after 4.45pm, I heard the sound of a train approaching at relatively slow speed though accelerating steadily. A plume of grey smoke appeared beyond the top of the bridge. Then suddenly a bright

Bournemouth West terminus was closed in 1965 in readiness for electrification, which included converting the nearby carriage sidings into an EMU maintenance depot. On 21 April 1956, 35018 *British India Line* makes a sure-footed start with the Up Bournemouth Belle.

malachite green 'Merchant Navy' 4-6-2 burst through the bridge, billowing clouds of dense smoke and followed by twelve clean brown-and-cream Pullman coaches. This was my first sighting of the Bournemouth Belle, and I was hooked!

The 'Belle' had been reintroduced in 1946. Its purpose was to tap the wealth of many of Bournemouth's more affluent citizens by offering a luxury style of travel for which they would pay a premium on top of the normal train fare. The train left London Waterloo seven days a week at 12:30pm, calling at Southampton Central on the way and taking two hours ten minutes to reach Bournemouth Central station, site of the 108 milepost. The train then went forward for the three-and-a-half miles to Bournemouth West where it terminated at around 2.55pm.

After the clientele had disembarked at Bournemouth West, the station shunting engine, usually an Adams O2 or Drummond M7 0-4-4T, headed the train up the 1 in 90 gradient to the carriage sidings for servicing (banked by the train engine); after 1956 the approach included a slow haul through the new carriage washing plant on the way. After banking the heavy train to the sidings, and as the 'Belle' was due to leave Bournemouth West at 4.34pm on its return journey to London Waterloo, it was deemed that there was insufficient time to send the 'Merchant Navy' Pacific off to Bournemouth Central depot for servicing and turning, as was normal practice with other train engines. The locomotive was instead run up the hill light engine to Branksome for turning on the triangle there, the Branksome sub-depot's turntable being too short to turn such a big locomotive. There was time then to service the engine and take on water before its return journey.

After the train had been prepared for its Up journey, the station shunting 0-4-4T hauled it back into Bournemouth West

On 23 March 1957, the Bournemouth Belle's Pullman cars are slowly propelled through the new carriage washing machine outside Bournemouth West.

This view across the Up end of Bournemouth Central station on 21 August 1951 shows the day that 'Britannia' 4-6-2 70009 *Alfred the Great* was rostered to haul the Up Royal Wessex service from Weymouth to Waterloo. The opposite, Down, platform end was the point where the town's fish traffic was unloaded at night from railway wagons for local distribution. (*Alan Trickett collection*)

ready for departure, and the 'Merchant Navy' backed on and coupled up. Departure at 4.34pm was assisted by the 0-4-4T pushing manfully at the rear until that engine could ease back and stop before reaching the starting signal at the outer end of the platform.

By 4.42 or 4.43pm, the train had arrived in Bournemouth Central. That station had well-prepared its passengers by announcing three times which carriage would stop where, for example '…coach C opposite the subway, coach D by the main entrance, coach E by the refreshment rooms…'. With between nine and twelve heavy twelve-wheeled Pullman cars on the train and the front few standing tight on the curve, getting that lot under way, all with plain bearing axleboxes, was no mean task. Bulleid's Pacific had to be carefully coaxed by the driver to keep wheelslip to a minimum. Nonetheless, this train was scheduled to reach Waterloo in the same two hours and ten minutes as the other fast trains on this route. Indeed, from the mid-1950s, the schedule of all these fast trains was cut to a straight two hours, a challenging timing that was regularly kept.

In the days of steam, Bournemouth Central was a railway observer's paradise. All Up departures could be watched from the main Down platform, the second longest in the UK after that which linked Manchester Victoria and Exchange stations; if one then walked westwards along the platform to what we knew as the 'western extension' beyond the scissors crossing that facilitated train movements into and out of either section of the long platform, we could watch all the movements of locomotives in and around the depot as well. Many of the Up trains provided their own spectacle. The first portion of a fast train to arrive would be that from Bournemouth West, which usually consisted of one of the excellent Bulleid six-car sets that included restaurant and buffet facilities. The station shunter, normally M7 0-4-4T 30112 or occasionally 30318, would attach to the rear and drag the carriages, complete with passengers on board, into the long siding between the Up main line and the engine sheds. The portion from Weymouth would then arrive, usually hauled by a Bulleid Pacific, rolling in with between four and seven coaches behind it. The M7 would then attempt to attach the West portion to the rear of the Weymouth portion by propelling it gently. A key difficulty was that the buckeye couplings occasionally refused to engage at the first impact, necessitating one or more extra attempts, usually resulting in an almighty 'clang' as the portions came together – I never heard of any passengers claiming for whiplash, though!

Most of the Up semi-fast trains on the other hand were complete trains of ten or eleven coaches from Bournemouth West, which was just as well as they didn't then have to spend so much time on the portion-joining process, but their timings to Waterloo were slower

From the Down platform extension at Bournemouth Central observers could watch almost everything going on at the steam locomotive depot there. This view on 28 March 1959 shows the former L&SWR engine shed; the Southern Railway attached a similar length extension to the west end of the engine shed, off left in this picture. To the right, also off the picture, are the sidings for ash disposal, coaling and watering locomotives and the turntable which was powered by vacuum created by the locomotive being turned. On the left in this view is 34065 *Hurricane* and a rebuilt version, 34045 *Ottery St. Mary*.

as they included about eight more stops en route than did the expresses. Their locomotives were a mixture of anything from a Bullied Pacific or 'Lord Nelson' to a Maunsell 'King Arthur', and from the early 1960s 'Schools' class 4-4-0s released by the Kent Coast electrification. BR class 5 4-6-0s joined the team in the late-1950s.

There were two principal cross-country trains as well, loading to between nine and twelve carriages. One came south from Newcastle (or just York in the winter) and the other from Birkenhead Woodside.

Local enthusiasts looked out for the through Brighton train which often had an Atlantic at its head. Summer Saturdays brought many extra trains to the resort, and more unusual locomotives appeared from time to time. H15s and S15s were not so unusual on relief trains, but the occasional appearance of a 'Remembrance' N15X 4-6-0 raised excitement levels.

By comparison, Bournemouth West was a much quieter station at which to watch train movements. The extra interest here was that it was the southern terminus of the Somerset & Dorset line's services from Bristol and Bath. Chapter 17 tells more about the S&D line.

The 'Beeching era' saw several closures of train services that used to use Bournemouth West. No longer did stopping trains arrive from Salisbury via West Moors. The M7-worked push-pull trains from Brockenhurst via Wimborne and Poole ceased as well. The S&D closed in 1966. Bournemouth West itself succumbed to the cuts, as did Boscombe station, between Central and Pokesdown.

Map 13 – Bournemouth.

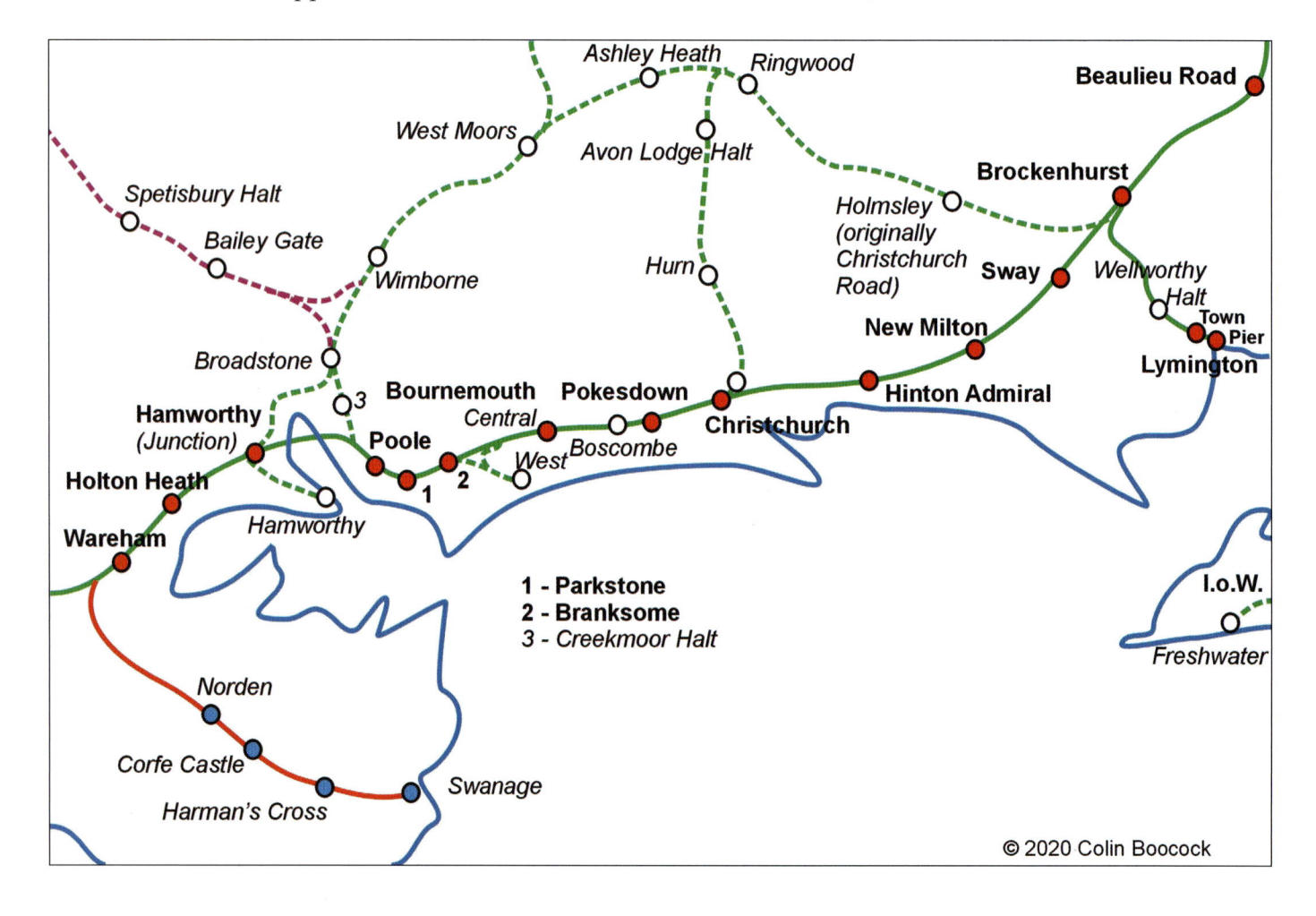

RAILWAY HUB – BOURNEMOUTH • 117

Electrification brought big changes to the railway scene in Bournemouth. The Central station's two through tracks were taken up, the Up main line approach was shifted to take the place of the siding on which the portions used to wait prior to coupling up. This in turn made space for two dead-end sidings between the main lines that could each take two four-car electric multiple units to act as a turn-back facility. Using multiple units and push-pull operation, the pattern eventually settled into a four-car REP power set, sometimes with a 4TC trailer set, waiting in the Up platform until a four or eight-car TC train arrived from Weymouth propelled by a class 33/1 diesel. Electrification to Weymouth took place in the late-1980s, whence brand new five-car express class 442 EMUs usually worked these trains. Later, Siemens five-car class 444s replaced the 442s, and four-car 450s replaced the unloved 4VEPs on slower services.

Bigger changes took place at what was Bournemouth West in readiness for electrification in 1966-1967. The former carriage sidings and depot were demolished and replaced by a new purpose-designed electric multiple unit maintenance and servicing depot.

At electrification in 1966/1967, the through tracks at the west end of Bournemouth Central were converted to turn-back sidings with facilities for train interior cleaning. This 1993 view shows a Network SouthEast class 442 EMU (left) being prepared for the next Up train to Waterloo, and a Midland Cross-Country HST undertaking its brief turnround before heading back to the north of England. On the right, a class 442 arrives from Weymouth on a London service; at this point, the Up main line is on the site of the former siding used in steam days for holding the rear portions of Waterloo-bound trains ready for propelling towards and coupling to the front portion that had just arrived from Weymouth.

At Bournemouth Central, the overall roof has been fully refurbished and new glazing and end screens installed. On 10 November 2007, a South West Trains class 444 from Weymouth (left) is about to couple to a strengthening unit to form an Up service to London. At the Down platform is another 444 on a working to Weymouth.

Branksome sub-shed was no longer needed, and neither was a complete triangle of lines there. The eastern side of the triangle was closed, illogically in my view since the direct route's lofty brick viaduct over the Bourne valley remains intact as a listed structure. This enabled closure of the signalboxes at Gas Works Junction and Bournemouth West Junction. Electric units needing access to the depot have to stop in Branksome station first, then reverse down the branch to the depot. Until the 1988 electrification to Weymouth, Branksome was the westernmost end of the South Western's conductor rail system.

The Bournemouth West station site is now largely occupied by the A338 Wessex

Over twelve years later, Bournemouth Central is still in pristine condition, thanks to Network Rail's efforts at maintaining its structures. On 14 December 2019, a class 221 CrossCountry 'Voyager' was ready to start away with the 12.46 to Manchester Piccadilly, part of the hourly service to the north that Bournemouth now enjoys.

Way arterial road that was built to link the A31 at Ringwood with points west into Dorset and cuts a swathe right through the middle of Bournemouth, mainly for the convenience of the motor car.

At about the time of electrification, the station at Poole was moved further west round the sharp curve that takes the Bournemouth-Weymouth line through the town centre. By then, the Poole Quay branch line that brought Adams B4 0-4-0Ts through the streets to the quayside had closed, as had the pottery behind Parkstone station that used to grace the former goods yard there with its little green Peckett 0-4-0ST *George Jennings* that dated from 1902. From Hamworthy Junction, a single line branch line still runs towards an industrial site around Hamworthy Quay, on the opposite side of the estuary from Poole Quay. The branch used to be shunted by a B4 tank, with any

The town of Poole used to become jammed with traffic when trains blocked two roads at level crossings. The 1960s road bridge in the background of this summer 1983 view of the station enabled the crossings to be closed to road vehicles. 33108 arrives with two 4TC trailer units destined for Weymouth.

SR goods engine working the trains down the branch. The quay itself was the haunt of two 1949-built Robert Stephenson & Hawthorne 0-4-0STs, *Bonnie Prince Charlie* and *Western Pride*. Nowadays, the observer mainly sees class 66 Co-Co diesels taking freight along the branch, or the occasional class 60 or 70, though traffic can be very sporadic with nothing for months on end.

The South East Dorset conurbation consists today of the former boroughs of Bournemouth, Christchurch and Poole. With a 2018 population of 396,000, more than many cities in the UK, it is still strange to contemplate that the first railway builders ignored Bournemouth completely, focusing on getting to Dorchester and beyond, throwing off a desultory branch line to reach Poole Harbour and another even less significant branch along the Avon valley to Christchurch. In the arch above the exit from the main Up platform at Bournemouth Central station is inscribed the date 1885. Actually, it wasn't until 1888 that Bournemouth's direct railway route to London was completed along the alignment that exists today. Only then would Bournemouth Central's cavernous overall roof echo to the hiss and clatter of main line trains direct from London Waterloo. Initially, both platforms were of equal length. The western extension to the Down platform was a later addition to cater for the growing number of trains as traffic increased.

So the remote fishing village that was clustered around the mouth of the short stream that locals called the River Bourne has grown in less than 200 years to become the centre of one of the south coast's biggest urban areas. We have to thank the railway for its part in making that growth possible.

RAILWAY HUB – BOURNEMOUTH • 121

The eastern approach to Bournemouth was via Christchurch, Pokesdown and Boscombe stations. This is Pokesdown, near the top of the 1 in 99 bank from the Stour valley. Class 47 Co-Co D1719 displaying the headcode for an unfitted freight train was in charge of the Down Bournemouth Belle in this 1967 view. In the 1970s, the centre through tracks here were lifted and the loop tracks realigned for fast running.

On 13 March 1955, 34109 *Sir Trafford Leigh Mallory* restarts an Up Bournemouth West to Waterloo semi-fast service from Christchurch station. At that time, the foreground siding, since lifted, still had a cattle pen.

34106 *Lydford*, calling at Branksome on 14 April 1957 with the Weymouth portion of a train to Waterloo, is routed to the right hand tracks which lead towards Bournemouth Central. The left hand tracks are for Bournemouth West.

CHAPTER 12

RAILWAY HUB – SALISBURY
THE CITY OF SARUM

Every centre has its claim to fame and most claims are positive. The cathedral city of Salisbury unfortunately became a negative victim to its station's track curvature with the Plymouth boat train accident referred to in an earlier chapter. The curve is at the east end of the station and affects all of its four main line platforms and also the former bay at the east end of the Down platform. Apart from the accident there, the curve also posed a challenge to steam locomotive drivers starting heavy Up expresses from the station. The binding of wheels on the sharp curve, combined with the 'stiction' effect of trains having plain bearing axleboxes, often made it hard for Pacific locomotives to get away from Salisbury without wheelslip, a situation similar to that at Bournemouth Central.

The main station buildings at Salisbury are on the south side of the railway and

On 27 April 1957, Bulleid 'Merchant Navy' class 4-6-2 35006 *Peninsular & Oriental S.N. Co.* restarts an Exeter to Waterloo express out of Salisbury, the tightness of the curve causing the carriages to bind such that the driver has the steam sanders working to help control wheel slip. In the bay platform on the left, T9 4-4-0 30702 awaits departure with a stopping train to Bournemouth West via West Moors.

At the other end of Salisbury station, WR 'Hall' class 4-6-0 6946 *Heatherden Hall*, has taken over the 5.2pm train to Cardiff from a Southern engine that brought the train from Portsmouth.

are Grade II listed as a fine example of L&SWR large station architecture. Before Salisbury tunnel was built in 1859, the railway from London terminated at a station at Milford in the south-east of the city. The tunnel enabled trains from the east, including those from the Southampton and Eastleigh directions, to reach the new station adjacent to the city centre. Milford station became a goods depot and survived as such until BR closed it in 1967.

East of Salisbury tunnel is Tunnel Junction, where the line from Romsey joins the main line. Romsey in turn receives trains from Southampton via Redbridge and from Eastleigh via Chandler's Ford. This junction also used to receive local trains from Bournemouth that meandered via Poole, Wimborne and West Moors to join the Romsey line at Alderbury Junction not far from Salisbury. The latter route succumbed when Dr Beeching was around.

The Great Western Railway confused matters back in the in the 1850s by building a 7ft 0¼in gauge branch line from Westbury to Salisbury, terminating in its own covered station parallel to and north of the L&SWR station. The GWR line ran parallel to the South Western main line from Wilton to Salisbury but made no connection with the main line until it arrived in Salisbury. Common

RAILWAY HUB – SALISBURY • **125**

Arriving at Salisbury from the former GWR tracks on 30 July 1954 is Churchward 2-8-0 2879 with a long train mainly of coal wagons from South Wales. Some would be domestic coal, and some for the two locomotive depots.

Map 14 – Salisbury

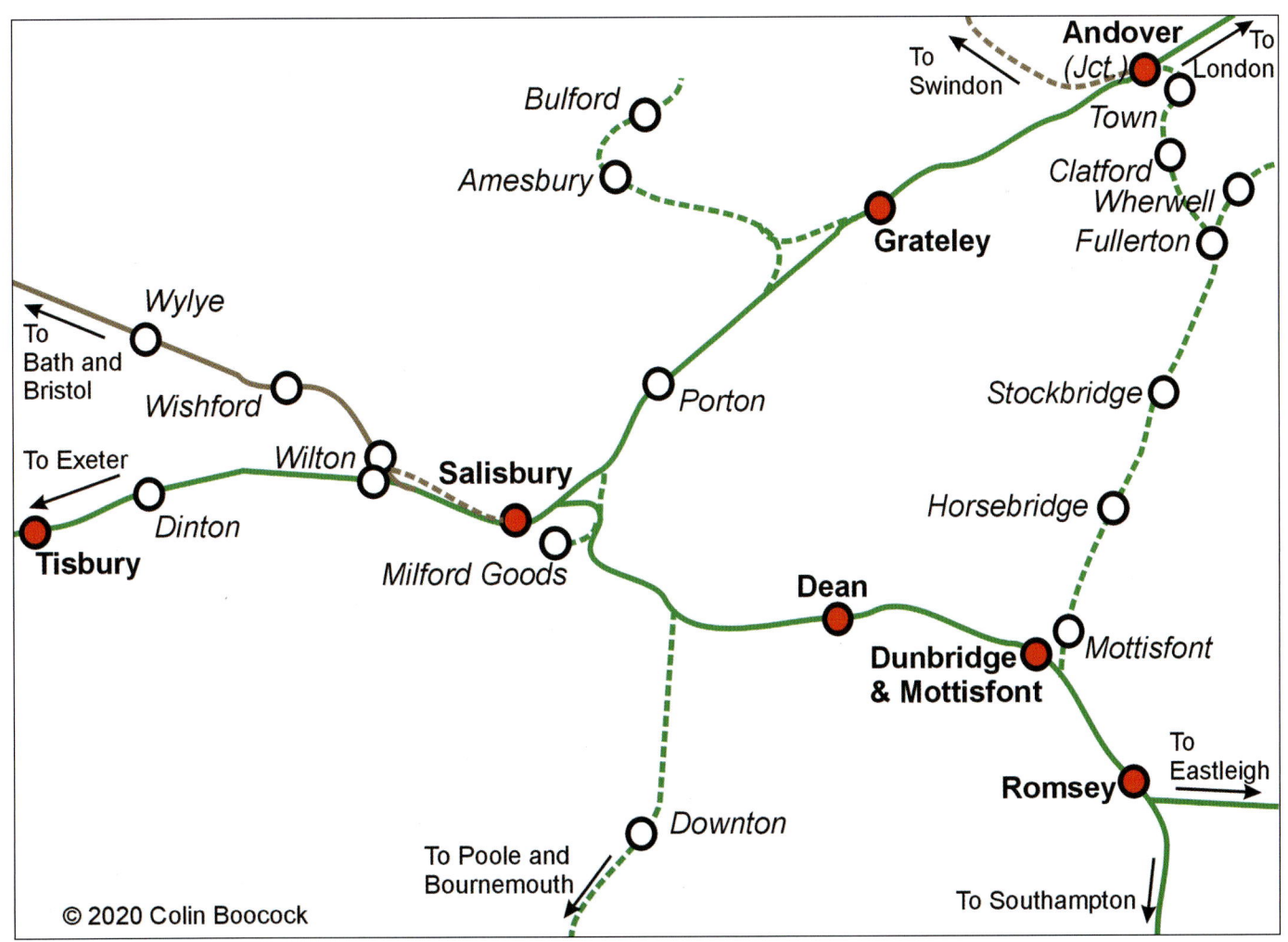

© 2020 Colin Boocock

sense eventually held sway; by 1874, the GWR had converted its branch to 4ft 8½in gauge, and the two railways began to co-operate by running through trains between Cardiff, Bristol and Portsmouth and by exchanging freight trains between their systems in the Salisbury station area. BR finally sorted out the Wilton situation by laying a junction there allowing trains to come off the Westbury line straight on to the former SR main line tracks. The parallel running then ceased with the lifting of the former GWR tracks into Salisbury.

Salisbury station has four through tracks arranged two Up and two Down; there was a bay platform set into the east end of the main Down platform from which trains for Bournemouth and Portsmouth used to arrive and leave. At the west end there was also a bay platform alongside the main Down platform; that is now a siding.

North of the main station the former GWR station became a goods depot, so Salisbury had goods facilities well scattered around the city, *viz* Milford, Fisherton where there were once passenger platforms east of the main station, and the GWR station area. They all disappeared as BR got to grips with rationalising its assets here. Now the area north of and parallel to Salisbury station is a modern depot for the maintenance and servicing of SWR's classes 159 and 158 DMU fleet.

To many enthusiast visitors watching steam operations it was the Cardiff-Portsmouth trains that made Salisbury station interesting. Even in BR days, the two Regions' steam locomotives did not work through. A train arriving from the Bristol direction would stop in the northernmost Up platform and its ex-GWR engine, usually a 'Hall' class 4-6-0, would uncouple and run off, eventually to reach the former GWR depot for turning and servicing. Meanwhile, a member of the station shunter staff would walk along the side of the train 'pulling the strings', railway shorthand for releasing the vacuum trapped above the piston in each vacuum brake cylinder. This was essential because the GWR, alone in the UK, worked its trains with 25inches of vacuum (measured theoretically as the height of a column of mercury that that vacuum could support).

In 1991 the Up bay platform is host to a 'Hampshire' DEMU stopping service from Portsmouth & Southsea while a pair of WR class 155 and 158 DMUs leaves on a Cardiff to Portsmouth Harbour limited-stop working. The sharpness of the curve along which the WR train is leaving was the cause of the well-known accident in 1906 when a Drummond L12 4-4-0 overturned because it was travelling at 60mph, around three times the speed limit.

Everyone else used 21inches of vacuum. If a Southern engine took over a train which had not gone through this operation, the driver might not be able to release all the brakes on the train. An SR locomotive, frequently a Maunsell U class or BR standard class 4 Mogul, was ready to back on to the train, couple up and take it away, so long as the brake continuity test proved the engine's ability to apply and release the brakes. At this distance I cannot recall how long this process took, but it seemed to be anything up to fifteen minutes, a serious obstruction to competitive running times!

After all these decades of daftness, common sense had appeared by the time these trains were dieselised, initially with DMUs, and later with mark 1 coaches hauled by 'Hymek' B-B diesel hydraulics, all of which worked right through between Cardiff, Bristol and Portsmouth. During the 1960s, the SR had surplus BRCW Type 3s, class 33s in more modern parlance, and these took over the workings enabling the trains to be electrically heated, not before some had been worked by 'Hampshire' diesel electric sets, though. Also in steam days there were the two through trains from Brighton that appeared at Salisbury behind Bulleid light Pacifics. The one bound for Plymouth would carry on happily westwards with the SR locomotive, but that going to Cardiff had to endure the engine change at Salisbury in both directions.

Nowadays the Cardiff-Bristol-Portsmouth and Brighton services are run by the Great Western Railway franchise using 165 and 166 DMUs. So Salisbury today is pretty well a 100 per cent diesel multiple unit railway. The current train service is very popular and well used.

I should have mentioned earlier the two steam locomotive depots at Salisbury that continued into BR days until sensible rationalisation closed the GWR one and moved everything across the line to the larger SR one south of the main line. After its closure, two steam locomotives sat temporarily stored in the GWR shed for a year or so, namely the preserved Adams T3 4-4-0 563 and the Stroudley 'Terrier' A1 0-6-0T 82 *Boxhill*. These were later moved away and kept at Tweedmouth depot (target practice for the pigeons there) until cosmetically restored at Eastleigh

The former GWR locomotive depot had closed by the time this photograph was taken in 1954. It shows two preserved locomotives in temporary store there. On the left is Stroudley A1X 0-6-0T 82 *Boxhill*, and in front of that, L&SWR Adams 4-4-0 563. By then all working locomotives were serviced at the former SR depot across the main line.

Locomotive Works and put on display in the new railway museum at Clapham, London.

The SR depot was by far the bigger of the two and served not only the Waterloo-Exeter main line but contributed locomotives such as early H15 4-6-0s for cross-country freights. Its final, sad, duty was to be one of the two collecting points for redundant steam locomotives on the evening of 9 July 1967, part of the Southern Region's publicity bid to ensure that from the next morning most travellers would never again see a steam locomotive on their 'modern' railway!

This 2006 view of the west end of Salisbury station shows in the left background the new maintenance depot for DMUs that was built in the early 1990s on the site of the former GWR station and yard. On the right, two class 159s have arrived from London Waterloo.

The approach to Salisbury from the east is through Salisbury Tunnel, from which is emerging DMU 155329 on a Portsmouth to Cardiff working. The date is 17 September 1991.

CHAPTER 13

RAILWAY HUB – EXETER
EITHER WAY TO LONDON

Exeter and Plymouth were the places where the L&SWR depended on the Great Western for short distances of running rights to get its trains to their ultimate destinations. Both provided passengers and enthusiasts alike with some potentially confusing directional eccentricities.

Exeter Central, the Southern station in the city centre, was well placed for potential passengers arriving by bus or foot, being close to the shopping and commercial areas. The former GWR station, down in the adjacent valley, was on the edge of the city, not so well placed, except perhaps in modern times when motor car ownership enables people to park outside the city centre and catch trains without having to negotiate what can be quite difficult traffic conditions.

When the L&SWR's main line was being extended westwards, the GWR's London Paddington to Plymouth main line was in the way at St David's station[9]. The L&SWR already owned the Exeter & Crediton Railway, which turned off the GWR westwards at Cowley Bridge Junction north of the city, so it was logical to link the two stations to create a through route that would serve mid-Devon and eventually reach Plymouth. The difference in levels between the two stations necessitated a steep gradient of 1 in 37 between the two, and the topography of the area required much of that gradient to be in tunnel, so linking the stations in this way wasn't a cheap option, neither to build nor to operate.

Exeter Central station began life as Queen Street, but its present size was established in 1933 when the SR rebuilt and extended it following a fire in the timber buildings, at the same time renaming it Exeter Central. Until 1969, there were four tracks between the two long through platforms and a bay platform at the east end of each, making four platforms in all. The two centre tracks were removed in 1969.

By the time BR inherited the Southern Railway's system in 1948, trains to London Waterloo from Exeter were mainly expresses made up of around ten to thirteen coaches and hauled by Maunsell 4-6-0s of 'King Arthur' type or by Bulleid's new Pacifics. The longest train was the Atlantic Coast Express which often left London with up to fifteen coaches, many of which were to be detached en route to serve multiple destinations.

Local and stopping trains going east towards Yeovil and Salisbury were headed by S15 4-6-0s, 'Woolwich' Moguls or Drummond 4-4-0s. Most expresses came from further west but arrived with much shorter formations of two to eight coaches with extra vehicles being added at Exeter Central while the train engines were being changed. These trains had come variously from Plymouth Friary, Ilfracombe, Bude,

---

9. Organisations differ as to whether to include the apostrophe. The National Rail website shows it in place, but the GWR website omits it as do most maps. I include it because it is almost certain that the station's name refers only to one St David.

In 1951, but still in the former Southern Railway malachite green livery although built by BR in 1948, 'Merchant Navy' 4-6-2 35023 *Holland-Afrika Line* waits at Exeter Central with a couple of strengthening coaches to take over the Up Atlantic Coast Express for its journey to London Waterloo. Portions from Plymouth, Ilfracombe and Padstow are yet to arrive to make up this quite complicated train. (*Robin Russell/David Peel collection*)

On 4 September 1964, 34015 *Exmouth* has taken over the Padstow portion of the Down Atlantic Coast Express at Exeter Central. The two 0-6-0 pannier tanks on the Up through track are banking engines awaiting a path back down to St David's station. (*John H. Bird/Anistr.com*)

Torrington or Padstow, headed in the main by Maunsell 2-6-0s or T9 4-4-0s, but the new 'West Country' class locomotives were rapidly gaining ground here as this was the original purpose of their construction. As BR progressed, standard class 4 4-6-0s appeared on secondary trains on the main line.

To get these trains up the hill from St David's station required them to be banked, for which duty there was a small fleet of class E1/R 0-6-2Ts; these were Stroudley E1 0-6-0Ts that had each been extended with a new cab and bunker and a pair of radial wheels in the extended frame. These would sit in a siding north of St David's station until a SR train arrived from Cowley Bridge Junction, and one would then buffer up to the rear of the train in readiness for the climb. The

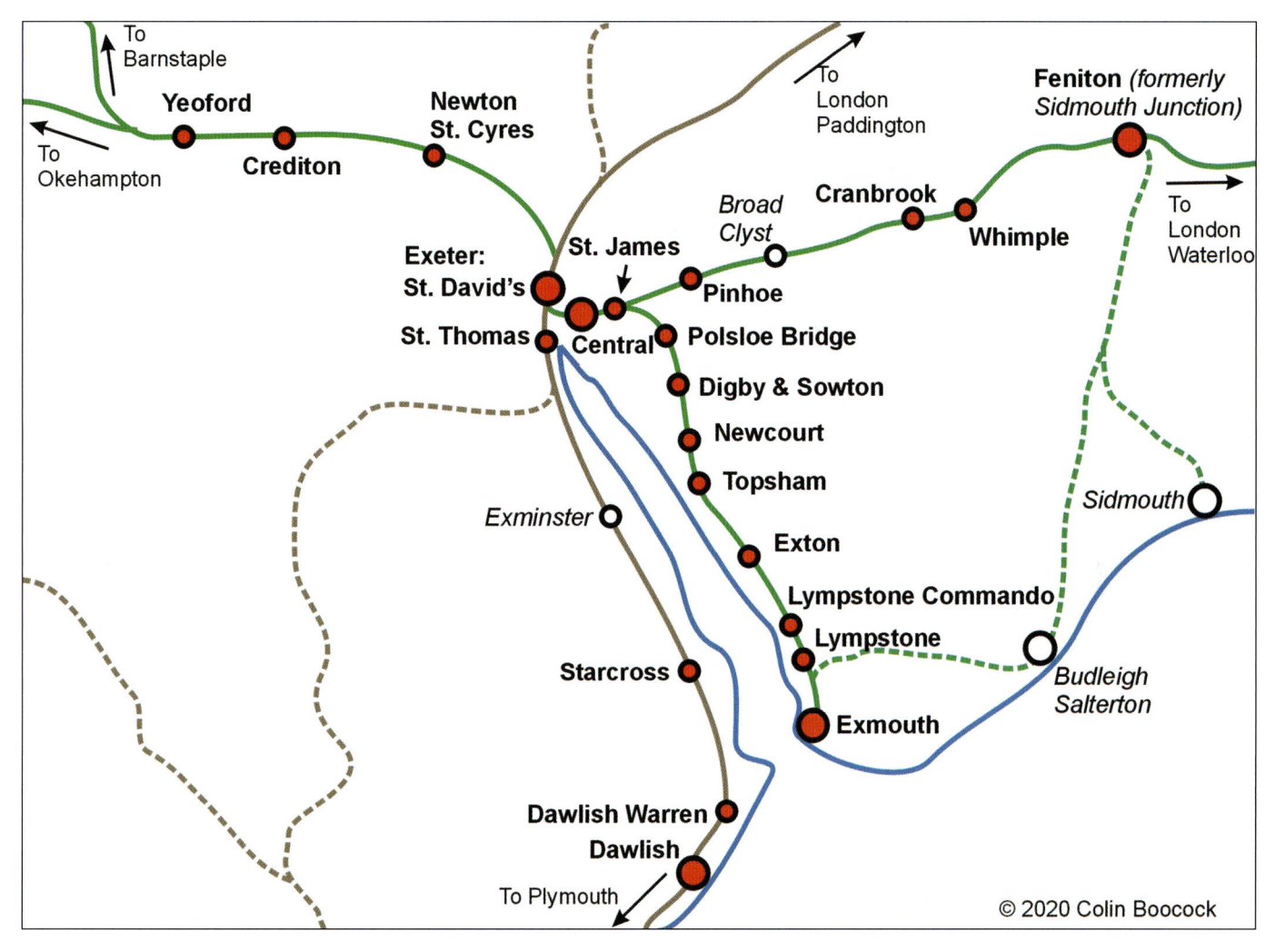

Most closed local stations omitted for clarity.

observer would watch with awe as the two engines, one at the front and one at the rear, roared away round the sharp curve and up the incline towards the tunnel. At Exeter Central, the banker(s) would wait in one of the centre tracks before being signalled back down the hill to regain their siding at St David's. Or they would nip up to Exmouth Junction shed for servicing.

When the E1/Rs became worn out, they were replaced by beefy Z class 0-8-0Ts that had been displaced by diesel shunters from marshalling yards elsewhere on the SR. The Zs' end came when heavy overhauls were due in the mid-1960s, to be replaced by W class 2-6-4Ts, but the crews would tell you that the Ws weren't a patch on the Zs as bankers! When the Western Region replaced steam locomotives by diesel hydraulics on the Waterloo services, the need for banking engines ceased.

West of Exeter, the train services were rapidly being cut in accordance with Dr Beeching's plan. What services were left were given over to WR diesel multiple units after that Region took over from 1963.

Local services east of Exeter included those to Exmouth, which the Southern Railway had served mainly with M7 0-4-4Ts, supplemented in BR days by the useful Ivatt and BR 2-6-2Ts and

Map 15 – Exeter.

The fireman of class E1/R 0-6-2T 32697 is between the buffers as he uncouples this engine from the rear of an express to Waterloo after arrival at Exeter Central. The engine has just banked this train up the 1 in 37 incline from Exeter St David's.

The Z class 0-8-0Ts replaced the old E1/R 0-6-2Ts on banking duties around 1960. 30955 is well into helping an Up freight train away from St David's up the 1 in 37 to Central station. (*Alan Wild*)

On 20 April 1963, W class 2-6-4T 31914, one of the short-term replacements for the Z class bankers that were due for overhaul, has coupled in front of light Pacific 34070 *Manston* for the run down to St David's. The train is the 4.21pm to Torrington. (*John H. Bird/Anistr.com*)

BR 2-6-4Ts. These made use of Central station's bay platforms.

The first diesel hydraulics used on the Waterloo trains were B-B 'Warships', by then in maroon livery with yellow ends. In turn, these were replaced by class 50 Co-Co diesel electrics, and later by Network SouthEast (NSE) class 47s, both these periods using good quality mark 2 stock.

As NSE developed into a fully multiple unit railway, it was not surprising that the longer-term solution for the Waterloo-Exeter line, which still holds sway today, was the introduction of class 159 air-conditioned 90mph DMUs.

Exeter used to handle quite a lot of general freight, for which the S15 4-6-0s were ideal. There was once a small engine shed and turntable at Exeter Queen Street, but the much bigger depot at Exmouth Junction opened in 1887 and this became the SR's principal shed in the west country. Its allocation included most key types from 'Merchant Navy' 4-6-2s down to the 2-6-2Ts used on local services.

It is worth mentioning that the SR had a civil engineering depot at Exmouth Junction that specialised in concrete products. Right across the SR, as modernisation continued between and after the wars, one would become aware of standardised fencing, lampposts, station nameboards, lineside sheds and footbridges, all of which had been cast in reinforced concrete at Exmouth Junction. Much of this has survived to modern times, indicative of the quality of design and materials used.

But a lot has disappeared. Exmouth Junction depot is no more, the land having gone over to an industrial estate, car parking and a supermarket. At Exeter Central the centre through tracks have gone, as has the Up side bay platform. The signalboxes that covered the route into Exeter from Exmouth Junction have gone, everything now being controlled from a panel at St David's control centre.

Nonetheless rail travel, at least on the line to Yeovil, Salisbury and London, is still booming here, which is good to see. One hopes this can continue.

Fifty-four years later, on 3 June 2017, South West Trains DMU 159019 approaches Exeter Central from St David's with a London Waterloo train. The steepness of the gradient between the two main stations is evident.

In the diesel-hauled era, on 7 July 1987 50034 *Furious* accelerates past Exeter St James's Park with the 09.38 from St David's to London Waterloo. The Network SouthEast branding is beginning to take hold, but in decidedly piecemeal fashion! (*Colin J. Marsden*)

CHAPTER 14

WAY OUT WEST
THE 'WITHERED ARM' AND ALL THAT…

The L&SWR was in direct competition with the GWR over its London to Plymouth route. The SR route from Waterloo to Exeter was a fast main line despite its gradient profile, and the GWR Berks & Hants line possibly less so, but the tables were turned west of Exeter. The GWR route round the coast and over the Devon banks was certainly difficult to work, but it was more direct than that which the L&SWR managed to develop through its acquisitions and extensions. The latter's frequent curves and the weight restriction over Meldon viaduct were also hindrances to really fast running.

As explained in the previous chapter, the SR's Exeter-Plymouth trains left Exeter St David's station facing north on the Up GW main line. They then turned off left at Cowley Bridge Junction. Weather patterns have changed with the effect that

On 24 July 1957 Plymouth Friary terminus was graced by light Pacific 34035 *Shaftesbury* which was awaiting departure with an afternoon train to London Waterloo, which it would haul via North Road, Devonport and Okehampton.

136 • SEVENTY YEARS OF THE SOUTH WESTERN

34061 *73 Squadron* leans to the curve as it brings a freight train from Meldon through Yeoford on 11 October 1960. (*Alan Wild*)

Twenty-four years later, on 2 October 1984, 33017 calls at the much-rationalised Yeoford station with the 15.00 from Exeter St David's to Barnstaple. (*Colin J. Marsden*)

in recent decades this area has been subject to repetitive flooding from the River Exe, so Network Rail has raised the track in an attempt to keep the rails above flood level. Climbing out of the flood plain, the train heads through Newton St Cyres before calling at the small town of Crediton. Beyond here is Yeoford, following which the line to Barnstaple turns off to the right at Coleford Junction. The railway has an undulating profile, having to cross the valleys of the Rivers Tawe and Okement, the latter just after calling at Okehampton. None of these places is a large centre of population, both Crediton and Okehampton having around 7-8,000 residents each.

Map 16 – The far west

Local stations in the Plymouth area are omitted for clarity, as are those on the Lynton & Barnstaple narrow gauge line.

In modern times, the station at Okehampton has seen passenger traffic at summer Sundays only with a Sunday train service by First Great Western from Exeter St. David's. This was met by a Dartmoor Railway shuttle service to Meldon, but that did not run in 2020 because the DR went into administration early that year. In happier times on 22 June 2014, the heritage railway's 'tub-thumper' DEMU 1132 awaits custom at Okehampton station. (*Colin J. Marsden*)

Meldon viaduct still stands as a Scheduled Monument. The slender lattice-steel bridge was photographed on 27 July 2014. (*Colin J. Marsden*)

Beyond Okehampton, the trains have to cross the slender Meldon viaduct. The Southern Railway and Region used to operate a ballast quarry here, and indeed the railway is still open to Meldon for any freight that may be on offer. Also, the Dartmoor Railway operated at weekends between Okehampton and Meldon, being the proud owner of two working 'Hampshire' type DEMUs[10]. The Yeoford to Okehampton line is the first to be resuscitated under the Government's 'Reopening closed railways' scheme, aiming at hourly trains in 2022. These trains are run from Exeter by Great Western Railway. Beyond Meldon, the railway was closed during the 1960s rationalisations. This line skirted the northern edge of Dartmoor before dropping through Lydford towards Tavistock, at 13,000 inhabitants quite the biggest intermediate town on the line and now without a railway. This area was also contested by the GWR in its heyday, the two railways running roughly parallel between Lydford and Tavistock, but there was not enough traffic here to satisfy even one railway according to the Beeching calculations, and certainly not two.

It is only when we get to Bere Alston that we are on a working railway again. Now heading south along the Tamar estuary, DMUs from Gunnislake to Plymouth serve all the remaining open stations before joining the former GWR main line just beyond St Budeaux, now heading towards Plymouth on the same tracks as GWR trains that have come over

---

10. Regrettably the Dartmoor Railway went into administration in February 2020. The two DEMUs have been relocated to Brechin in the north of Scotland.

140 • SEVENTY YEARS OF THE SOUTH WESTERN

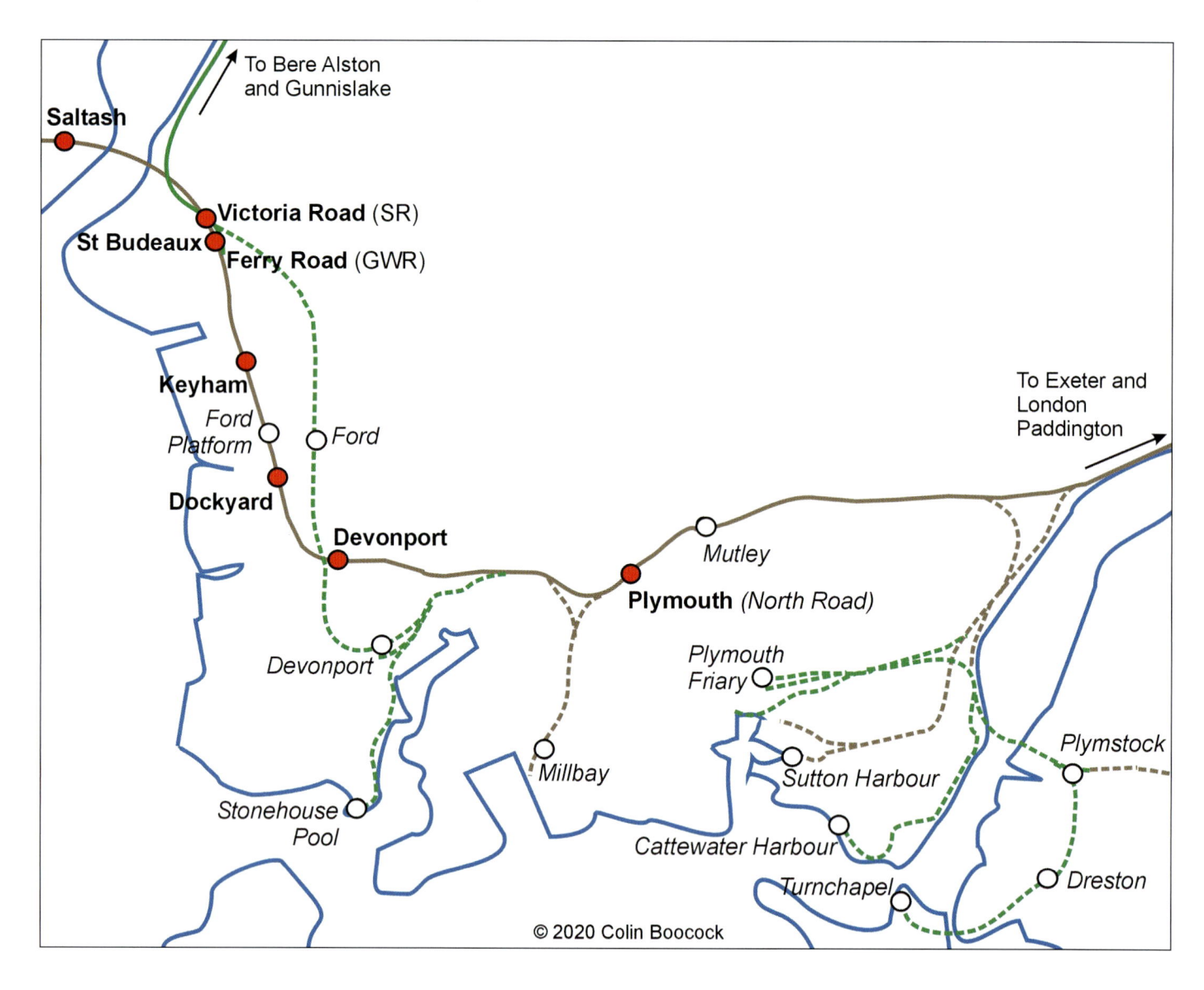

Map 17 – Plymouth

the Saltash bridge from Cornwall. Before BR's rationalisation, the SR's route ran further south through Devonport, in some places nearer to the docks, before joining the WR line west of Plymouth North Road station.

The SR ran a couple of short passenger and freight lines around Plymouth linking the docks at Devonport as well as short branches terminating at Cattewater and at Turnchapel. Adams O2 0-4-4Ts worked push-pull trains to Turnchapel with ancient gated L&SWR carriages here until closure came in BR days.

Plymouth North Road station is the main station in the city and until 1948 was jointly owned by the GWR and SR. After calling there, Down Southern trains then headed further east along the Up line before turning sharply south on the triangle near the WR's Laira depot, and then sharply west to terminate in Plymouth Friary station. Friary was the L&SWR's terminus in the city, only a short distance south of North Road, but quite a long way round by rail! The station had four platform tracks alongside the two island platforms. I put Friary in the past tense because BR closed the station in 1958 along with much of the railway infrastructure around there. There had been a locomotive depot there that maintained the SR's locomotives that worked out of Plymouth. The station and depot site is now rail-less, the station area being occupied by modern retail units.

I recall distantly a journey a friend and I made from Friary station on our way back to Exeter, having decided to go the whole way via the SR route. Our engine was a 'West Country' class light Pacific, with about five coaches behind the tender. Despite the long way round, the trip round to North Road station did not seem too long in the making. I recall that running was brisk once we had cleared the Plymouth suburbs, and a Pacific with that light load had no problem with the gradients as the train headed north and began to skirt Dartmoor. Earlier that day we had watched a Drummond T9 4-4-0 leave North Road station with four coaches for the same route.

The line via Devonport that the L&SWR occupied was originally part of the Plymouth, Devonport and South Western Junction Railway. This route today is worked by GWR diesel multiple units, covering the stretch between Plymouth and Bere Alston before turning left onto the PD&SWJR branch line proper. The train then calls at Calstock and Gunnislake, beyond which the line is no longer there. Originally it went on to terminate at Callington. The PD&SWJR operated the outer part of this line independently for many years until the L&SWR took it all over. The small railway company had two 0-6-2Ts and an 0-6-0T, all outside cylinder machines supplied by Hawthorn Leslie. The 0-6-2Ts ended up in the late 1950s as works shunters at Eastleigh, and the 0-6-0T had a stint shunting at Nine Elms depot. In modern times, this line has outlived the main line which is closed beyond Bere Alston. Dr Beeching's, *The Reshaping of British Railways* (HMSO, 1963), showed all this route, from near St Budeaux through to Callington, as proposed for closure, but only the stub end from Gunnislake to Callington actually closed. The rest is now an active commuter line for people working in or visiting Plymouth.

On 24 July 1957, T9 4-4-0 has four coaches in tow as it approaches Plymouth North Road station with a train from Friary to Waterloo, which it will haul as far as Exeter Central.

At the branch terminus in Callington, a track maintenance gang of six men is at work on a siding track. Meanwhile, Ivatt 2 2-6-2T 41295 runs round its train, which it has propelled into the loop to the right of the photographer. *(Ray Oakley/Colour-Rail 305974)*

Heading west from Meldon Junction was the straggling line that ended up at Padstow in Cornwall. Padstow was the farthest point west reached by the L&SWR, and the Southern Railway after it. This line first headed north-west from Meldon Junction until it reached Halwill. Northwards from there it threw off two branches, the line to Bude on the Cornish coast and the less trafficked line that meandered north to Torrington, Bideford and Barnstaple.

The stretch from Bideford to Barnstaple, now a cycle trail, featured a few years ago in two television shows that attempted to lay OO-scale model track the whole way and then to run model trains the full nine miles distance. Alas, they are the only trains to have run that way since the early 1960s.

On leaving Halwill, the Padstow train turned to a south-westerly direction to meander through Launceston, a town with 9,000 people, then headed west to join the River Camel briefly but missing Bodmin entirely, climbing and then dropping south-west to Wadebridge, before heading west along the south shore of the Camel estuary to terminate in the small station at Padstow. Even far-distant places like this had through carriages to London Waterloo, which were sent first to Exeter, joining up on the way with portions from Bude, Plymouth and Ilfracombe, to form important trains at Exeter Central such as the Atlantic Coast Express.

I should have added that, after leaving Launceston, an Exeter-Padstow train would call at the small station at

The double junction west of Barnstaple Junction station is now gone, though the station remains as a single platform for DMUs from Exeter. On 5 September 1964, Ivatt 2-6-2T 41208 arrives with a train from Torrington. The lines coming in from the right are from the Ilfracombe line, and became single track to cross the river bridge between the two Barnstaple stations. (*Alan Trickett*)

On 1 July 1961, class U1 2-6-0 31904 rolls into Launceston with the Padstow portion of a train for Waterloo. (*Alan Wild*)

Egloskerry to be met by what must have been the most famous duck in the UK. In 1960, on the only journey I made along this line, I saw it there, waddling and quacking along the platform. I remember reading a few weeks later in our national newspaper that the duck apparently met every train and had become a local celebrity!

Wadebridge had a depot which was host to BR's three oldest ex-L&SWR locomotives. At one time, a large fleet of Beattie 2-4-0 well tanks worked suburban trains out of Waterloo station until displaced by larger engines towards the end of the nineteenth century; all were withdrawn before 1910 except three, which were seen as ideal for working a branch line that struck north from Bodmin to collect wagons of clay from the Wenford Bridge quarries. These locomotives, built in 1874 and 1875, received their last general overhauls at Eastleigh Locomotive Works at the end of the 1950s. When the Western Region took over everything west of Salisbury in 1963, they were replaced by 1366 class pannier tanks, and later on by Drewry diesel shunters. Thankfully, the two 1874-built Beattie well tanks are preserved, one locally at the Bodmin & Wadebridge heritage railway.

Eastwards from Wadebridge station was the SR's Bodmin branch that terminated at Bodmin North. Just before there, at Boscarne Junction, a GWR line branched off south-east to go via its own Bodmin station with a reversal there, and then to terminate in a bay platform at Bodmin Road alongside the GWR Cornish main line. All the railway from Boscarne Junction to Bodmin Road is now the Bodmin & Wadebridge Railway.

West of Boscarne Junction station on the former track bed is the Camel Trail which enables walkers and cyclists to reach both the preserved Wadebridge station building (home of a Sir John Betjeman display) and Padstow. I can confirm that while the outward journey by bicycle from Bodmin to Padstow is relatively straightforward, when returning to Bodmin one realises late on in the journey that the 1 in 50 gradient up into that town is actually quite a steep challenge for a by-now very tired cyclist!

If we had left Exeter on a train bound for Ilfracombe we would have turned right at Coleford Junction and headed north-north-west, dropping into the Tawe valley at Eggesford and following it through small places such as Portsmouth Arms towards the town of Barnstaple. Nowadays the town has a population of around twenty thousand. Today an hourly DMU service operates from Exeter as far as Barnstaple, which is on the site of the former Barnstaple Junction station. In older times, a GWR line used to trail in from the right just before this station; that was the line from Taunton, one of many in the west that succumbed to the cuts in the 1960s. Beyond the station today is the Tarka Trail, a public pathway that follows the track bed of the former Torrington line and which goes south beyond there as far as Meeth, not so far from the former junctions at Halwill. There is a shorter stretch of trail north of the river estuary. This water used to be crossed by a curved railway bridge with a single track that linked Barnstaple Junction and Barnstaple Town stations. Fortunately, the old Town station buildings are still intact and preserved.

The Town station was where one could once alight to catch the Southern Railway's only narrow gauge trains, those that crossed undulating farmland to reach a spot overlooking the cliff-top town of Lynton. That railway closed in 1935, but a preservation group now runs a short length of it, based at Woody Bay, and is making progress towards its target of an eventual full reopening. What has been achieved here is superb and augurs well for the future, however long it may take to reach the railway's long-term objective.

Also from the Town station one might have remained in the train we caught in Exeter and continued along the winding and eventually steeply descending line to the terminus station that overlooked the seaside resort of Ilfracombe. This was one of the railways that later developments have enabled people to challenge whether the logic of total closure was always correctly applied. It's less than ten miles from Barnstaple to Ilfracombe and for the cost of keeping that bit of railway open, the resort of Ilfracombe suffered quite a period of decline. Modern times have been kinder as the continuation of train services to Barnstaple has shown, but Ilfracombe has since 1970 had to rely on visitors being able to bring their own transport with them.

In steam days, working trains out of Ilfracombe was expensive in that heavy summer holiday trains needed to be double-headed out of the resort because of the steep gradient of 1 in 36 necessary to gain the tableland above. This was regarded as the steepest climb out of any UK railway terminus with the exception of Folkestone Harbour. The use of Bulleid light Pacifics helped, but even they needed assistance with the heaviest trains. In the mid-1960s, diesel multiple units replaced steam, with diesel locomotive haulage of the heavier summer trains, but the line did not pay and was closed in 1970.

In spite of the railways west of Exeter having a largely rural nature, holiday destination towns brought traffic from afar including a daily Pullman train from London. The Devon Belle observation car needed to be detached and turned on arrival at Ilfracombe using the depot's locomotive turntable. (*Robin Russell/David Peel collection*)

It was foggy on 2 June 2017 when the author visited the re-constituted Lynton & Barnstaple Railway. This heritage line has the long-term objective of reopening the whole length of this two-feet gauge railway. The 0-4-2T *Isaac* is seen (just) with its authentic carriages approaching Woody Bay station from the south.

CHAPTER 15

SOMERSET & DORSET HILLS
THE 'SLOW AND DIRTY' OR THE 'SWIFT AND DELIGHTFUL'?

Echoing my childhood surprise at seeing LMS engines in Bournemouth, I suppose, was the continued lift in excitement in later years when observing the traffic that came off the former Somerset & Dorset Joint Railway's route from Bath. Under normal circumstances, locomotives and

On 19 May 1956, BR 5 4-6-0 73050 has just breasted the summit of the 1 in 90 gradient out of Bournemouth West with the northbound Pines Express and is passing Branksome locomotive sub-depot (left). The junction in the background was with a pair of tracks that crossed a viaduct over the Bourne Valley and joined the Weymouth to Bournemouth Central line at Gas Works Junction, the north-east corner of Branksome triangle.

The small depot at Branksome was within the triangle of lines. It had a short, two-road shed and a turntable that was not long enough for the bigger engines that came for servicing – these turned via the triangle. 34043 *Combe Martin* and 73052 were stabled there on Sunday 27 June 1954.

stock from the S&D line did not venture round into Bournemouth Central station or depot, so one had to make the effort to get to the West station or to Branksome, Parkstone or Poole to see them.

Since 1930, the Somerset & Dorset had been a jointly-owned railway between the LMS and the Southern Railway, hence the different locomotives the line brought to Bournemouth.

A Sunday afternoon was a good time to make unauthorised visits into the triangle at Branksome and so gain access to the small two-road engine shed there. The engine for the following (Monday) morning's Pines Express would always be inside, usually an LMS or BR class 5 but sometimes one of Bath's 'West Country' Pacifics. There would also be one or two older engines, normally a 2P 4-4-0 or 4F 0-6-0. Only stopping trains ran on Sundays. These went to Bristol Temple Meads via Bath Green Park (reverse) and Mangotsfield and were made up either of an SR Maunsell three-coach set or about four ex-LMS coaches, and headed by a 2P, a 4F or occasionally one of the S&D 2-8-0s. There was also one diagram that took an Eastleigh-based BR4 2-6-0 to Bath over the S&D, and for a time in the very early 1950s we saw Bristol-based Ivatt 4 2-6-0s with double chimneys, rather ugly in the eyes of local enthusiasts who dubbed them 'doodlebugs'. So, the variety was limited, even in later years when the older engines were replaced by BR standard types, themselves displaced from other parts of the UK. Around 1961, transfer in of former Cambrian BR class 4 4-6-0s wiped out all the 2Ps on the S&D at a stroke. BR 2-6-4Ts from the LT&S line infiltrated the local trains. Ivatt 2 2-6-2Ts took over trains on the Highbridge branch, making the 3F 0-6-0s and 1P 0-4-4Ts redundant there. Once the WR had taken over most of the line, that Region's Collett 0-6-0s replaced the ex-LMS 4Fs, Stanier 8Fs took over freight from the unique 7F 2-8-0s, and pannier tanks ousted the few remaining 'Jinty' 3F 0-6-0Ts.

But it was summer Saturdays that were the main attraction for S&D train watchers and travellers. In addition to the 'Pines', the Saturday service to the Midlands and North was augmented by relief trains to Liverpool, Manchester, Sheffield, Nottingham, Leeds and Bradford. A real oddity that Bournemouth observers would not see was the Cleethorpes to Exmouth train. That reached the S&D via Birmingham and Bath Green Park; it was later in the day's sequence of southbound trains arriving at Bath, and so received whatever engines could be rustled up to get it over the Mendips as far as Templecombe, where the S&D crews thankfully handed it over to the Southern for transit over the main line westwards. Engines for these long-distance trains were predominantly from Bath Green Park depot, but SR depots such as Bournemouth, Nine Elms and Eastleigh contributed, and Bath was quite adept at 'borrowing' Stanier 5s from depots further north. The great additional type that came in 1960 was the 9F 2-10-0, a few of which belonging to Cardiff Canton were loaned to the S&D for the summer seasons to the end of the 1962 one. These were the only engines that were authorised to take more than ten coaches unaided over the Mendips, their limit being twelve coaches. Twelve vehicles was the maximum length of the Pines Express and any of

While the Southern provided some coaching stock for S&D trains, other local trains had former LMS stock. It was unusual for a former LNER articulated twin to be in such a formation, seen on 10 September 1960 as ex-LMS 4F 0-6-0 44558 lifted the 5.30pm Bournemouth West to Templecombe stopping service past Broadstone golf course.

Ex-LMS class 5 4-6-0 45440 arrives at Templecombe SR station with a Bristol to Bournemouth stopping train. This train will need to reverse back out to rejoin the S&D main line that bypasses the main station. An assisting locomotive will be attached to the back of the train to undertake that duty.

the weekend trains. The sedate 7Fs were allowed ten coaches unaided, but the class 5s and Pacifics had to be helped by a pilot engine north of Evercreech Junction if the load was more than eight.

One could divide the S&D main line into two in terms of differing characteristics. South of Evercreech, the line undulated gently across farmland and through small towns and villages. North of there was the long climb at mainly 1 in 50 or 60 to get the railway over what must have been the highest railway summit in the south of England at Masbury, some 811 feet above sea level. Coming south, the climb out of Bath was initially just as ferocious. While there was a break in the climb to cross the valley over the viaduct at Midford, the nearby tunnels with their tight, single track bores were unpopular with engine crews, particularly those on the second locomotive of a double-headed train who had to contend with smoke from both engines swirling back into their cab.

I remember a friend joining me one day for a run over the S&D on the northbound Pines Express. We had a 'West Country' Pacific at the front of our ten ex-LMS Stanier coaches. The climb up the 1 in 90 out of Bournemouth West was energetic, and my friend was surprised that we were soon dropping quite fast down the 1 in 60 of Parkstone bank before we swung across the causeway by Poole Park and slowed round the sharp curve through the level crossings to stop briefly at Poole. The 4-6-2 made light of all the undulations and the short climb up to Broadstone station, through which we slowed to join the junction with the line from Hamworthy before turning left onto the single track S&D line proper. We then galloped along, calling at Blandford before carrying on across the grasslands to reach Templecombe. Here, S&D trains that stopped at Templecombe station used to take on a shunt locomotive on the rear of the train to drag it round the curve into the station which was actually at a lower level about a quarter of a mile away on the West of England main line which we had just crossed on a bridge. All this cost time, and the 'Pines' was

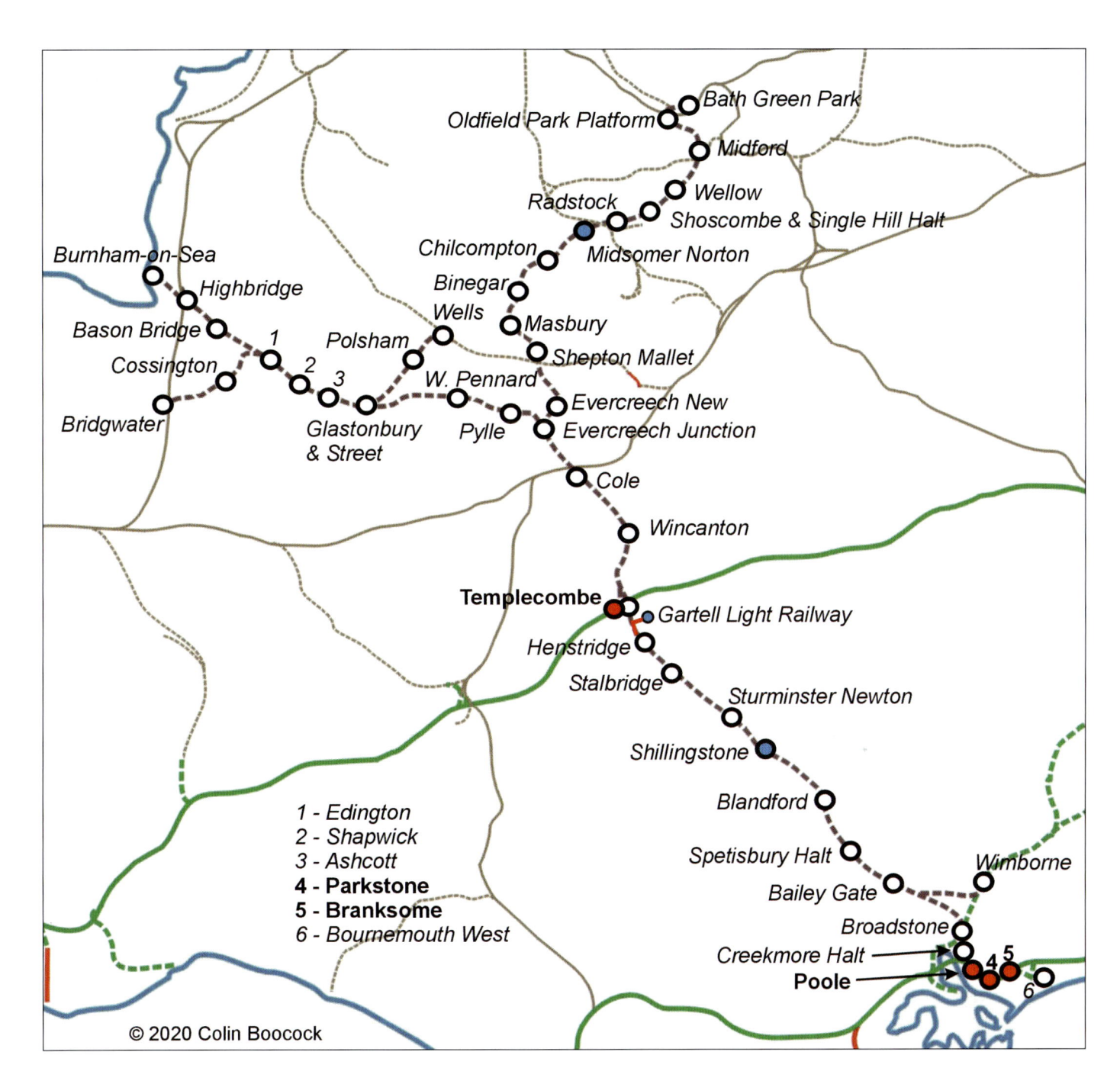

Map 18 – Somerset & Dorset line

Summer Saturdays transformed the S&D line into a busy main line. About a dozen heavy through trains used the line linking the Midlands and north of England with Bournemouth and other south coast resorts. This train is the 10.05am Bournemouth West to Bradford on 4 August 1962 with BR 4 4-6-0 75072 piloting 34046 *Braunton* on the climb past Winsor Hill. The BR 4s had been transferred to the S&D a couple of years earlier to replace the erstwhile ex-LMS class 2P 4-4-0s that had done most of the piloting over the Mendip Hills during the previous three or more decades.

regarded as a train in a hurry and so did not deign to stop at Templecombe. The next stop was Wincanton, but only on race days. Then the train arrived at Evercreech Junction. A centre track hosted the row of pilot engines, one of which was drawing forward promptly so that it could gently back onto our train's locomotive while the latter was taking water.

So, with the 2P and 'West Country' combination at the front looking visually at odds with each other, we set off up the first part of the climb. The branch line to Highbridge turned off left as we pulled out of the station. The Highbridge branch was the original main line that went to the harbour at Burnham-on-Sea on the coast of the Bristol Channel. The S&DR's early objective was to get people and goods from southern England to South Wales using the ferry from Burnham-on-Sea, and to match that with holiday traffic and coals from South Wales to the English south coast. That that was a bit of a non-starter soon became evident, but the railway boldly then went north to Bath and thus linked up with the Midland Railway to make up the thoroughfare between that railway and the Poole/Bournemouth area.

SOMERSET & DORSET HILLS • 153

By 1957, the branch line to Burnham-on-Sea had been partially curtailed and passenger trains were terminating at Highbridge. Class 3F 0-6-0 43218 is ready to leave there with a train for Evercreech Junction on 6 April 1957. The footbridge in the left background links the S&D station with the ex-GWR one on the line from Bristol Temple Meads to Taunton and Exeter.

On the same day, 3F 43216 poses by the water tower at Highbridge depot. Outside the shed stands an Ivatt 2 2-6-2T, and inside rests a Johnson 0-4-4T.

The Burnham-on-Sea branch of the S&D crossed the Western Region main line just north of the latter's Highbridge station. By 6 April 1957, the branch line was used for freight only beyond Highbridge.

Soon after our train was well under way on the climb, we reached Shepton Mallet, a small but important community in the middle of Somerset. After calling there, we crossed the fine stone viaduct across the town before resuming the upwards grind; the deep slow beat of the 2P 4-4-0 sounded quite harsh compared with the lighter chattering exhaust of the Bulleid engine. Speed was slow all the way up to the cutting at Masbury but the summit was crossed on time and the rest was easy.

People forget that there were coal mines around at Radstock, which generated traffic for both the GWR and S&D lines there, the latter employing one of the 'Jinty' 3F 0-6-0Ts that were based at Bath but sub-shedded here. The long drop down towards Bath needed the brake blocks working most of the time, and warm they were when the train curved right to join the ex-LMS line from Bristol and rolled into the covered station at Green Park. At least the first few coaches were covered, the overall roof not being very long and most of the train stopped out in the rain! At the buffer stops, the two locomotives were uncoupled from the train ready to move back to the depot for servicing. A rebuilt 'Scot' had backed onto the other end of the train for the departure for Birmingham and points north.

My comment about the 'Pines' being thought of as a train in a hurry was relative to the slow speeds on that line generally. Some wags called the S&D line the 'slow and dirty'. The fact was that it took two and a quarter hours for an express train to cover the seventy-three miles from Bournemouth to Bath. Rerouting the Pines Express to run via Basingstoke, Oxford and Banbury to reach Birmingham was logical and came in 1962. While a longer way round, it certainly wasn't slower than the S&D! The local trains soldiered on reluctantly with no prospect of dieselisation until the axe finally fell in 1966.

Then there was just one train a day between Bournemouth and Manchester. Today there is one every hour! But that is a subject for the next chapter of this book.

The S&DJR served collieries at Norton Hill and Radstock. At the former on 19 July 1963, S&D 7F 2-8-0 53810 is ready to leave with a coal train for the north while 'Jinty' 3F 0-6-0T 47557 shunts past a notice banning BR engines from doing just that! (*Alan Wild*)

In April 1960, 34102 *Lapford* has its maximum load of eight coaches that it is allowed to take over the Mendips unaided by a pilot engine. It is leaving the former Midland Railway route to Bristol and Gloucester at Bath Junction and is heading up the initial 1 in 50 climb on the S&D main line, on its way eventually to Bournemouth West. (*Colour-Rail SD169*)

Ivatt 2 2-6-2T 41241 sits at Bath Green Park terminus on 6 April 1957 with a local train for Mangotsfield and Bristol Temple Meads. Note the Southern Maunsell three-car set that forms the train. This terminus station roof still stands, as a cover for a supermarket car park.

CHAPTER 16

CROSS-COUNTRY
FROM THREE TRAINS A DAY TO HOURLY; AND A LOT OF OIL

As highlighted in Chapter 15, the Pines Express was the only all-year-round long-distance train to traverse the Somerset & Dorset line. Its transfer to the South Western route via Basingstoke and then Oxford, Banbury and Birmingham came in 1962.

There had previously been a Bournemouth to Birkenhead train, which was an interesting aberration in a way.

The Newcastle to Bournemouth through train leaves Eastleigh behind WR 'Hall' class 4-6-0 6970 *Whaddon Hall* on 11 June 1958. This is the SR train set of largely green-painted coaches, though it does include a Gresley buffet car.

On the first Saturday after the Pines Express was re-routed off the Somerset & Dorset line to run via Basingstoke, 15 September 1962, rebuilt 'Battle of Britain' 4-6-2 34085 *501 Squadron* heads the northbound train through Christchurch. The locomotive would be replaced by a WR one at Oxford.

It was originally the GWR's attempt to catch some of the Liverpool to south coast traffic potential, but as the GWR did not reach Liverpool itself, Birkenhead was the nearest option, being but a short ferry journey across the River Mersey, or a brief Mersey Railway journey under it. That the Birkenhead-Bournemouth train survived as long as it did is surprising. The stock for the train was formed of two sets, one Western and one Southern, each set doing one single journey in a day, and back the next. Thus, SR green coaches were seen in the Wirral, which perhaps added some colour to their day! Locomotives were usually changed at Oxford, a Southern 'King Arthur' or 'Lord Nelson' being the norm south of there, and the WR provided a 'Hall' or other 4-6-0 for the onward journey north. The route would have been the former GWR one via Oxford, Banbury, Birmingham Snow Hill, Wolverhampton Low Level and Chester; I have read that the train was cut back to Wolverhampton in 1961. From 1962, most of the Birkenhead train's former calling points were served by the re-routed Pines Express. Passengers from the south for Merseyside would catch the Pines Express which normally included a couple of carriages for Liverpool Lime Street. These long-distance trains used to bypass Reading General station by calling at Reading West and then using the west curve to reach the main line towards Didcot and Oxford, convenient for the railway operators but a deterrent for Reading passengers.

While the 'Pines' was usually SR Pacific-hauled as far north as Oxford, dieselisation soon came and facilitated more joined-up thinking; the London Midland Region class 47s employed on this train were rostered for the complete

Manchester-Bournemouth and return journey. Initially this was still with the BR standard mark 1 stock, now increasingly in blue-and-grey instead of maroon. Later the cross-country trains graduated to mark 2 stock, then mark 2 air-conditioned coaches once enough 47s had been modified for train electric supply to support electrically heated coaches. For a few years their destination moved west to Poole.

The Bournemouth-York and Newcastle service was one that in steam days brought a 'Hall' or 'Grange' 4-6-0 to Bournemouth, the locomotive returning to the WR with an evening stopping train heading towards Reading. The York train also needed two train sets, one owned by the North Eastern Region (later Eastern) and one by the Southern[11]. The closure of the Great Central route via Nottingham Victoria, Leicester Central, Rugby and Banbury forced the train's diversion to run via Birmingham New Street with a reversal there to reach Banbury and points south, instead of the previous more direct routing. For a time in the mid-1960s ex-LMS class 5s worked the southbound train between Birmingham and Bournemouth, thus bringing LMS-type engines back to the resort once more but this time to Bournemouth Central station. Dieselisation followed the same principles as for the 'Pines'. With diesel

After dieselisation, additional cross-country trains were introduced over the years. WR 'Hymek' B-B diesel hydraulic 7068 roars through Eastleigh station in 1969 with a Southampton to Birmingham Snow Hill service.

---

11. Six journeys a week for a set of coaches in the 1950s compares with today's DEMU utilisation of some twenty to thirty journeys.

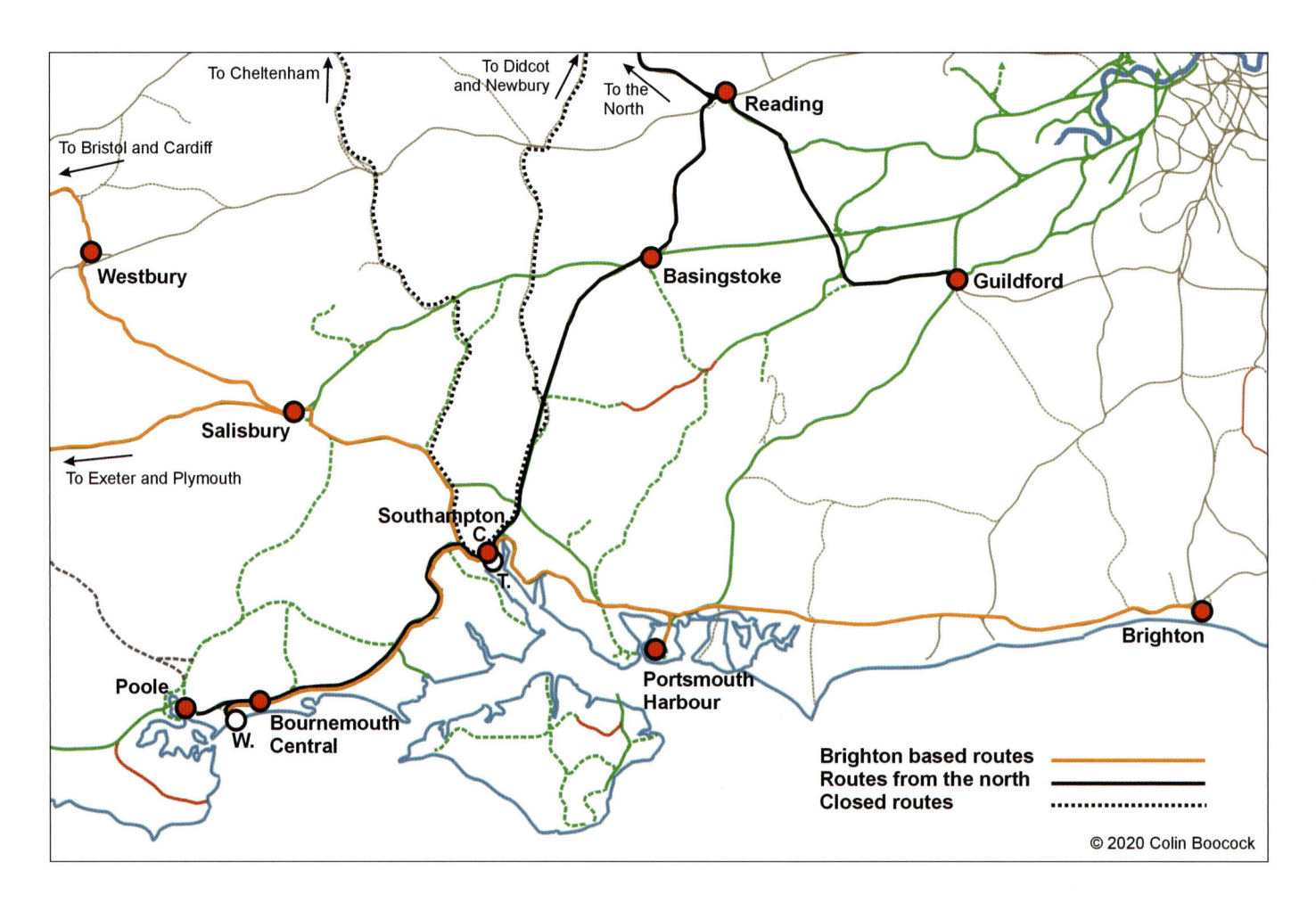

Map 19 – Cross-country.

locomotives in charge, BR took the sensible decision to run these trains into Reading's main station, the locomotives running round their trains there for the onward journey.

BR set up its business organisations in the early 1980s. The Midland Cross-Country part of InterCity made efforts to improve frequencies and timings on the Bournemouth trains, locomotive haulage giving way steadily to an increased use of HSTs (InterCity 125s). Privatisation changed everything in the twenty-first century. For a few years after 2001, Bournemouth had an hourly service to the north for destinations that alternated between Newcastle and Manchester. More recently, that changed to an hourly service to and from Manchester Piccadilly with connections at Birmingham for Sheffield, York and Newcastle. There was also an hourly service from Newcastle to Reading, which in the last few years has had alternative trains extended to Southampton Central. One of the Reading terminators is currently extended to end its journey at Guildford.

The rolling stock offer by the privatised Virgin Cross-Country franchise was a fleet of four- and five-car 'Voyager' classes 220 and 221 diesel electric multiple units. The five-car sets of class 221 were equipped with tilting so that they could take some designated curves faster; tilting was employed only on the West Coast Main Line and on the cross-country route between Coventry, Banbury and Oxford. When that franchise was replaced by Arriva CrossCountry, the tilt facility on

CROSS-COUNTRY • 161

An Up InterCity cross-country train is lustily starting away from Bournemouth behind 47638 *County of Kent* in December 1993. By the 1990s these trains were made up largely of air-conditioned mark 2 stock.

In the last few years of BR, the 11.20 Bournemouth to Edinburgh received the name Dorset Scot, seen passing through New Milton with HST power on 12 June 1999. By this time Virgin had won the new CrossCountry franchise, though some power cars still needed repainting in that company's colours.

The Brighton to Bournemouth daily through train was of local interest because it often came to Bournemouth with an Atlantic at the head. Right on cue, 4-4-2 No 32426 *St Alban's Head* approaches Bournemouth Central with the Bournemouth West to Brighton train on 31 August 1953.

the Arriva sets was locked out of use; the argument was that the relatively minimal time saving between Coventry and Oxford did not justify the cost of maintaining the tilt equipment.

The upshot of all this is that Bournemouth now has an hourly fast through train service to Birmingham and Manchester, with access to a two-hourly one to York and Newcastle at Southampton Central, or an hourly one from Reading or Birmingham. What a change from the so-called 'good old days' when there were at most three trains a day to the north! People still complain, however. Over seventy train carriages a day linking Bournemouth and Manchester each way today compares with a maximum of twelve a day in steam days. Yet the rise in railway passenger traffic in the UK has been so strong that 'Voyagers' are often overcrowded north of Birmingham.

Other trains that South Western passengers used to enjoy that could be dubbed 'cross-country' were the Brighton to Bournemouth, Cardiff and Plymouth trains. These have been described in previous chapters. These trains all traversed the north side of the triangle between Cosham and Havant and so avoided the need to reverse at Fratton or Portsmouth. Suffice it to say here that east of Bournemouth and Salisbury all these trains were powered by locomotives allocated to Brighton depot; in the 1960s these were usually Bulleid light Pacifics. Earlier on, the Brighton-Bournemouth train was a regular Brighton Atlantic duty, but in the absence of one of these, the depot could use anything from a U1 2-6-0 to a 'borrowed' ex-works BR 2-6-4T. The other trains were normally Pacifics but could turn up with lesser engines from time to time. In modern times, the only trains from this group that still survive are the GWR DMUs that ply from Cardiff and Bristol to Southampton, Portsmouth and Brighton, which are mostly now classes 165 and 166. There is also the class 377 EMU service from Southampton Central to London Victoria via Fareham, the south coast line and Three Bridges; this is an hourly 'Southern' service that partly replicates the once-a-day former Bournemouth-Brighton train.

That summary leaves out two cross-country routes that are easily nowadays forgotten. For example, there used to be trains that linked Southampton and Cheltenham. These travelled via Romsey and Andover Junction and then turned north off the west of England main line at Red Post Junction to call at Savernake, Marlborough and Swindon Town and finally catching traffic at Cirencester and Andoversford before arriving at Cheltenham Spa St James station, not far from the Midland's Cheltenham Spa Lansdown station. These trains brought Southern engines to Cheltenham, mainly Maunsell or BR standard Moguls. In addition to ex-GWR Moguls on the line, I did see a 45XX 2-6-2T arrive on one of these services at Southampton Central, so there was indeed some variety there. This was the route of the former Midland & South Western Junction Railway.

Members of the Bournemouth Railway Club used to travel that way each year on their annual Sunday visit to Swindon Works. We would join the WR train at Andover Junction and the Churchward 2-6-0 would hustle us northwards,

In 1958, WR 2-6-2T 5509 was working a service from the M&SWJR line when seen pulling away from Southampton Central on its last leg to Southampton Terminus with a train from Cheltenham. This line was more usually worked by Maunsell or ex-GWR 2-6-0s.

occasionally being uncoupled to shunt at what seemed like a wayside station, such as Marlborough. It was a slow journey but quite interesting. Our train would leave the M&SWJR line at Swindon Town by turning off and dropping down to join the main line west of Swindon Junction station and terminating in a bay platform there. It was then just a short walk to the works main entrance. The whole route closed to passengers in 1961 and freight in 1969.

But the other route north from Southampton could claim more variety, both of train types and engine power. The tracks of the former Didcot, Newbury & Southampton Railway led what outwardly seemed a tenuous existence in the late 1950s. Local stopping trains headed by T9s or SR Moguls, or ex-GWR 2251 0-6-0s or 2-6-0s (even 3440 *City of Truro* for a season or two) passed or overtook pick-up goods trains in the many passing loops on that single line railway. Goods trains brought Q1 or Q 0-6-0s, Moguls and BR standard class 4 2-6-0s to the route. Heading north from Southampton Terminus, the DN&S line trains would call at Eastleigh and Shawford and then branch right to stop in the ex-GWR Winchester Chesil station close by the city centre. The line then turned due north to dive under the SW main line, underneath the junction from which the Alton line sprang, the eponymous Winchester Junction which the DNS line at its lower level ignored for most of its life. Among the stops on the way was Highclere, home to the grand house that gained recent television fame as Downton Abbey. Joining the ex-GW 'Berks & Hants' line just west of Newbury, the trains would call at the main station there and then immediately turn off left to head north-west to Didcot, always the limit of where DN&S passenger trains went. Any idea of a fast Southampton to Oxford service that way didn't happen.

However, fast freight trains did rattle along that line in the late 1950s up to 1965. The growth of the oil refinery at Fawley

On the day that the last passenger train ran on the Didcot, Newbury & Southampton line, 5 March 1960, ex-GWR 0-6-0 2240 calls at Winchester Chesil with the 5.12pm from Eastleigh to Didcot.

opposite Southampton spawned a regular flow of heavy trains of refined oil in 45ton four-wheeled wagons, the trains being heavy enough to command LMR-based class 9F 2-10-0 haulage. The sight of one of these impressive trains threading its way along the single track through the fields and dales was an odd scene. They were heading eventually for the West Midlands distribution depot at Bromford Bridge. Routing them over the DN&S line kept them off much of the main line, but under the BR closure programme the DN&S line in any case was doomed. Passenger trains ceased in 1960, and freight in 1965. By that time the Fawley-Bromford Bridge oil trains were headed by pairs of BRCW Type 3 Bo-Bo diesels that were better able to keep up speeds on the main cross-country route via Basingstoke and Reading. Subsequent construction of pipelines put paid to the Fawley oil trains for good.

Although not related to any cross-country railway route, while on the subject of oil trains I should mention that there was for a time a flow of oil by rail in the 1970s from Furzebrook sidings on the Swanage branch that came from the oil field at Wytch Farm near Wareham in Dorset, said now to be the biggest on-shore oil field in Europe, which opened in 1973. The field stretches eastwards from the shores of Poole Harbour across part of Bournemouth Bay. I also saw oil wagons awaiting dispatch from the yard at Wareham in 1967 which related to a smaller oil well near Wareham itself. The oil trains of crude oil from Wytch Farm went to the Fawley refinery. A pipeline ended rail's involvement in the movement of this oil, too. Methane gas is piped to the national gas grid near Christchurch, and oil is now moved by pipeline and also by road.

The heaviest trains to work over the DN&S line, routed that way to free up capacity on the main line through Basingstoke, were the Fawley to Bromford Bridge oil trains. On 17 March 1962, 2-10-0 92211 heads one of these trains up the main line, ready to branch off at Shawford. With about twenty 45ton gross laden weight tanks in tow, the 9F's load was over 900 tons.

CHAPTER 17

HAMPSHIRE BY-WAYS
PUSH-PULL TERRITORY, AND MORE

One might not associate the phrase 'crossing the Alps' with anything other than Hannibal's army and elephants, or with the railways in Switzerland and Austria that crossed western Europe's grandest mountain range. But South Western train crews did use this term for when their trains were diverted off the main Waterloo to Southampton line to traverse the railway from Brookwood to Alton and then over the steep gradients that

The rule of the M7 0-4-4Ts and push-pull sets on the Southampton Terminus to Alton trains was virtually at its end when 30029 was pictured arriving at Alresford with a southbound train on 2 November 1957, with railway enthusiasts having a last ride. It is crossing an Ivatt class 2 on an Up service. 'Hampshire' diesel units took over this service soon afterwards.

HAMPSHIRE BY-WAYS • 167

eventually brought the train back down to the main line north of Winchester. Modern heritage railway enthusiasts will be familiar with half of this line; the section from Alton westwards as far as Alresford forms the Mid-Hants Railway, also known as the 'Watercress Line' on account of the cress beds on the valley floor that used to be visible from the trains on this route. The early electrification from London ended at Alton station. Beyond there, Edward Heath's government deemed the railway ready for closure, and shut it in 1973.

However, back in 1948 when BR was created, push-pull trains usually formed of ex-L&SWR two-coach sets pulled or propelled by M7 0-4-4Ts plied between Southampton Terminus and Alton, connecting there with semi-fast electric

Map 20 – Hampshire byways.

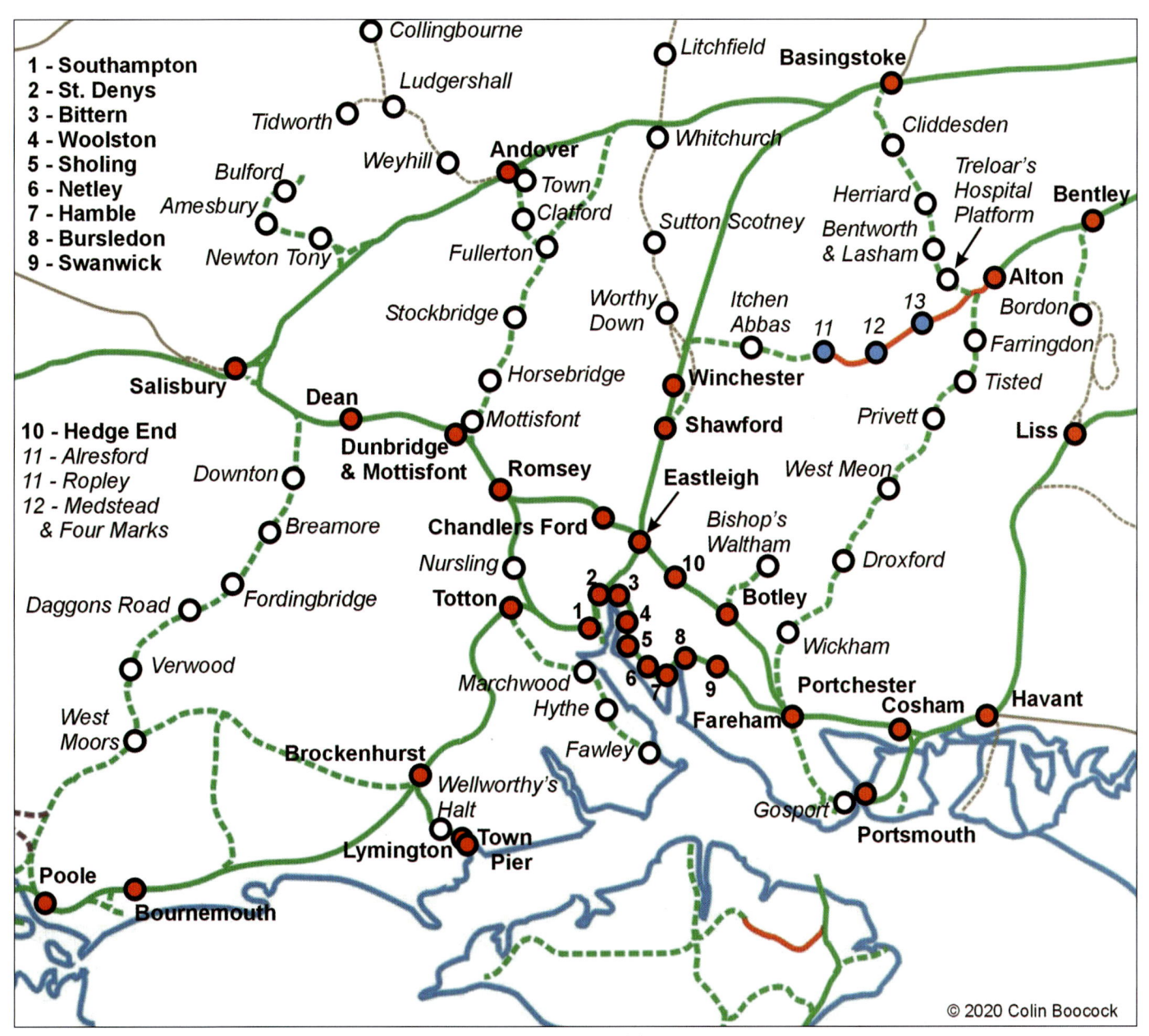

1 - Southampton
2 - St. Denys
3 - Bittern
4 - Woolston
5 - Sholing
6 - Netley
7 - Hamble
8 - Bursledon
9 - Swanwick

10 - Hedge End
11 - Alresford
11 - Ropley
12 - Medstead & Four Marks

Local stations on the main lines, on 'Castleman's corkscrew', and around big towns and cities are omitted for clarity. They are included on the appropriate maps elsewhere.

On a Branch Line Society tour of freight-only branch lines on 7 March 1959, 30111 has arrived at Droxford on the Meon Valley Line (Alton to Fareham). BR had a more relaxed attitude to 'organised trespass' in those days!

trains to Waterloo. In the mid-1950s, the M7s were supplemented by Ivatt class 2 2-6-2Ts transferred to Eastleigh depot at the BRHQ operating department's behest. Unfortunately, that august body didn't understand that the SR's push-pull system was worked by compressed air and that these class 2 locomotives were either fitted with vacuum push-pull equipment or none at all. Thus, the practice of running round their trains at the journey ends had to be reinstated to keep the trains running. The Ivatts were strong little engines, however, and were perfectly happy climbing loudly up the 1 in 50-ish inclines on this route. Hampshire diesels took over after 1957; they were less happy but coped.

Alton was also the northernmost terminus of the Meon Valley line that branched off just west of Alton station to head south-west through small farms and villages with just six stations before joining the Eastleigh to Fareham line. In this case, the push-pull trains terminated at Fareham connecting there with trains to Portsmouth in one direction and Southampton in the other. It was my misfortune not to have travelled the full length of this line before it closed its passenger services in 1955. After that, odd freights ventured from Fareham as far as Droxford, and from Alton an even shorter distance to Farringdon, until these ceased in 1968. The Meon Valley line had brief fame when it was used as the backdrop for television's first attempt at E. Nesbitt's story of *The Railway Children*, in black-and-white, which showed Drummond 4-4-0s, M7s and 700 class 0-6-0s at work on the line.

Another line that branched away west of Alton station was the line north to Basingstoke that the Southern Railway closed in 1933 to passenger trains and 1936 to goods, apart from two short sections at either end that survived until 1967. On this line, the closed Cliddesden station was used for filming the Will Hay 1937 comedy film *Oh, Mr Porter!*, the station being renamed Buggleskelly for the production. Before this, *The Wrecker* film of 1929 had also been filmed on this line.

The Botley to Bishop's Waltham branch was covered during the same railtour. Bishop's Waltham station was later demolished to make way for a roundabout on the B2177 Winchester Road.

The final call for 30111 on the BLS railtour on 7 March 1959 was the derelict station at Gosport with its overall roof and architecturally fine buildings still intact. Gosport was the original L&SWR station for Portsmouth, with a ferry connection to that city.

On 7 March 1959, the Branch Line Society chartered a special push-pull train to visit the remains of several of the Hampshire branch lines as well as one in Sussex. Starting from Portsmouth Harbour, apart from the line from Chichester to Lavant which was outside the scope of this book, the train visited the Botley to Bishop's Waltham branch off the line from Fareham to Eastleigh, then the Meon Valley line where it called at Wickham and Droxford stations, and finished up reaching Gosport with a call at the intermediate station of Fort Brockhurst on the way. At least I took enough photographs to help illustrate something of the character of these places, showing that the L&SWR was generous with its station designs even in outposts like these.

There was another branch line that struck south from Bentley on the electrified line east of Alton. This went south to Bordon. It had been opened in 1905 to connect the army camp at Bordon with the national railway network. BR eventually decided to close the line with passenger services stopping in 1957, goods trains ceasing nine years later.

Bordon was interesting because it was also the northern terminus of the Longmoor Military Railway that had been built to train Royal Engineers and other army personnel in the techniques of running railways to assist in the war efforts. The Bordon end of the line had been opened as an eighteen inch gauge railway in 1903 and was relaid to standard gauge in 1905 and 1906. A southern extension to Liss on the Portsmouth Direct Line opened in 1933. There was a roughly circular loop line from Longmoor Downs station that penetrated part of Woolmer Forest. The whole railway ended its usefulness with closure in 1969.

Moving west of Portsmouth, we come to the railways that linked that city and Southampton with Salisbury and Andover. In BR's early days, the service pattern was principally from Portsmouth to Salisbury via Southampton and Romsey, and Portsmouth to Andover Junction via Eastleigh and Romsey, the idea being that passengers could change at Romsey for the alternate destinations. The Salisbury services were largely worked by Drummond 4-4-0s and 'Woolwich' Moguls, the latter's duties incorporating the Bristol and Cardiff trains already described. The meandering double track to Andover Junction was usually worked by push-pull trains with M7s.

Together with the Southampton Terminus to Alton trains, the Portsmouth-Southampton/Eastleigh-Salisbury and Andover group were targeted for the new 'Hampshire' diesel electric multiple units (DEMUs), beginning in 1957. This turned out to be a more challenging story than perhaps many people understand and deserves its own chapter in this book.

Oil trains were not the only trains to venture along the Fawley branch line that turned south off the Bournemouth main line just west of Totton station. There was a sort of passenger service as well, aimed at getting people to work and back again. Fawley branch trains used M7 0-4-4Ts or BR standard class 3 2-6-2Ts. Stations along the single line were Marchwood and Hythe. At Marchwood, there was a new coal-fired power station, built in the 1950s, as well as a large army camp with its own internal railway system that was worked by steam 0-6-0STs and a few diesel shunters. Hythe boasted its own narrow gauge pier railway which continues today. The present pier railway replaced an earlier one in 1922 and claims to be the oldest pier railway in the world. Fawley station was a single platform with just a run-round loop and a set of buffer stops. The branch line opened in 1925 and closed to passenger trains in 1966. Freight continued only as far as the Esso refinery, and the last train serving that was in 2016, with only the Marchwood sidings remaining in use since then. Local bodies are adamant that there is a case for reinstating passenger trains along the Fawley branch because of the new housing in the area. A scheme for this is being pursued with the Department for Transport.

Further west still, beyond Brockenhurst, was a three-way junction called Lymington Junction where the 'Old Road' to Dorchester via Wimborne branched to the right and the Lymington branch peeled off to the left. The branch to Lymington still operates and is single track, but the Junction has gone; the branch line is now worked as a single line from Brockenhurst's Down loop platform running parallel to the main line and diverging south where the junction used to be. A factory on the way to Lymington, Wellworthy's who used to make engineering items such as cylinder liners and piston rings, managed to persuade BR to build a small halt alongside the factory for trains to call by request. In Lymington itself, Lymington Town station has a substantial building and just a single platform, and the stub end of the branch line leads across a bridge to the Pier station where trains connect directly with ferries to Yarmouth in the Isle of Wight.

The original Chandler's Ford station was closed in May 1969 and later demolished, the Eastleigh to Romsey line being singled. A new Chandler's Ford station was built and opened in May 2003. 170308 calls there with a train from Totton to Romsey on 2 December 2005. The 170s were soon replaced by 158s as SWT rationalised the number of classes.

Fawley line passenger services were timed mostly for the movement of workers at Fawley and Marchwood to and from their home towns of Southampton and Eastleigh. Class M7 0-4-4T 30032 had just arrived at Fawley's single platform with the 3.43pm from Southampton Terminus when photographed on 25 May 1957.

Lymington Junction was seriously remodelled during the electrification works, and indeed was eliminated in favour of running the branch single track to Brockenhurst station as an independent track parallel to the main line. In the 1980s, a pair of 2HAP (class 416) units forming an afternoon service to Lymington Pier is seen where the branch line curves away from the main line.

On the Lymington branch, BR inherited a service of L&SWR style push-pull trains, M7-worked. It later replaced the 0-4-4Ts with Ivatt class 2 2-6-2Ts. Weekends were more exciting because there were holiday trains from London Waterloo to Lymington Pier, usually ten coaches headed by 4-6-0s or 'Schools' 4-4-0s. For transit along the branch a Q or Q1 class 0-6-0 was provided to shuttle these trains between Brockenhurst and Lymington Pier while the train engines were turned.

Many people were surprised when the Lymington branch was electrified in the first thrust of electrification of the Bournemouth main line in 1967. The Hampshire diesels that had replaced steam a decade before were themselves replaced by 2HAP electric sets. In the early part of the twenty-first century, 'heritage' EMUs in the form of two specially refurbished three-car CIG units were supplied to Bournemouth depot to work the half-hourly interval service. More recently, due to stock shortages, a class 158 DMU worked all weekday services on the branch with class 450 EMUs working it only at weekends. Now 450s work it all week long. The half-hourly shuttle service of course leaves no room on the branch for through London trains, but the change for passengers at Brockenhurst from main line services is not too burdensome, particularly since a new footbridge with lifts was built there recently.

The only other by-way of significance that perhaps needs reference in this chapter is the single line from West Moors towards Salisbury. This was part of a through route from Bournemouth via Poole that followed the 'Old Road'

On boat train duty on 12 July 1958, Maunsell Q class 0-6-0 30532 stands ready to leave Lymington Pier with a ten-coach train for London Waterloo. A main line locomotive will take over at Brockenhurst. The ferry berth is right alongside the station.

This 2005 view of Lymington Town station shows one of the two 3CIG EMUs that SWT ran for a couple of years as 'heritage' trains. By then the service was half-hourly between Brockenhurst and Lymington Pier, and sharp turnrounds enabled the branch line to be run with one unit. As main line EMUs provide frequent connections at Brockenhurst, the need for separate boat trains has long since passed. The current service is maintained by modern class 450 EMUs.

through Broadstone and Wimborne as far as West Moors. It then turned off to the north-east, calling at several small country stations until it joined the Romsey to Salisbury line at Alderbury Junction. In fact, very little of this route was actually in Hampshire; more of its length was in Dorset and Wiltshire, so perhaps it does not really qualify as a 'Hampshire by-way'. In any case it closed in 1964.

CHAPTER 18

DORSET AND DEVON BRANCHES
TO HARBOURS AND HOLIDAY RESORTS

In the former borough of Poole is the branch line from Hamworthy Junction to the various sidings and quays at Hamworthy on the opposite side of an arm of Poole Harbour to Poole Quay. Goods trains used to traverse the branch and shunt their wagons into the several different groups of sidings. A B4 class 0-4-0T was regularly resident on the branch, and often acted as train

During the lifetimes of BR and the privatised railway, Hamworthy station has not had a passenger service. The branch line continues to survive on freight, the trains serving the nearby quays and industrial sites. In steam days the line was served by a Bournemouth-allocated ex-L&SWR B4 0-4-0T, 30093 being seen there on 17 March 1956 after arrival with wagons from Hamworthy Junction on the main line.

In later years, all train movements on the branch were done by the train engines. On 21 May 1993, Co-Co diesel electric 56073 *Tremorfa Steelworks* pulls away from Hamworthy with empty bogie bolster wagons having delivered steel products. (*Patrick Fitz-Gerald*)

engine to shift wagons up to the yard at Hamworthy Junction to be picked up by a local freight. More recently, there has been international steel and stone traffic along the branch using air-braked block trains hauled by Co-Co diesels, though in the third decade of this century freight is just about petering out.

Further west was the Swanage branch, its recent history being dominated by its resuscitation as one of the UK's more successful heritage railways. When BR inherited the Swanage branch in 1948, it hosted two types of regular passenger train. The more frequent was the service of push-pull trains to and from Wareham on the main line which connected with trains on the London to Weymouth route. The branch trains were worked by Drummond M7 0-4-4Ts until Ivatt 2-6-2Ts and BR 4 2-6-4Ts took over in the 1960s.

Other trains to Swanage included through carriages from London. From 1951, the Royal Wessex main line train included two Swanage coaches in its formation. These were detached from the Down main line train in the evening at Wareham and taken to Swanage as part of the formation of the push-pull service. Likewise, the two coaches were worked up to Wareham next morning to be shunted on the back of the Weymouth to Waterloo 'Wessex' service. Similarly, but on summer weekends only, other through

Map 21 – Dorset and Devon branches

Stations:
1 - Polsloe Bridge
2 - Clyst St. Mary & Digby Halt
3 - Digby & Sowton
4 - Newcourt
5 - Topsham
6 - Exton
7 - Lympstone Commando
8 - Lympstone Village
9 - Littleham
10 - Budleigh Salterton
11 - East Budleigh
12 - Newton Poppleford
13 - Colyton
14 - Colyford
15 - Westham Halt
16 - Rodwell
17 - Sandsfoot Castle Halt
18 - Wyke Regis Halt

© 2020 Colin Boocock

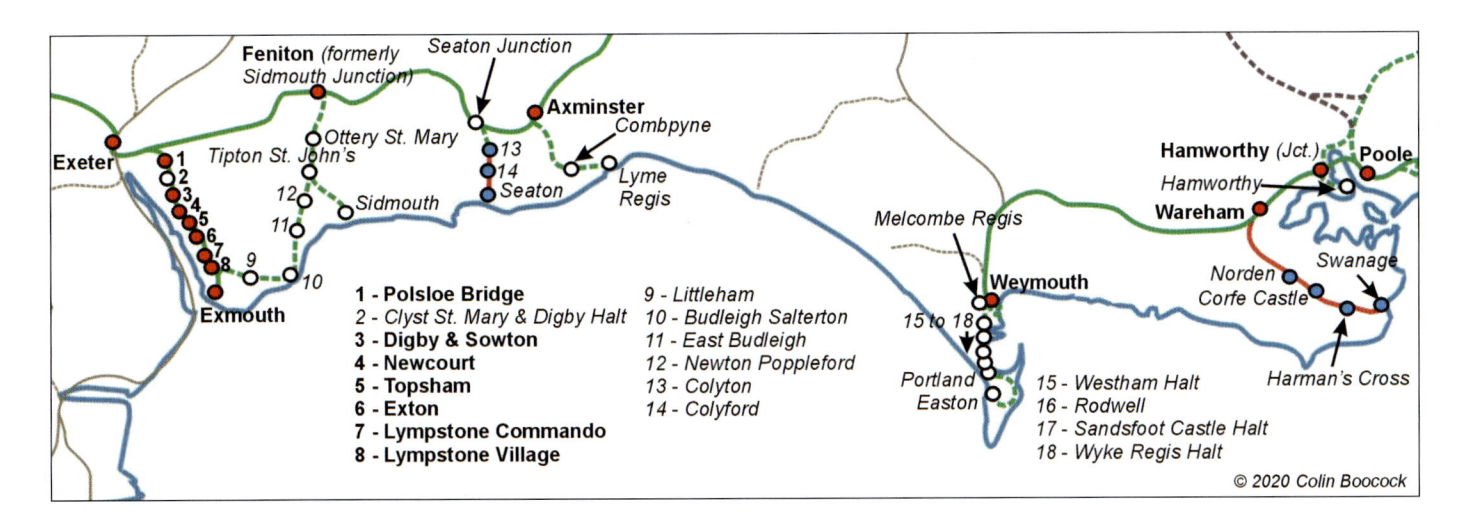

carriages, or even full excursion trains, worked to Swanage for holidaymakers. These trains sometimes brought light Pacifics to Swanage, though these could not be turned on Swanage depot's small turntable, so light engine movements to and from Bournemouth or Weymouth were needed.

A journey on the branch was interesting. The train left the main line at Worgret Junction from where it headed south, soon passing the oil sidings at Furzebrook, or in earlier days crossing the narrow gauge clay railways there and at Norden a little further down the line. The one intermediate station in those days was Corfe Castle, a site dominated by the remains of the Norman castle keep on its high mound, a very attractive scene at the edge of a notable village. With the Purbeck Hills in view to the west, the single line soon descended into the seaside resort of Swanage.

Dieselisation took place in the early 1960s using 'Hampshire' diesel electric units, but the railway's economic performance led British Rail to propose closure of the passenger services which happened eventually in 1972; this had not been a recommendation of the Beeching report which showed the line continuing. This closure left a stump of the branch line open from Worgret Junction to Furzebrook for freight, mainly oil from the Witch Farm oilfield. After the Swanage closure, BR soon lifted the track from Swanage through to Furzebrook.

Preservation however was supported by Dorset County Council (DCC) who bought the track bed, enabling the nascent Swanage Railway to make its first moves towards laying track again and opening the railway. This activity happened in several stages from 1975, reaching its climax early this century with Network Rail reinstating a physical connection with the national network following DCC granting £1 million towards the signalling works required. Spasmodic summer services between Wareham and Swanage by the Swanage Railway and as far as Corfe Castle by South Western Railway have happened recently. The heritage railway is now close to achieving its aim to operate a regular service with its restored and refurbished ex-BR DMUs between Wareham and Swanage connecting with SWR EMUs on the Weymouth-London run. A star feature of the Swanage Railway is the large 'park-and-ride' car park at its new station at Norden. This enables visitors to Corfe Castle and Swanage to leave their cars and take the steam train to these places, thus

Map 21 – Dorset and Devon branches.

One of the attractions of the Swanage Railway since preservation is the classic L&SWR minor station at Harman's Cross, unusual because there never was a station there before! M7 30053 calls on 14 June 2004 with a train from Swanage to Corfe Castle and Norden.

avoiding potential traffic chaos in the village of Corfe Castle. Another gem is the station at Harman's Cross that was opened in 1989. This is based on a L&SWR country station with passing loop and looks as if it has always been there, not like the twentieth century addition it actually is!

Down in Weymouth, further along the coast, the line through to the Quay used to be visited daily by boat trains, initially from Paddington but switched

DORSET AND DEVON BRANCHES • 179

The Weymouth Quay street tramway's sharply curved track led to the GWR using short wheelbase 0-6-0PTs such as 1368 seen on a boat train in July 1959. These locomotives hauled both freight and passenger trains connecting with Channel Islands ferries. The BR ferry alongside the Quay is the 1,885 ton displacement *TS St Julien* which was built in 1925, took part in the Dunkirk evacuation in 1940 as a hospital ship, and was withdrawn in 1960. (*T.B. Owen/Colour-Rail BRW623*)

by BR to Waterloo by the early 1960s. These trains were worked along the quay mainly by ex-GWR 0-6-0 pannier tanks until Drewry diesel shunters took over. After electrification had reached Bournemouth, class 73 electro-diesel locomotives usually worked the boat trains from Waterloo as far west as Bournemouth, being replaced there by class 33 diesels that by then had been passed to traverse the Weymouth Quay branch line. Along the Quay line, boat trains were escorted by a traditional 'man with red flag' together with a police car whose driver carried a huge key ring in case anyone had left their car or van blocking the railway, a common occurrence. Suffice it to say that recent years have seen cessation of the through Channel Island boat trains and switching of some ferries from Weymouth to Poole. The branch line single track, which had been laid along streets in the town, was

One of the difficulties of operating a street tramway in modern times is road traffic getting in the way of trains. 33101 waits patiently in summer 1983 as a policeman tries to open the door of a Vauxhall Viva that is parked over the hatched markings while its owned goes shopping. Eventually the constable was able to drive it away, and the train proceeded to allow its passengers to join the waiting Channel Islands ferry. The Quay tramway is now closed and the track lifted.

mothballed for many years before being decommissioned. The track was lifted finally during 2021.

Another, longer branch line ran further south from Weymouth along the spit that linked the mainland with Portland Bill. There was a station platform near Weymouth Junction called Melcombe Regis for the class O2-worked push-pull trains. The passenger train locomotives were maintained at Dorchester shed and were well looked after. After crossing the bridge over the Fleet onto the Bill proper, the train called at four small halts before arriving at Portland station near the naval dockyard. Then it climbed steeply up and around the cliffs on the east side of the Bill and rounded a long right-hand curve to reach the single-platform terminus at Easton. A feature of the decorations at this station was the collection of fossils in rocks on display around the station platform. An important traffic source here was

DORSET AND DEVON BRANCHES • 181

Another branch line that ran south from Weymouth was that to Portland and Easton. Portland station was photographed on 15 February 1956 from the brake van of a freight train, four years after passenger trains had ceased running on the branch.

The Portland branch traffic to the end was Portland stone, loaded one or two blocks per wagon at Easton. Ex-GWR pannier tank 7782 was working the roster on 15 February 1956 and would take water at Easton station before bringing its train down to Weymouth yard.

Synonymous with the Lyme Regis branch were the three Adams 'Radial' 4-4-2Ts that worked it for many decades until the early 1960s when Ivatt 2-6-2Ts took over. 'Radial' 30583 is pictured on the climb up from Axminster to Combpyne with a train for Lyme Regis on 22 October 1960.

Portland stone from the nearby quarry. This was loaded into open wagons, one or two large blocks per wagon, and taken to Weymouth for onward shipment. Ex-GWR pannier tanks of the 57XX type based at Weymouth depot worked these trains in their later years. However, passenger services had ceased in 1952 and freight ended in 1965.

One branch line that was popular among railway enthusiasts left the West of England main line at Axminster in Devon, turned south and then east, crossing the boundary into Dorset just before reaching its terminus on a bluff above the resort of Lyme Regis. Trains started from a bay platform at the north side of Axminster's Up platform. The line climbed with a ruling gradient of 1 in 40 from the start. Soon after leaving the station, the single track crossed the main line on a bridge and headed south, meandering through and round fields to gain height without resort to major earthworks. The only intermediate station was at Combpyne which had a single platform and a siding or two on the west side. The summit of the line was near, or on, the only major engineering feature of the line, the Cannington viaduct, which crossed a valley in which that hamlet nestled. It has been said that the railway did not build a station at Cannington because no safe location could be found for it!

Lyme Regis station was also a single-platform affair but with adequate wooden buildings on the south side and a small yard which accommodated a single road engine shed. Some subsidence in later years had caused a wall of the shed to sink slightly, giving it a lop-sided appearance when viewed from the east! The line's locomotive was kept here overnight ready to take the first train of the day out of Lyme Regis to connect with an Up express at Axminster.

The motive power that will be for ever associated with this branch line was the Adams 'radial' 4-4-2Ts. The L&SWR had tried other types, including Stroudley 'Terrier' 0-6-0Ts and O2 0-4-4Ts, but only the 4-4-2Ts were flexible enough to cope with the curves and had enough power to master the steep gradients on the line. BR was still overhauling these engines at Eastleigh Locomotive Works as late as 1960, even though later that year the SR drafted in Ivatt 2-6-2Ts after trials that showed that one of these competent locomotives was able to haul six carriages unaided along the branch, one more coach than the maximum number allowed for two 'Radial' tanks double-heading on summer Saturday portions from London. When it took over from 1963, the Western Region tried a 14XX 0-4-2T but that was found wanting, and diesel multiple units soon replaced steam altogether. The railway closed in 1965. The station building at Lyme Regis found new use at Alresford on the Mid-Hants Railway. The Cannington viaduct is a listed structure and survives intact.

The next station three miles further along the main line west of Axminster was Seaton Junction. From there, another branch line struck south heading for the coast at Seaton. This was also a spot for push-pull operation using M7 0-4-4Ts. The line offered scope for through holiday trains, or portions of trains, at summer weekends as it was not severely graded. Seaton, however, began to decline in popularity such that the railway, which the WR had run with DMUs for a few

Between Combpyne and the resort of Lyme Regis is this viaduct at Cannington, now a Grade II listed structure.

184 • SEVENTY YEARS OF THE SOUTH WESTERN

On the line from Sidmouth Junction was the small station at Tipton St John's, junction for Budleigh Salterton and Exmouth. On a few occasions each day, Tipton St John's could be quite busy. 41321 and 41318 have arrived there on 20 April 1963 with a train for Sidmouth and Exmouth which will divide here. 41270 waits in the Up platform. (*Alan Wild*)

years, was closed to all traffic in 1966, including the junction station on the main line.

Closure, however, was not the end of the story. In 1969, the Eastbourne Tramway in Sussex, a small concern that carried holidaymakers on half-size replicas of old UK tramcars, decided to move its operation entirely to Seaton and to lay its narrow gauge track on the trackbed as far north as Colyton, not far from the former Seaton Junction. This project has brought additional interest to the area and has developed its range of miniature trams so that a journey in high season is actually more interesting than one might imagine. The terminus area at Seaton has been upgraded and is a credit to that town.

Further west on the main line, a few miles beyond the summit near Honiton tunnel, was Sidmouth Junction. Branch trains headed off south from here bound for two destinations, either to Sidmouth, mainly a push-pull operation, or to the resorts of Budleigh Salterton and Exmouth, the dividing of the ways being at Tipton St John's station. M7 0-4-4Ts and later Ivatt or BR 2-6-2Ts and BR 4 2-6-4Ts were seen on these lines. Sidmouth station was over a mile from the beach and over 200 feet above it. Train services were mainly direct between Sidmouth Junction and Sidmouth, and between

Exmouth and Sidmouth with a reversal at Tipton St John's; some Exmouth trains ran through to Sidmouth Junction. Summer weekends saw through trains and portions from Sidmouth to London Waterloo. By 1964, now managed by the WR, DMUs were in use on the Sidmouth branch and the Tipton to Exmouth line. All these lines closed in 1967; Sidmouth Junction was then renamed Feniton after the nearby village, thus regaining its original L&SWR name.

The only South Western branch line that survives today in Devon is that from Exmouth Junction east of Exeter Central. Fortunately, that line not only serves as a holiday branch line but also as a commuter route for people living by the sea and working in the city of Exeter. Despite it having been marked in the Beeching report for complete closure, today it carries a healthy service of Great Western Railway DMUs. In older times, it followed the usual pattern of being familiar with M7 0-4-4Ts and modern 2-6-2Ts and 2-6-4Ts, like most of the other branches described in this chapter, these being eased out by DMUs after the WR took over these lines from the Southern in 1963. The Exmouth branch keeps near to the coastline down the east side of the Exe estuary, site of several small towns of 'desirable' residences, eateries, pubs and other facilities. Exmouth marina adds to the seaside attractions of the area.

Looking very business-like, 2-6-4T 80039 rolls into Exmouth with the 2.15pm from Exeter Central. The train is made up entirely of BR standard stock. (*Alan Wild*)

CHAPTER 19

THE ISLANDS
FROM PORTSEA TO WIGHT AND HAYLING

Three islands graced the Portsmouth area, laid out close to the south coast. I have already charted the railway fortunes of Portsea Island with its stations past and present including Portsmouth Harbour, Portsmouth & Southsea, Fratton and Hilsea. To its east was another island, also accessed by bridges from the mainland, namely Hayling Island. And to the south of both Southampton and Portsmouth lay the much larger Isle

Ryde Pier Head station is sited sufficiently out into the sea to enable ferries conveniently to tie up alongside. This was the scene on Sunday 25 June 1961. Adams class O2 0-4-4T 16 *Ventnor* is pulling out with a six-coach train destined for its namesake town, while 25 *Godshill* awaits departure with a train for Newport and Cowes. To the right is the BR paddle steamer *Ryde*, withdrawn from service after its last season in 1969.

of Wight, linked to the mainland even today by no bridge at all but by sea-borne ferries from Lymington, Southampton and Portsmouth. Southsea also has its sea front departure point for the only regular hovercraft service in the UK which crosses the water of the Spithead to the beach alongside Ryde Esplanade. All three islands had railways. Two were distinctly part of the South Western in one form or another, and one wasn't but is included here because of its proximity to South Western rails; it is also interesting in its own right.

I was born in the Isle of Wight but was far too young to remember our house move from Ryde to Addlestone in Surrey in 1939. After our next move, to Bournemouth in 1945, my parents took me to the Isle of Wight on occasional short holidays. I still remember the malachite green of the beautifully turned out Adams O2 0-4-4Ts with SOUTHERN or later on BRITISH RAILWAYS emblazoned on their tank sides above their red nameplates. I was most fortunate at the age of eleven to be let loose with a child rover ticket to enjoy the Island trains, the only restriction being '… be back in Ryde in time for tea!'

Thus I had a compartment to myself on the Ventnor train, glimpsed the engine

Map 22 – The Islands.

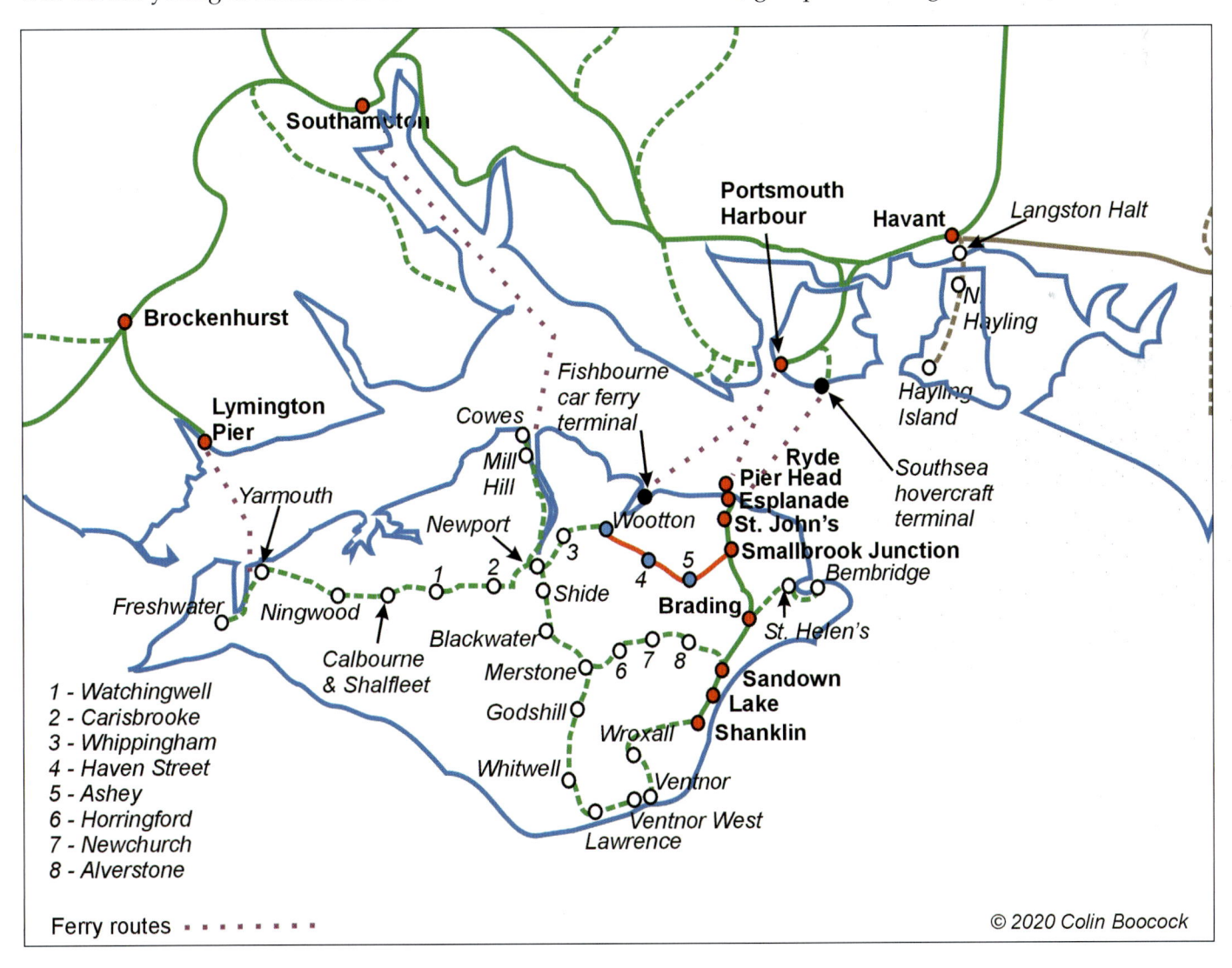

1 - Watchingwell
2 - Carisbrooke
3 - Whippingham
4 - Haven Street
5 - Ashey
6 - Horringford
7 - Newchurch
8 - Alverstone

Ferry routes · · · · · · · ·

© 2020 Colin Boocock

Most mainland stations are omitted for clarity.

Ryde depot was just south of St John's station and across the main line from the works. This scene on 2 August 1958 shows from left to right 33 *Bembridge*, 21 *Sandown*, 29 *Alverstone*, 36 *Carisbrooke*, 17 *Seaview* and 4 *Wroxall*. The depot closed when steam working finished in 1966.

sheds at Ryde St John's Road, saw the Bembridge branch push-pull at Brading and watched at Ventnor as the crew eased our engine onto the short sector plate that enabled it to reach the run-round track, but not until the fireman had shovelled quite a lot of ash out of the smokebox. Back at Sandown, I changed trains and joined a shorter one that headed off to Newport also with an O2 in front. We called at Merstone where a green A1X 'Terrier' 0-6-0T with another push-pull set waited in the loop platform to run south to Ventnor West. In Newport, I saw a second A1X, a war-time black one this time, waiting at a more distant platform with the train for Yarmouth and Freshwater; but I didn't have time to go and catch that one. I had to head back on a direct train as far as Ryde Esplanade, just in time for tea.

Ryde actually had three piers, alongside each other. On the left looking out to sea from Esplanade station was the pedestrian pier that also permitted motor vehicles along its timber-slatted roadway. Next was the pier tramway, two independent tracks, each occupied by a petrol railcar and trailer, all four-wheeled vehicles owned by the railway. British Railways re-engined the petrol cars with diesels in 1959. To the right of the tram pier was the railway, two tracks leading along its pier to the terminus station of Ryde Pier Head with its four platforms. All three piers linked with the end section

THE ISLANDS • 189

On 2 August 1958 W14 *Fishbourne* has run round its train at the Cowes terminus and is ready to depart for Newport and Ryde Pier Head.

Newport is the county town of the island and there is local pressure to reopen the railway to it. W14 *Fishbourne* has arrived with a train from Ryde Pier Head to Cowes.

Between the railway and pedestrian piers at Ryde is the tramway pier, though the latter is now derelict. In summer 1961 the tramway was still operating as two independent tracks with trams 1 and 2 shuttling to and from the Esplanade. No 1 in its final condition as a diesel vehicle is seen leaving Pier Head while PS *Ryde* is moored in the background.

against which the ferries to Portsmouth Harbour berthed. Today the tramway pier still stands, rusting away, but the outer two piers are in regular use.

While Ryde Pier saw the largest number of people being ferried to and from the mainland, the port of Medina at the south end of Cowes was the busiest for freight. The Island's goods engines were four Stroudley class E1 0-6-0Ts. Goods traffic included household and locomotive coal, and general goods and construction materials. One duty that an E1 locomotive undertook from time to time was the tourist train that linked Ventnor with Newport, Yarmouth and Freshwater. This was almost certainly the only regular passenger duty of these engines. One locomotive I did see, arriving at Ryde Esplanade much to my surprise in 1947, was E4 class 0-6-2T 2510. I learned later that this was on trial as a proposed substitute for the ageing O2s, but it wasn't liked by the crews and was soon sent back to the mainland. In normal service, the O2s nearly always faced south out of Ryde. When I saw it the E4 was facing the other way.

Under British Railways, the existence of so many small railways in one area was clearly uneconomic. In 1956, BR closed the lines from Newport to Freshwater, Newport to Sandown, from Merstone to Ventnor West and the Bembridge branch. The Ryde to Newport and Cowes line and the southern extension from Shanklin to Ventnor closed in 1966. That left just the Ryde Pier Head to Shanklin section which was also recommended in Dr Beeching's report to be closed. Local interests claimed this would cause great hardship and persuaded the authorities to retain the line. BR decided, in view of the prevalence of by then ancient rolling stock and locomotives, to modernise the Ryde to Shanklin line as cheaply as was reasonable to ensure the line's continued future.

THE ISLANDS • 191

The island's railways had four Stroudley class E1 0-6-0Ts for freight work. No W1 *Medina* was under repair outside Ryde Works on 11 July 1954. The locomotive is named after the wharf near Cowes through which most freight used to be handled.

This view of Ventnor station from St Boniface Down in 1960 shows 0-4-4T W29 *Alverstone* waiting to depart with a train for Ryde Pier Head. The caves in the cliff face opposite the station were used among other things as garages for road vehicles. The station area is now a small industrial estate.

In early 1990, one of the first batch of ex-LUL trains to work on the island, unit 043, calls at Sandown on a working from Shanklin to Ryde Pier Head. By this date, the island's railways were part of Network SouthEast.

Clearly influenced by the SR's operators and M&EE officers, it was decided to use second-hand trains on the Island Line, as it became known, with conductor rail electrification on the standard Southern system feeding former London Underground units. These were already forty years old when transferred, but they did breathe new life into the Island's railways. Their replacements came when London Underground released some of its 'more modern' 1938 stock. These units arrived as individual vehicles on the island loaded on road trailers carried from Portsmouth on the car ferry to land at Fishbourne. They were the oldest trains on the national network when they were replaced by Class 484 two-car electric units from Vivarail in 2021.

During the time that the Island's main railway was part of Network SouthEast, BR opened a new station at Lake between Sandown and Shanklin to serve the suburb of that name. By then the line was marketed under the Ryde Rail brand. In more recent years, the branding has changed again, this time to Island Rail which makes much more sense when viewed from the perspective of residents in Sandown and Shanklin.

Through the franchisee South Western Railway, a project has been completed to secure the future of the railway on the Isle of Wight. The track and ballast has been relaid to a better standard than the shingle-ballasted bullhead rail track that has survived so long there. Remedial work has been carried out to the railway pier at Ryde. A new passing loop has been laid for Brading, which allows the train service to run at a regular half-hourly interval instead of the previously unsatisfactory twenty/forty minutes service.

THE ISLANDS • 193

Ryde Esplanade station sits on a curve at the landward end of the pier. Transport connections here include a bus station on the extreme left and the hovercraft landing point from Southsea out of the picture to the right. By this date, 15 June 2004, the eastward track on the pier had been abandoned. Unit 009 of the ex-London Underground 1938 stock leaves for Shanklin.

Approaching Wootton on the Ryde to Newport line is class O2 No W24 *Calbourne*. This is actually a modern picture, taken on 25 September 1983, and shows how the Isle of Wight Steam Railway has managed to recreate an authentic memory of how the railways there looked when the Ryde to Newport line was functioning in the late 1950s into the 1960s. The locomotive and the coaching stock it is hauling are genuine IoW vehicles.

The line from Sandown to Newport was closed in February 1956. In August 1958, the signalbox, water tower and island platform at Merstone were still intact though deteriorating slowly. This station used to be the junction for the branch line to Ventnor West and was photographed when the author walked the line.

Meanwhile, I must mention the excellent heritage railway that has grown out of the remains of the Ryde to Newport line. With a connection at Smallbrook Junction just a mile or so south of Ryde St John's, the Isle of Wight Steam Railway has steadily worked to reopen as much of the line as it can without actually being able to extend into the county town of Newport. The line runs through Ashey and Havenstreet as far as Wootton on the outskirts of Newport. It operates a range of trains from a set of really old four-wheeled carriages to the more recently recognisable pre-grouping bogie stock that populated the IoW trains of the Southern Railway and Region before electrification. It has the only surviving Adams O2 0-4-4T in existence and has lovingly restored that to working order as well as two of the Stroudley A1X 0-6-0Ts that worked on the Island in steam days. These are supported by some of the War Department 'austerity' 0-6-0STs of the type that worked at Marchwood or Longmoor, as well as a couple of Ivatt 2-6-2Ts, a class that BR once planned to send across to the Island but which in the event didn't happen because the island's railways were at the time expected to close. The steam railway's working centre and depot is off Haven Street station[12].

In summer 1958, an Island friend and I decided we would walk the full lengths of the trackbeds from Brading to Bembridge and from Sandown to Newport. This was some nine years after my childhood journeys and enabled me to photograph the remains of the stations, in particular those at Bembridge and Merstone, which I had previously not done. Borrowing my father's car for half a day enabled us also to reach and photograph the railway extremities at Freshwater and at Ventnor West. It was all a strange reminder that an island little more than twenty miles long once

---

12. The village is variously written as Havenstreet or Haven Street. The railway station boards show the latter, but the railway's web site gives its address as the former. Villagers are divided on the issue.

supported a railway system of fifty-five miles at its greatest extent.

The last stop for many main line trains from London or from the south coast line before crossing onto Portsea Island is Havant, a junction station that used to have an east-facing bay on the south side of its Down platform. This was the starting point for trains bound for Hayling Island. The island is both a seaside resort and a dormitory town for commuters to Portsmouth. It is connected to the mainland by a road bridge. The LB&SCR built a railway bridge and causeway across Langstone Harbour to reach the island. The line terminated in a small station in Hayling town in the south-west of the island. There were two halts on the line, Langston (always omitting the 'e' at the end of the name) which was north of the bridge, and North Hayling, south of the bridge.

Leaving Havant for Hayling Island on 26 July 1958 is Stroudley 'Terrier' 0-6-0T 32677 with the summer Saturday 3.40pm train made up to three coaches.

The 5.40pm from Havant is seen crossing Langstone Harbour bridge behind 32640. The weakness of this bridge imposed a severe weight restriction, forcing BR to use small and old locomotives on this line.

The bridge imposed a serious weight limit on the operating railway and this led to the use of small locomotives throughout the branch line's life. It was one of the haunts of the Stroudley 'Terrier' A1X class 0-6-0Ts. A SE&CR P class engine was tried, but the sprightly A1Xs prevailed. A summer Saturday would see up to three 'Terriers' in use, one on the branch and one being serviced at each end to take over when the next train arrived there. Otherwise the less frequent weekday service could be run with one engine in steam. The non-corridor carriages were normally pre-grouping vehicles, but there was one interesting exception. BR Eastleigh, noted for its use of resin-bonded fibreglass construction for components such as carriage doors, put together on a BR underframe from a damaged vehicle a new ten-compartment suburban coach body to BR mark 1 outline, the body made almost entirely of plastic. After its trials the design was not perpetuated, but the vehicle saw out its days as a regular carriage in the Hayling Island branch consist. S1000 is preserved and is used on the East Somerset Railway.

The Hayling Island branch line succumbed to the swathe of cuts in the early 1960s by closing to all traffic in 1963. A scheme to convert it to a tramway using a second-hand Blackpool tram eventually gained no official support, and the track was lifted from 1966. The bridge over Langstone Harbour was dismantled, leaving the piers intact. North and south of the bridge the railway has been surfaced as a walkway and cycle track. The train, which everyone locally knew as the 'Hayling Billy', has gone. However, the name lives on in the Hayling Billy public house in the centre of the island. It has rave reviews, so that cannot be bad!

CHAPTER 20

HAMPSHIRE DIESELS
THE 'TUB-THUMPERS'

As delivered, the first twenty-four diesel electric multiple units in the 'Hampshire' group were 500bhp two-car sets. Two vehicles were adequate for the loadings on the Alton route and helped with the necessary hill climbing. Unit 1114 leaves Eastleigh in the evening of 13 May 1959 with a service from Alton to Southampton Terminus.

Like the Western Region's early preference for diesel hydraulic locomotives, the Southern Region had its own ideas for the type of diesel multiple unit it wanted to own, operate and maintain. By the early 1950s, the SR had developed, in close cooperation with the English Electric Company, a set of design and construction parameters for electric multiple units that worked well on its conductor rail infrastructure and had established a long-term contractual agreement with the company. The Southern wanted to use the same standards for its diesel multiple units, which would thus be diesel electric multiple units, or DEMUs for short. Its first essay into this field produced the slab-sided 'Hastings' units, delivered as six-car express corridor sets, each set with a power car at each end. Each power car rode on two EMU standard motor bogies, the innermost one being motored with two EE507 axle-mounted dc commutator motors that were geared for 90mph running. The outermost bogie was not motored but was strong enough to carry the weight of the power unit above it, which a standard trailer bogie would not have been. Behind the driving cab in each power car was a compartment containing a cooling unit with two side radiators; beyond that was the power unit of 500 brake horse power (bhp), the EE 4SRKT four-cylinder in-line engine that was a member of the supercharged RKT series of reliable, floor-mounted engines that English Electric had developed over the recent decade or so. Behind the engine room was the guard and luggage space, then a half-length passenger saloon. The trailer coaches were to all intents and purposes BR mark 1 coaches with narrower bodies but riding on BR single bolster bogies that had been designed to be used under suburban stock.

Introduced in 1957, the 90mph 'Hastings' sets proved the DEMU concept. Designs were quickly developed for a fleet of similar but shorter sets based on outer-suburban type EMU stock for local and regional work. The 'Hampshire' units as first delivered late in 1957 were two-coach sets on 63ft 6in underframes, non-gangwayed, each with one 500bhp power car and built to the full standard mark 1 carriage width of nine feet. In effect they were a DEMU version of the 2HAP EMUs to be built for North Kent but, being for local stopping services, these DEMUs were geared for 75mph maximum speed, the speed that the Southern had adopted as the top limit for most of its secondary routes.

Each 'Hampshire' power car had a half-length five-bay saloon, each bay with an outward opening slam door on each side. The seating was arranged two-plus-three across with an off-centre walkway. A similar saloon graced the inner end of the trailer car. Centrally in this vehicle there were two small toilet compartments, one linked to the second class saloon and one to the corridor that passed to one side of the two first class compartments. There was also one full-width second class compartment just behind the driving cab. Each driving cab on each unit had no side doors but was linked by a central door to a cross vestibule with side doors; this arrangement was to avoid the profusion of cab draughts that had bugged early Southern Railway electric units; the new arrangement was standard across all BR EMUs with electro-pneumatic brakes (EPB), the braking system adopted also for the Southern's DEMU fleets. The slam doors were timber-framed and clad in steel plate with sprung drop light windows in vertical slides and had internal slide door handles as well as external turning ones.

The units were introduced first on Southampton Terminus to Alton trains and on the Salisbury to Portsmouth route via Southampton Central. This was the first time that these services had been scheduled to operate to a clock-face hourly timetable. The use of two-car DEMU sets had been thought by Regional management to have been adequate provision for the traffic then on offer. This soon proved to be erroneous. Passengers flocked to these trains, so much so that overcrowding quickly became endemic – local newspapers reported around a thirty per cent increase in traffic in the first six months due to the introduction of DEMUs and the new timetable.

Thankfully a rescue operation was imminently possible. Eastleigh Carriage Works was building the next batch of 'Hastings' sets. Underframes were therefore available to be diverted for additional carriages to strengthen the 'Hampshire' units to three cars each. Design and construction of twenty new bodies to the standard outer suburban profile was straightforward, too. The main

Within a few months of DEMU operation of a regular hourly service on the Portsmouth-Southampton-Salisbury axis, the popularity of the trains caused significant overcrowding. A third carriage was added, at a stroke almost doubling the standard class accommodation. To haul the extra load, the power cars were re-equipped with more powerful engines of 600bhp. On 19 September 1959, soon after its additional carriage had been inserted, unit 1118 approaches St Denys on a Salisbury to Portsmouth Harbour semi-fast service. Four DEMUs were left as two-car units for the Alton line.

issue was how to raise the engine output, because 500bhp, while adequate for a two-car unit, would not be suitable to accelerate a three-car set from frequent station stops and maintain existing schedules. English Electric stepped in quickly with a proposal to boost the turbo-charger output so that the 4SRKT engine output could be raised to 600bhp. Twenty new engines intended for

'Hastings' units were modified to 600bhp and diverted to the 'Hampshire' upgrade programme. The still fairly new 500bhp engines already in the two-car DEMUs would be transferred to new 'Hastings' sets currently under construction.

The new intermediate trailer cars each had two five-bay second-class saloons which occupied the full length of the coach. This provision almost doubled the second class capacity of these units. However, anyone wanting to use a lavatory on the train who was travelling in the power car or intermediate coach would need to change carriages at a convenient station stop and move to the driving trailer. The new intermediate carriages were introduced into the units as one by one their power units were exchanged for the 600bhp ones, beginning in 1958, such was the urgency to reduce overcrowding, particularly on the Southampton-Portsmouth section.

It soon became apparent that the extension to three cars was not really suitable for those sets working the Alton line. The additional horsepower was less useful at slow speeds on the hills because the two traction motors were only able to deliver a certain amount of torque, and with three carriages on steep gradients they risked being overloaded. Four of the next batch of new 'Hampshire' units, Nos 1121 to 1124, were supplied as two-car sets and mostly dedicated to the Alton trains which had not been experiencing the heavier passenger loadings seen elsewhere.

Riding in a 'Hampshire' power car was an interesting experience. In the first few years, the ride of the bogies was quite hard. Braking from speed was particularly strange because the bogie bolsters that slid vertically between the frame transoms would tilt slightly forward and lock up, shorting out the secondary suspension springs and giving the passengers a thumping hard ride, apparently hitting each rail joint with such force as to make the carriage side doors rattle in their frames! It wasn't quite so bad on accelerating from a stop, but the undamped ride at speed could appear to the trained person to be somewhat out of control. Riding in a power car was, for an engineer such as me, also interesting because the engine vibration came through the floor and one could hear and feel exactly when the various stages of traction motor field weakening were activated. It was not dissimilar in experience to riding on a diesel electric locomotive!

Because of late deliveries of new DEMUs, the new regular interval hourly timetable on the Portsmouth to Andover Junction line was in jeopardy. BR took an unusual and bold step in deciding to operate the new, faster timings with steam locomotives until the new units arrived. The service was temporarily divided into two connecting legs. Portsmouth to Eastleigh trains would be three-coach corridor sets hauled by T9 4-4-0s, and the Eastleigh to Andover Junction leg would revert to M7s on two-coach push-pull trains in view of the short turn-rounds. The results were surprisingly good. In particular, the T9s performed well, keeping close to the diesel timings and living up to their 'greyhound' nickname. However, the M7s, which were clearly being driven enthusiastically to keep to the diesel timings along the curvaceous Test Valley line, began to suffer hot leading axleboxes, necessitating them being lifted at Eastleigh depot for speedy attention and remetalling. There always seemed to be one of these up in the air under the depot's lift hoist! Arrival of the required DEMUs soon rectified the situation.

The urgent need to improve the ride of the DEMUs led to a modification to fit wider spring planks in the bogies to accommodate a more appropriate type

HAMPSHIRE DIESELS • 201

The initial bogie ride of the 'Hampshire' units was hard and swinging. An early modification with wider spring planks was applied to alleviate this; what was known as the 'mark 2' version of the BR single bolster MU trailer bogie is seen here under a unit in the yard at Eastleigh Carriage Works. The wider and deeper spring plank is between the wheelsets.

'Hampshire' units had to be withdrawn from service to enable the bogie modifications to be done, and again later when the power cars were being re-engined with 600bhp engines. On the first occasion, the Portsmouth to Eastleigh leg of the Portsmouth – Andover Junction service was worked by T9 4-4-0s with three coaches, keeping quite well to the diesel timings. 30726 approaches Eastleigh from the Fareham direction on such a working.

When DEMUs were withdrawn for modification, M7-worked push-pull trains had to substitute for DEMUs on the Eastleigh to Andover Junction line. They managed to keep time, but at the cost of several hot axleboxes on the 0-4-4Ts, repairs to which kept Eastleigh depot's mechanical staff very busy. 30249 was working the 7.40pm Eastleigh to Andover Junction when photographed approaching the stop at Chandler's Ford.

of secondary coil spring. Because one or two sets were out of service in summer 1958 for this to be done, the Eastleigh to Andover Junction leg once again found itself being worked by M7s with push-pull trains, though diesel units were able to work the Portsmouth-Eastleigh section this time.

Indeed, the ride of these units and particularly of the express EMUs built for the first phase of the Kent Coast electrification gave a real headache to engineers, not only on the SR but also at the M&EE design headquarters in Derby. A series of trials based from Lancing Carriage Works near Worthing in 1960 led to a further range of modifications to the BR standard single bolster multiple unit bogie, with theoretical technical guidance from HQ engineer Jury Koffmann. The result was a set of changes within these bogies that revolutionised the vehicle ride. The changes included long vertical swing links supporting the spring planks, with so-called 'knife-edge' rocking ends to reduce friction, anti-roll bars to control lateral vehicle body roll (a 'first' in a BR bogie design), and vertical and lateral hydraulic dampers. The vertical rubbing plates that had caused the hard vertical ride were eliminated by the use of longitudinal torsion bars, one either side, linking the ends of the spring plank to the bogie frame. Softer secondary coil springs were fitted. The changes brought the ride up an acceptable standard and substantially reduced the internal vibrations in the passenger compartments as well. The mark 4 bogie modification was applied almost across the whole fleet of SR EPB EMUs and DEMUs, except for the later 'Oxted' DEMUs which were being built at the time when the mark 3 bogie modification version was the latest one available.

Meanwhile, Eastleigh Locomotive Works had been pioneering production of a carriage exterior slam door made out of resin-bonded fibreglass. This proved to be stronger and also lighter than the timber-framed standard variety and very much less in need of structural maintenance at overhauls. The 'plastic doors' were introduced across the SR's EPB fleet of EMUs and DEMUs and immediately almost eliminated the noisy vibrations that had plagued riders in the DEMU power cars in particular.

The last seven of the outer-suburban type of DEMUs were intended for Reading to Salisbury services and were nicknamed the 'Berkshire' units. Externally, the main difference from the 'Hampshire' sets was that the guard's van was longer to enable more luggage to be carried. To compensate for this, the passenger saloon lost one bay and was thus four bays long.

Electrification of the Bournemouth line in 1967 and the WR later taking over responsibility for the Basingstoke-Reading service enabled many of these units to be redeployed, and others to be withdrawn. In later years, such as those when BR's Network SouthEast business was up and running, the various types of DEMUs became much more common-user in their areas of operation. 'Oxted' sets were seen in Hampshire. 'Hampshire' and 'Berkshire' units joined 'Oxted' sets on the services out of London Victoria and London Bridge to serve the commuter lines south to Uckfield and to East Grinstead, and also the Hastings to Ashford (Kent) services, until they were all replaced after privatisation by Connex South Central's 'Turbostar' class 170 (later 171 after fitting Dellner couplers) DMUs. One or two of the 'Hampshire' sets were modified with through corridors and gangways within the sets to facilitate conductor-guard ticket collections on the Ashford (Kent) to Hastings line.

There are at least five full DEMUs in preservation around the south of England as well as various odd vehicles from former sets. Three units are on former South Western lines at the time of writing. The Mid-Hants Railway has 205 025 formed, sensibly in view of its gradients, as a two-car unit. The Caledonian Railway (Brechin) has 205 028 and 032.

In later BR years, after there had been branch line closures in Sussex and Kent, a few of the narrower-bodied DEMUs of the 'Oxted' group moved to the South Western and shared some of the Salisbury to Portsmouth workings. Resplendent in new BR blue livery, unit 1302 was entering St Denys station on such a working in 1968.

A small number of SR DEMUs has been preserved, including 1132 which went to the Dartmoor Railway, seen in traffic at Meldon Quarry station on 22 June 2014. This unit is now at Brechin in Scotland. (*Colin J. Marsden*)

CHAPTER 21

ELECTRIFICATION AT LAST
WORTH WAITING FOR!

On the Isle of Wight, electrification began with second-hand London Underground stock which was the first south of the Thames to appear in the new BR rail blue livery. A 4VEC+3TIS formation arrives at Ryde Esplanade from Shanklin in August 1979.

As I have already written, the Southern Railway's long-term strategy had included eventually eliminating steam traction by extending its electrified network to include the railway from Woking to Bournemouth and from Worting Junction to Salisbury. Diesel locomotives would work trains beyond these points as traffic further west was believed not to justify electrifying these lines. Three electric locomotives were already working on the Central Division and would have been seen as prototypes for future schemes. Three 1Co-Co1 diesel electric locomotives were delivered in the first decade of BR's life and these were given duties that included the railway west to Exeter. The three diesel electric shunting locomotives built by the SR before the war were also prototypes for future elimination of the smaller sizes of steam locomotive. So one can see with the benefit of hindsight that, early on, the Southern Railway had deliberately sown the seeds for elimination of steam locomotives when the time eventually became right to do so.

British Railways was however strapped for cash from its earliest years, having to spend quite a lot in continuing the recovery from war damage and associated restraints on maintenance expenditure, for example on working to remove the many temporary speed restrictions across the nation. However, by the middle of the 1960s, the time began to look right to resurrect the plans to electrify the railway at least to Bournemouth. The Kent Coast electrification scheme had been completed in 1962 and was attracting considerable extra passenger business with its clockface timetable and shorter journey times. The natural choice was clearly more of the same.

But there was a snag with the Bournemouth line that made it different from north Kent. While Southampton and Bournemouth were clearly traffic sources of useful size, west of Bournemouth the towns of Poole, Wareham, Dorchester and Weymouth were smaller, the last two in the list already being served by trains of the Western Region as well as the Southern. Splitting electric multiple unit trains at Bournemouth might seem the obvious answer, but how do you get EMUs to Weymouth when there are no plans to electrify the infrastructure?

The SR's Chief Operating Officer and Chief Mechanical & Electrical Engineer were in charge of departments that were able to provide an innovative solution to this dilemma, a unique solution that was never copied by any other railway to my knowledge. It was actually quite simple. Instead of every four-car unit in a Waterloo to Weymouth electric train being motored, as was conventional EMU practice, all the power needed would be concentrated in the motors of the unit at the London end of the train; this powered four-car set we can call a tractor unit. Other four-car sets would be trailer units, still set up with the driving controls and braking systems that were standard on SR EMUs, but without any traction motors under them.

A train from Waterloo to Weymouth would leave the London terminus with the tractor unit propelling one or two trailer units and this formation would be designed to run up to 90mph where sensible on the way to Southampton and Bournemouth. At Bournemouth, in the off-peak season, the front trailer unit would be uncoupled from the rest of the train and coupled to a diesel locomotive to be hauled to Weymouth. In the high season, the locomotive would need to manage two trailer units to and from Weymouth. On the way back, the diesel locomotive would be at the back of the train working push-pull and totally unmanned, the driver being in the leading cab of the front trailer unit. On arrival at Bournemouth, the Weymouth portion would be propelled gently onto the back of a tractor unit (with or without another trailer unit already attached) ready and waiting for it and the locomotive would be uncoupled from the rear. The tractor unit would then haul the trailer unit(s) to Waterloo. The maximum train formation on the Bournemouth-London stretch would be twelve coaches, the minimum eight. Some would be eleven, allowing for an electro-diesel locomotive to work the train instead of a tractor unit.

In the UK, no railway had at that time attempted to propel push-pull trains of more than three coaches, nor had such operations been at speeds as high as 70 to 90mph. Testing was needed to prove the concept and to convince Her Majesty's Railway Inspectorate (HMRI) that such operation would be safe. The first significant push-pull trials were carried out with a prototypically-modified class 33 Bo Bo diesel electric locomotive, D6580. To provide a train for it, a six-coach set was made up of former Portsmouth 4COR type carriages, six vehicles in all with a former driving motor coach at each end but without traction motors. The traction control system on this set was replaced by one like that used on the SR's EPB groups of EMUs. D6580 was similarly equipped and was visually changed by the addition of two sets of jumper connections and air pipe hoses on each cab front. Trials were successful enough for this train to be used for a season or two on the Clapham Junction to Kensington Olympia service.

The electrification scheme laid conductor rails on all main line and slow line tracks between Woking and Branksome including most recess loops. At Branksome, the station beyond Bournemouth, empty units would need to reverse to access the new maintenance depot down the hill towards the former (closed) Bournemouth West terminus. Line voltage was set at 750V dc, the same as was becoming standard on the SR following introduction of the Kent Coast electrification. The Waterloo to Woking end was still at 660V dc, but upgrading was programmed to follow.

In readiness for the Bournemouth electrification scheme, in which push-pull operation of up to twelve coaches at speeds up to 90mph was planned, class 33 diesel locomotive D6580 and a six-coach set of ex-4COR vehicles was modified and assembled for trial running. After the trials, set 601 found regular employment on the Clapham Junction to Kensington Olympia shuttle train; it is seen at Clapham carriage sidings in 1967.

Between Beaulieu Road and Brockenhurst lies Woodfidley curve which had a 75mph speed restriction. 4REP 3009 with one 4TC unit rounds the curve in the New Forest while working an Up semi-fast from Bournemouth to Waterloo in August 1967.

In summer 1983, 33108 propels two 4TC units up the 1 in 60 above Parkstone station with a Weymouth to Waterloo service. The units will couple to a 4REP at Bournemouth with the 33/1 released there to collect the next train for Weymouth.

Chapter 22 describes in more detail the tractor units, classified 4REP, and trailer units which were 3TC and 4TC; it also introduces the 4VEP units that worked stopping services between London and Bournemouth. Chapter 22 also describes briefly what happened to the class 74 electro-diesel locomotives that were converted from class 71 electric locomotives to work boat trains and other services.

The services these push-pull units worked had easily-remembered operating codes that were displayed externally on roller blinds within the gangway ends. Code 90 was the Weymouth boat train (locomotive hauled), 91 marked an express train with stops only at Winchester and Southampton on the way to Bournemouth, and code 92 was for the hourly semi-fast services that called at Clapham Junction, Basingstoke, Winchester, Eastleigh, Southampton Central, Brockenhurst, New Milton, Christchurch, Pokesdown and Bournemouth. Code 93 denoted stopping trains.

The 91s started off as two-hourly and most had Weymouth portions. The early success of this electrification soon led to the 91s becoming hourly, needing additional REP and TC units to be supplied and the 3TCs that had been used mainly on the semi-fasts (92s) were extended to 4TCs. Once the 91s became hourly, they conveyed all the Weymouth portions and the 92s all terminated at Bournemouth.

The residents of Weymouth had to wait another twenty-one years before electric trains began working to their town. The year 1988 saw the culmination of works to lay conductor rails to the by then much reduced station at Weymouth, power supplies being specified that were sufficient only for trains of up to

Electro-diesel locomotives were delivered for trains that used non-electrified sidings and yards. The class 73 series proved to be very reliable machines. A 73/1 passes Brockenhurst with an Up Channel Islands boat train from Weymouth in 1983.

210 • SEVENTY YEARS OF THE SOUTH WESTERN

The 8VAB unit was hurriedly assembled to help plug the gap in traction availability soon after the Bournemouth electrification started. Unit 8001 lasted to 1975; it is seen near Southampton Airport in 1968 on a Waterloo to Bournemouth semi-fast with a 4VEP attached to the front.

The class 74 electro-diesels were converted from redundant E5000 series electric locomotives. E6104 propels two 4TCs on an Up semi-fast train through St Denys in 1968.

five coaches to operate under electric power. This fitted the design of the new express units that were commissioned for this service to replace the REP+TC formations which were withdrawn. By this time, however, the unreliable class 74 electro-diesels had already been scrapped, the last being withdrawn in 1977. The Channel Islands boat trains had been withdrawn in 1987. Future travellers to the Islands would have to use the regular EMU train services plus bus connections to the ferries. Most however soon fled to the short-hop airlines.

Two years later, the Solent Link electrification scheme got the conductor rails laid between St Denys and the west and north sides of the Portsea triangle, and between Eastleigh and Fareham. A new station appeared at Hedge End between Eastleigh and Botley, the first new station to be opened in Hampshire since Southampton Airport in 1966. For these services, refurbished EMUs,

New EMUs being delivered early this century by BREL to Connex South Central and SouthEastern had displaced sufficient older units to enable South West Trains to run the newly-electrified Southampton and Eastleigh to Portsmouth routes without acquiring new stock. On 8 March 2003, 4CIG (class 421) 1315 leaves Southampton Central with a London-bound stopping train while 4CEP (411) 1565 arrives from Portsmouth. Both are in the colours first adopted by Stagecoach, owners of the South West Trains franchise.

A step change in passenger comfort came with the arrival in 1988 of the new class 442 five-car units based on the mark 3 carriage body design. At a later overhaul, these units received a much advanced livery in which the firm Best Impressions used the Stagecoach colours imaginatively. Unit 2409 at Waterloo in 2009 looks superb!

mainly 4VEPs, replaced the DEMUs that had worked the Southampton to Portsmouth stopping trains. The services from Salisbury to Portsmouth became dependent on the hourly WR DMU services from the Bristol direction to maintain the link from Salisbury to Portsmouth and Brighton. A brand-new hourly EMU service from Portsmouth to London Waterloo via Fareham and Eastleigh was an innovation that gave the residents of Fareham their best ever train service to London.

Another new service was established in the twenty-first century by Connex South Central. This was an hourly four-car class 375 EMU from London Victoria that came south via Three Bridges and the South Coastway, took the north side of the Portsea triangle, and reached Southampton Central via Fareham. When Connex was sent packing by the Department for Transport, the franchise was re-let, this time to Govia who branded it the Southern Railway which is how the trains are marked at the time of writing, though nowadays it is all part of the very much bigger franchise that also includes Gatwick Express, Thameslink and Great Northern. SWR tried to get in on the act in 2017 with a proposal to run a through hourly train from Weymouth to Portsmouth via Fareham instead of to Waterloo; understandably the burgers of Weymouth objected vociferously to this idea and managed to persuade SWT to continue with two trains an hour to London, a service which they had enjoyed for about a decade.

My only beef about the train service between London and Bournemouth is that timings today are not all that ambitious. There are stretches of Joseph Locke's beautiful main line that could support 125mph running, but SWT appears to have no aspirations in this direction. In steam days, expresses with one intermediate stop did the 108 miles in two hours. Nowadays, the faster electric trains take up to one hour fifty-five minutes depending on the stopping pattern, slower than the new electric service in 1967. I now live in Derby which is 130 miles from London and has two trains an hour doing that longer distance in one and a half hours (fasts) and one and three-quarters hours (semi-fasts), and this with diesel electric multiple units on a route that abounds with speed-restricted curves!

The 'Desiro' units enabled SWT to eliminate its last slam door stock. 444020 calls at Hinton Admiral on 14 November 2007 with a Down stopping service.

CHAPTER 22

NEW TRAINS
…. OR WERE THEY NEW?

From 1957 to 1968 virtually all trains serving the South Western main lines were replaced. This view at Eastleigh in 1968 reminds us of the Hampshire dieselisation, with an Alton to Southampton DEMU leaving; and of the Bournemouth electrification with 4REP 3002 arriving with an Up semi-fast. Semaphore signalling had also been replaced by multiple aspect.

To keep the cost of the 1967 Bournemouth electrification scheme as low as possible, the BRB insisted that almost all the vehicles for the express units had to be converted from early examples of existing mark 1 main line carriages. The interiors would be upgraded to current standards with double-glazed windows, full electric heating and wall and floor insulation for both heat containment and noise reduction. Coloured plastic walls were to replace the erstwhile timber decor of old. Lighting would be brought more up-to-date and brighter. Most standard class accommodation would be in open saloons using existing seating but with new, brighter moquette. First class would be in compartments with ergonomically shaped seats. The carriages would ride on modern coil sprung B.5 bogies.

The four-car class 508 units were among several groups of new trains that were based on the 4PEP prototype which had been trialled on the SR and had proved the concept of sliding doors in place of slam doors. Two trains of 508 units approach Vauxhall on 10 May 1981 while a 4EPB rolls past on the right.

The 508s were later transferred away to Merseyside, being replaced by class 455 units like 5825 seen here with another on a train bound for Chessington, near Tolworth on 29 May 1985. (*Colin J. Marsden*)

The tractor units were made up of two driving motor coaches, each riding on two mark 6 bogies of the same basic design as used under the SR's successful class 73 electro-diesel locomotives. These were in my view the best riding bogies in the whole train. The two motor coaches were the only carriages that were constructed new in these express trains and had harder, modern design seating. The motor bogies used the same EE546 traction motors as did the class 73s, the four of which together output 1,600bhp. Thus, a 4REP unit, as the tractor units were to be dubbed, would have 3,200bhp which was 200bhp more than other modern twelve-coach EMUs on the SR at that time. On many trains, one of the REP power cars was used as the restaurant car, supplied from the small kitchen in the adjacent buffet car. The other intermediate vehicle in the set was the guard's brake car with first class compartments included.

Most of the trailer units were four-car sets, but a few began life as three-car sets, only to be extended to four cars in later years. Each four-car trailer set had a driving open standard coach at each end, a full first class coach, and a standard class coach with guard's brake. These units were classified 4TC, the three-car ones with no first class being 3TC. The TCs were mainly converted at York Works and delivered in overall rail blue, an error in my view and one which was corrected the first time these units went through Eastleigh Works for overhaul, from which they emerged looking much smarter in blue-and-grey.

Stopping trains on the route were covered by twenty new four-car EMU sets designated 4VEP. These were slam door units with an old-fashioned interior layout that was similar to many SR suburban units, as well as having many doors along the sides. They started off with luggage racks mounted on brackets across the tops of the seats, a layout later deemed hazardous because of the risk to passengers of falling luggage after which normal ceiling side racks were fitted. Stopping trains were code 93 and could not work west of Bournemouth. It was not until the 1980s that the Bournemouth line received units with power operated sliding doors. In this first electrification phase, the Lymington branch was worked by existing two-car units of type 2HAP.

Late delivery of the last members of the 4REP type, and the SR's insistence on starting the summer timetable on time on 10 July 1967, led that summer to some interesting alternative train formations appearing, mostly on the 92 semi-fast services. Class 33/1s (push-pull fitted BRCW Type 3s) and class 73 electro-diesels could be seen in pairs hauling or propelling trains between London and Bournemouth. I saw one with a 33/1 at each end. Non-push-pull fitted 33s also appeared with TC stock but in haulage mode only. Occasionally, a train arrived at Bournemouth from Weymouth only to find the London train waiting with a 73 on the rear; thus the train went up to Waterloo with its locomotive in the middle! Tough luck on the Weymouth passengers hoping to visit the buffet car.

To ease the situation in 1968, while the SR was still waiting for all the class 74 electro-diesel conversions from class 71 Bo-Bo electrics to arrive, the Region cobbled together a special unit to act as a back-up to keep the service running. The 8VAB unit as it was dubbed (Vep And Buffet) was formed out of seven VEP coaches that included three power cars plus a borrowed RU loco-hauled kitchen buffet car modified with through control wiring. The unit usually ran with another 4VEP in multiple as a twelve-car train. Four power cars enabled it to keep to the tight schedules of the semi-fast 92 trains despite its 90mph maximum speed, which 'straight' 4VEPs would not have been able to do.

The aforementioned ten class 74s were derived from redundant Bo-Bo electrics that had originally been supplied for the Kent Coast electrification scheme's freight services, which regrettably had dwindled. Their new duties included working boat trains to and from Southampton Docks. South of Northam Junction, and west of Millbrook, one of these locomotives could switch from electric operation off the third rail by starting up its Paxman 650bhp diesel power unit. This could provide enough tractive effort to take the train off the conductor rail and on the non-electrified tracks leading to and inside the Docks areas. However, the diesel engine was insufficiently powerful to take a train west of Bournemouth all the way to Weymouth at any useful speed, and the same applied to the class 73s. When one of these locomotives worked a Channel Islands boat train bound for Weymouth, it was replaced at Bournemouth by a class 33 diesel. If the Weymouth line had been electrified, the 73 or 74 could have worked it along the Quay branch on diesel power at the very low speed limit in force.

The Weymouth line was indeed eventually electrified as I have described. New five-car class 442 EMUs were built for this service, based on BR mark 3 coach bodies riding on standard BX-series air-sprung EMU bogies fitted with yaw dampers enabling them to run up to 100mph. The formation included a buffet in the central brake coach. Each unit had four traction motors taken from withdrawn REP motor coaches, so a ten-coach train was able to muster the same 3,200bhp as a twelve-coach REP+TC formation. Trains from London would be ten coaches at peak times and just five off-peak. All ten-coach trains bound for

The BREL class 442s for main line workings were delivered in Network SouthEast colours and looked fine. These were the first mark 3 coaches in the UK to have automatic swing plug doors; these gave trouble at first. 2420 awaits departure on an Up working at Bournemouth's by-then rather decrepit Central station on 14 December 1991.

The class 159 DMUs used between Waterloo and Exeter are maintained at their dedicated depot at Salisbury and have gained a good reputation for reliability. The picture shows 159022 calling at Axminster on 30 January 2016.

Weymouth would split at Bournemouth and leave one of the two units behind.

The 442s were a considerable advance on what had gone before, with a smooth quiet ride, full air-conditioning, power-operated access doors and a well-designed exterior including gangwayed cab fronts in which the gangway looked to be an integral part of the vehicle rather than something added on as an afterthought (viz the original 458s and Scotland's 385s). They were delivered in the white, red and blue livery of Network SouthEast. 4VEP units soldiered on working stopping trains, looking all the more old-fashioned. When Stagecoach took over at privatisation, the 442s were repainted in more striking styles as seen in the photographs.

The UK government was insistent that slam door trains should be eliminated from our railways. Thus, from 2004 the franchisee South West Trains (SWT), owned by Stagecoach, obtained on lease forty-five new class 444 five-car express EMUs that were built by Siemens in Austria, as well as a fleet of 127 class 450 four-car outer-suburban units, also from Siemens but this time made in Germany. The 444s were initially shared between the Bournemouth and Weymouth line and the Portsmouth Direct line services. Later, SWT decided to move some 444s away from the Portsmouth line to increase seating capacity there using 450s (released by the retention of 458s on the Windsor lines) and to take the opportunity to use the 444s to replace all the 442s which were summarily withdrawn despite them currently going through a refurbishing programme at Wolverton which SWT had itself initiated. The political uproar that followed, led by a local Portsmouth MP, raised many eyebrows but did nothing to change things immediately. The 442s later went to work the Gatwick Express services.

In the second decade of the twenty-first century, new trains went into service on Gatwick Express and the 442s were once again redundant. Some refurbished ones re-entered service with South Western Railway in 2020, this

NEW TRAINS • 219

For outer-suburban work, Alstom delivered to SWT a series of four-car EMUs of class 458. Initially not truly reliable, these were later rebuilt into five-car sets with most of the same maker's Gatwick Express class 460s incorporated into them. Two 458s in their original form approach Vauxhall on 19 August 2005 on a Windsor service.

The main delivery of units for outer-suburban services came from Siemens in the form of the 450 class four-car units. On 6 December 2005, 450071 awaits departure from Bournemouth with an Up stopping train.

time on the Portsmouth Direct line to alleviate the apparent pain caused by having to put up with 450s on express services. However, the drop in passenger carryings caused by the pandemic led SWR to withdraw the 442 units permanently early in 2021, even those units that had received new traction equipment. They are currently off-lease and being scrapped.

The 444s soon settled down as SWT's flagship trains on the Bournemouth and Portsmouth lines. 444009 arrives at Hinton Admiral on 14 November 2007.

To maintain its classes 444 and 450 EMUs, Siemens built this brand new depot at Northam, Southampton. Seen on 8 March 2003 during its construction phase, the staff at this depot have ensured the continuing reliability of the 'Desiro' family of units.

The new generation of suburban EMUs that is sweeping away all the 455, 456, 458 and 707 units is the Bombardier class 701 units. 701002 passes Isleworth on 12 August 2020 on a Waterloo – Brentford – Richmond – Waterloo mileage accumulation run. (*Patrick Fitz-Gerald*)

Upgrading of earlier technology is an on-going feature of the modern railway. The South Western Railway 442s, for example, have been through a programme of re-tractioning at Wolverton, replacing their second-hand English Electric dc equipment by modern traction equipment from Kiepe including solid state controls. The picture shows unit 442414 being hauled from Wolverton to Eastleigh behind 47812, with 57312 at the rear, the consist including four barrier-translation vehicles. The train is seen passing Isleworth on 27 November 2020. These units have since been withdrawn. (*Patrick Fitz-Gerald*)

CHAPTER 23

WHO OWNS IT NOW?
'... AND THE FIRST SHALL BE LAST'

Five years into the South West Trains franchise and this 4CEP unit is still in BR's Network SouthEast colours! Unit 1553 hurries through Hersham working semi-fast from Basingstoke to Waterloo on 18 January 2001.

There were three quite different ideas going round in the early 1990s about how railway privatisation might be set up. Prime Minister John Major had a personal vision that BR could be divided up geographically into large companies something like the 'Big Four' railways that our forebears lived with from 1923 to 1948. The first Sir Bob Reid, Chairman of British Rail at the time, had already managed the dividing up of the operating railway into business sectors[13], each of which had its own profit-and-loss account and bottom line by which financial performance could better be judged; BR was keen to offer these business sectors, or their smaller sub-sectors, as potentially saleable stand-alone companies. Apparently, the Adam Smith Institute, which had the ear of government where it mattered, actively promoted the concept of franchises, a bit

---

13. InterCity, London & South East (later re-branded Network SouthEast), Regional Railways, Freight, and Parcels.

like the way television companies are competitively franchised out periodically.

By the mid-1990s, apart from the operating railway, those bits which could be sold off relatively easily had been disposed of. Railways no longer ran hotels and shipping, for example. Outfits such as British Rail Engineering Ltd. (BREL) and BR Maintenance Ltd. (BRML) were on the table as saleable, but eventually the sales were of the individual works rather than the companies as a whole, presumably to foster the idea of promoting some competition between them. Apart from Freightliner, which was an obvious sale item on its own, the freight sector was believed to be more saleable as three smaller competing companies. Thus, Load Haul, Mainline and TransRail were born, only to be snapped up by the Wisconsin Central team from the USA and merged to form English, Welsh & Scottish Railway (EWS). Other companies were formed later that entered the rail freight business with some energy, groups like the Atomic Energy Authority and GBRf. EWS eventually got taken over by Deutsche Bahn.

To get the passenger businesses into a form that offered something that looked like competition, they were split up into over twenty individual potential franchises. The main element of competition was not generally between operating companies but between those bodies that had to bid to own and operate the franchises. BR's former Southern Region perhaps was one of the easiest to define as it was naturally divisible into the three areas that were delineated by the three former Divisions, South Western, Central and South Eastern. The first round of franchise sales put the South Western into the hands of the Scottish bus company Stagecoach which took over in 1996 and managed to hold on to it for twenty-one

South West Trains pitched its second-generation liveries well, the 'blue trains' being outer suburban. A pair of five-car 458s arrives at Staines on a train from Reading on 4 July 2018.

By comparison, South Western Railway has opted for a uniform livery across all train types. Looking less colourful, 159006 brings up the rear of a Waterloo to Salisbury and Exeter service at Basingstoke on 25 January 2020.

years, losing it in 2017 to a consortium formed of First Group and Mass Transit Railway of Hong Kong (MTR) when it was renamed South Western Railway.

BR had set up a sub-sector within InterCity which it called Midland Cross-Country. This managed the Midland Main Line express services out of St Pancras as well as InterCity-quality cross-country services spanning the whole country except London. These two parts of the sub-sector were separated and became individual franchises. Richard Branson's Virgin company was successful in buying Cross-Country. Arriva got hold of it much later.

The ownership of passenger rolling stock was subject to serious study in the mid-1990s, and the BR Board obtained government agreement to dividing the assets up into three rolling stock leasing companies. These became the independent companies of Angel Trains, Eversholt Rail and Porterbrook Leasing. Later ownership moves included banks and investment groups taking over these companies, but they are all still there and have recently been joined by other new start-ups in the industry. The pattern is that franchise holders lease rolling stock from one or more of these companies for the duration of the franchise period. The rolling stock companies (ROSCOs) use their capital to purchase new trains when required and obtain a return on their investment from the lease rental. Most of them are also in the business of paying for the major overhaul of the trains they own, which also comes out of the rental.

A new situation emerged from this system. In BR days, when trains were withdrawn as life expired, they were almost always sold for scrap. Now, with short lease terms of seven to ten years being more common than long ones, trains that go off-lease are usually held in safe storage with the prospect that another lessee may come along and use them. It has only been recently when the

Department for Transport imposed tough demands for train replacement to meet legal requirements such as disabled access that ROSCOs have been sidelined a little. The InterCity Express project and the new class 700 trains for Thameslink, for example, were specified and ordered by government as a means of 'getting it done'.

In 1996, Stagecoach's South West Trains franchise took over all train services out of London Waterloo terminus. As with other franchises, it was constrained by the service commitments it had entered into as part of its franchise agreement. It did use its initiative a bit, particularly during the short period when SWT ran a service of four trains an hour between Waterloo and Southampton Central. That proved to be a little over-the-top and was soon thinned out.

By leasing trains from ROSCOs, SWT was able to meet the Government's franchise requirement to get rid of slam-door stock. The class 442 fleet was owned by Angel Trains as are the 444 and 450 fleets. Eversholt Rail owns SWT's 455 and 456 suburban trains, and Porterbrook has the 159 series of DMUs and the 458 EMUs. The Siemens fleets are maintained by the builder at its dedicated new depot at Northam. Most other SWT fleets are maintained at Wimbledon depot.

The CrossCountry franchise has brought 'Voyagers' to the South Western route since privatisation began. Firstly it was Virgin CrossCountry, and then Arriva took over. One of the latter's class 221 units arrives at Birmingham New Street on 30 January 2020 on a Bournemouth to Manchester Piccadilly working.

Many photographers comment that favourite railway viewpoints have disappeared as a result of encroaching trees or branches. Scenes such as this 1983 view of a charter train curving through Christchurch in later BR days are no longer available at some locations. Thankfully, Network Rail has begun to get to grips with clearing those trees that pose a danger to smooth train operating during the leaf-fall season.

Bournemouth depot, I understand, now looks after the 458s.

BR equipped the Cross-Country part of Midland Cross-Country with HST sets and class 47-hauled trains of mark 2 stock, latterly of air-conditioned varieties. When Virgin took these over, they quickly began to sport Virgin's bright livery of red with white stripes. From 2002, the Virgin Voyager fleet of four- and five-car diesel electric multiple units began to enter service, enabling some faster train timings to be set up. Unlike the BR/SR DEMUs, the Voyagers have one underfloor Cummings engine of 750bhp under each car. This drives an alternator that supplies current to traction motors suspended in the bogies. The performance of these units was quite a revelation when they were first introduced. Acceleration from a standing start was every bit as good as many EMUs. The high installed power also gives them excellent hill climbing and high speed performance up to their maximum of 125mph.

I mentioned earlier the Southern Railway service between Southampton and London Victoria via Fareham and the Coastway line. The class 377 trains used on this are the earlier standard four-car units that Bombardier built from 2001 for the Connex SouthCentral franchise. They were delivered as 375s, but the frequent coupling and uncoupling required in service prompted SouthCentral to replace their couplings with the more robust Dellner type for which they were reclassified 377. That franchise was lost when Connex left under a cloud as a result (officially) of poor timekeeping performance. Govia now runs the franchise.

Meanwhile, at the beginning of privatisation in 1994, all the railway's infrastructure was entrusted to a single company called Railtrack. Railtrack saw itself as a contracting body that bought in most of its services from outside companies such as Balfour Beatty, Carillion and so on. Those companies had already managed to buy up the technical bodies that BR had set up to manage track and signalling renewals and maintenance. A lot of knowledge and technical detail about the railway's track and structures as well as signalling was thus in the hands of Railtrack's contractors. Commentators were soon criticising Railtrack that the company didn't know much about its assets. A firm that was bidding for work was told (apparently) that it had to find out elsewhere what the infrastructure dimensions and details were because Railtrack could not give that information. This applied particularly for requests for gauging data. This lack of engineering expertise at a high level in the company must have been an element in the disasters that occurred at Hatfield, when a rail shattered, and at Potters Bar, when point blades had become misaligned. It is now a matter of history that Railtrack was forced into administration by the Government in 2002.

Network Rail (NR) was formed out of the rubble of Railtrack as a company with one shareholder, the government. NR quickly set up its asset register and has been measuring so much over the years that it is now very well informed about its infrastructure. NR's accumulated debt forced the government to take full ownership of Network Rail a few years later. Effectively it is now government-owned, and accounts for roughly half of the UK railway in turnover. It is also the source of over half of train delay minutes.

There are many critics of NR, but it has to be said that the standard of track and structures now being achieved, after a long period of steady investment and renewal, is higher than I can ever remember. At last, the increasing problem of trees dropping leaves on the railway is being slowly dealt with by tree lopping and felling at locations where wheel-rail adhesion problems have been registered. Drivers on South Western still comment that driving a train nowadays is like driving through a long green tunnel due to overhanging trees! This is gradually improving.

Railway photographers, of course, will not agree. The presence of trees blocking the view of passing trains at locations where the scene was wide open to view in steam days is a constant source of grumbles. It seems that it was ever thus!

Rail head condition is a 'modern' issue. When we still had steam trains, such as 34001 *Exeter* climbing the 1 in 60 of Parkstone bank pictured here on 9 September 1961, and rolling stock with cast iron brake blocks, rail heads were clean enough to ensure adequate adhesion. Modern trains with disc brakes do not clean the rail head in the same way. On this site on 28 November 2013, Stanier class 5 4-6-0 44871 slipped to a stand due to the contaminated rail head. (And the trees here are evergreens!) The class 5 was hauling a train no heavier than such engines used to pull daily and successfully with trains such as the Pines Express. A class 33 diesel was called to rescue the train and its passengers who arrived about an hour late for the Christmas markets at Bath and Bristol. So today's railways resort to 'defensive driving' with some extended timetables to allow for the low rail adhesions faced in the autumn.

CHAPTER 24

WHAT OF THE FUTURE?
I REALLY NEED A CRYSTAL BALL!

The Government's aim for Britain to be carbon neutral by 2050, and to ban diesel passenger trains a decade or more before then, will ensure that trains such as the 159 class DMUs on the London to Exeter run are replaced. But how much new electrification will actually happen? Hopefully, at least the line between Worting Junction and Salisbury. A pair of 159s is seen at speed through Winchfield on the way to London on 12 August 2010.

I have only once attempted to forecast future railway developments in a book. Having re-read that passage which I wrote in 1996, I realise that I did escape some of the severe pitfalls that most forecasters fall into. That must have been sheer good luck!

Nonetheless, I am writing this chapter at a particularly difficult time. As the Covid-19 pandemic reaches the end of its second wave, the railways are still running, but trains and buses are almost empty, certainly outside London and the big cities. Many businesses are failing, not just small ones either, as one airline collapsed just as this crisis began and others are looking fragile.

So what does the future hold for our railways?

My guess is that passenger travel levels will rise again, perhaps slowly, to much the same levels as before, though London commuting may take much longer to reach high levels. Eventually the same problems will arise again of overcrowded trains in the big cities and general congestion on northern railways. Planning for national de-carbonisation is under way. South Western Railway was forecasting in 2020 that its franchise results were not emerging as per the original plan and it would soon run out of money. Everything changed in 2020 with railways signing up to Government support though Emergency Rail Management Agreements (ERMAs), but what will replace these?

Let us assume for the time being that Great British Railways will be ready for action as planned in 2023 and will take account of the recommendations of the Williams-Shapps review. And let us then look further ahead to the next big changes in the South Western area.

The first big thing, which is happening now, is the introduction of the Bombardier Aventra class 701 EMUs that are intended to replace all the existing SWR inner suburban trains. That programme is expected to put the 455 and 456 EMUs off-lease. The plan was also to put the almost-new Siemens 707s off-lease because they, too, don't fit the 'homogeneous fleet' strategy of SWR. While the 455s and 456s may end up being scrapped, SouthEastern has accepted the thirty class 707 units. Despite the fact that the class 442 EMUs on the Portsmouth line have been withdrawn, the city's inhabitants will not have to put up with class 450 outer-suburban stock on their morning and evening commutes for very long. Twenty-eight class 458 units, reformed as four-car units and adjusted to a 100mph maximum speed, and with main line style seating spacing, are being drafted to the Portsmouth Direct line to improve the lot of travellers on that line, at least until 2027. However, new express units must be in the pipeline in about ten to fifteen years' time. Will there be the courage then to resurrect my suggestion that they be tilting EMUs so that they can speed up the Portsmouth Direct line services? I doubt if any other approach could be as effective in boosting passenger numbers and revenue on that route.

Then there are the erstwhile class 159 and 158 DMUs that keep the Waterloo to Exeter line going. Here, to get in line with electric train speeds east of Worting Junction, a new 100mph type would be useful. Maybe DfT may be tempted to transfer class 222 Meridians displaced from the Midland Main Line to the Exeter route. Assuming there would be enough of these, perhaps boosted by some displaced Voyagers from the West Coast Main Line, bear in mind these are all 125mph units. That raises the question again – should SWR and Network Rail jointly look at the potential for 125mph running on the Wimbledon to Worting Junction section of the Waterloo main line? Or at least 110mph? There are already ac versions of the Siemens 'Desiro' class 350 that can run safely at 110mph, and the 444s and 450s are also 'Desiros', so a speed uplift would be perfectly feasible with some technical tweaking if necessary of the behaviour of EMU collector shoes. The extra revenue potential from shorter journey times must be tempting.

Of course, DfT has recently been very keen to exploit bi-mode technology. A bi-mode multiple unit that can take current from the third rail and

What about raising the speed of Bournemouth fast trains to 110mph? Other members of the Siemens 'Desiro' fleets can do it! A pair of 444s races through Hersham on Joseph Locke's main line, a route that is well-aligned for higher speeds.

then switch to alternative power at Basingstoke would be a solution for a new fleet for the Exeter line, and could be designed with the necessary potential for higher speeds if such were wanted in future. Actually, building a fleet of electric pantograph-transformer cars to insert into the Meridian and Voyager fleets so as to extend and turn them into bi-modes would also be feasible and much more sensible as an economic way to turn these trains into bi-modes – or even convert some of the redundant mark 4 coaches to this use. That would not preclude electrifying the railway as far west as Salisbury as a way of preparing for the eventual full de-carbonisation of our railways. Alternatively, a 25kV ac scheme for Worting Junction-Salisbury-Exeter would be a useful way of ensuring proper de-carbonisation as it is a cheaper option to install than dc and west of Basingstoke an ac scheme would have a better business case. My guess is that, however, we will be saddled with bi-modes for the next generation of rolling stock replacement on this line.

Talking of third-rail electrification, the blatantly obvious case for an infill scheme is the Reading to Redhill line that has conductor rail sections at each end and in the middle but needs diesels to cover the rest. Let not the potential of bi-modes be used as an excuse to put this off any further!

All of this ignores the possibility that the Treasury might insist on railway cuts and closures to help rebalance the nation's finances after spending so much on the Covid-19 measures.

What of the heritage railway industry? We need to build on the success of regular summer steam excursion trains from the London area to Bournemouth, Weymouth and Swanage. With the advent of apprenticeships as a way of attracting dedicated and keen young people to the heritage industry, we have the opportunity to keep main line steam specials going into the foreseeable future. The same applies to the heritage railways, Mid-Hants, Swanage, Dartmoor (?), Seaton Tramway and indeed the little Lynton & Barnstaple. Eventually one or more of these might welcome owning a redundant 159 DMU! There is clearly not much else in the South Western area coming off-lease that such a railway could use, as EMUs are impractical.

I doubt if I shall be around to re-read this chapter to see what really happens in the next twenty years, but if I do reach 104 … then maybe!

Might heritage railways such as the Swanage Railway embrace the more modern world and operate trains with redundant 158s or 159s in future? It seems likely, based on the current long list of four-wheeled 'Pacer' trains being set aside for preservation! Hopefully there will still be room for preserved steam traction as well, such as Drummond M7 30053 that looked perfectly at home arriving at Corfe Castle with green mark 1 stock on 14 June 2004.

INDEX

660V dc / 750V dc, 51, 207

Alsthom/Alstom, 89, 109, 110, 219
Army/military, 41, 43, 54, 80, 170
Arriva, 69, 160, 162, 224, 225
Atlantic Coast Express, 9, 11, 47-49, 61, 129, 130, 142

Banking/piloting, 131, 150, 152, 156
Basingstoke, 11, 13, 18, 19, 21, 22, 36-38, 41, 49, 69, 81, 92, 93, 99, 107, 155, 157, 158, 165, 168, 198, 203, 209, 222, 224, 230
Bath Green Park, 148, 149, 156
Battledown, 22, 39, 41
Beeching, Dr. R., 26, 30, 33, 34, 109, 116, 124, 131, 139, 141, 177, 185, 190
Bombardier, 64, 81, 82, 89, 221, 226, 229
Bordon, 170
Bournemouth Belle, 25, 36, 37, 98, 112, 113, 121
Bournemouth Central, 30, 33, 34, 36, 37, 113-120, 122, 123, 147, 148, 159, 162
Bournemouth West, 32-34, 36, 37, 112, 113, 115-118, 121-123, 147, 149, 150, 152, 156, 162, 207
Branksome, 32, 34, 113, 118, 122, 147, 148, 207

Callington, 141, 142
Cannington, 182, 183
Castleman, 27, 28, 30, 31, 33, 36
Clapham Junction, 10, 19, 20, 37, 37, 54, 68-74
Connex, 203, 211, 212, 226
Containers, 13, 23, 28, 43, 91, 92, 94
Cunarder, 93, 94

Dartmoor Railway, 138, 139, 141, 203, 204, 231
DEMU, 40, 57, 100, 126, 138, 159, 198, 199, 203, 214
Devon Belle, 44, 47, 49, 145
DN&SR, 22, 26, 41, 101, 164
Docks, 10, 13-15, 18, 23, 24, 26-28, 50, 51, 53, 55, 84, 91-98, 101, 106-108, 140, 217
Durnsford Road, 20

Eastleigh Works, 15, 93, 108-111, 128, 141, 144, 183, 196, 198, 201, 203
Electro-diesel, 49, 102, 179, 206, 209-211, 216
Eurostar, 59, 61-63, 67
EWS, 223
Exeter, 9, 22, 30, 36, 39, 40-43, 47, 48, 65, 66, 68, 86, 123, 128-136, 138, 139, 141-145, 185, 206, 218, 224, 228-230
Exmouth Junction, 47, 131, 132, 185

Feltham, 13, 24, 85, 87-89, 91
First Group/MTR, 13, 19, 224
Freightliner, 92, 93, 108, 223

GBRf, 223
Govia, 212, 226
Guildford, 13, 20, 21, 51, 53, 54, 77, 80, 81, 84, 160

Hamworthy, 10, 30, 31, 35, 119, 151, 175
Hayling Island, 15, 54, 186, 195, 196
Highbridge, 148, 152-154

Isle of Wight, 13, 15, 30, 38, 51, 53, 55, 58, 96, 171, 187, 193-195, 206

Joseph Locke, 9, 17-26

Liss, 53, 170
Longmoor Military Railway, 54, 170, 194
Lynton & Barnstaple Railway, 144, 146, 231

M&SWJR, 163, 164
Meldon quarry/viaduct, 135, 138, 139, 142, 204
Meon Valley line, 168, 170
Midland Cross-Country, 117, 160, 224, 226

Necropolis cemetery, 14, 60, 64
Network SouthEast, 13, 40, 117, 133, 134, 192, 203, 217, 218, 222
Nine Elms, 17, 37, 59, 91, 104, 141, 149

Oil traffic, 13, 165, 170, 177
'Over the Alps', 81

PD&SWJR, 141
Pines Express, 14, 99, 147-150, 155, 157, 227
Plymouth, 27, 43, 47, 48, 98, 99, 123, 127, 129, 130, 135, 139-142, 162
Pneumatic signals, 19
Portland, 62, 180-182
Portsea Island, 51, 55, 186, 195, 211, 212
Portsmouth, 13, 18, 19, 21, 23, 24, 26, 38, 44, 50-58
Push-pull, 9, 12, 16, 24, 45, 46, 49, 69, 116, 117, 140, 166-168, 170, 173, 176, 180, 183, 184, 188, 200, 206, 207, 216

Reading, 21, 38, 40, 53, 68, 72, 80-82, 84-87, 90, 92, 144, 158-160, 162, 165, 203, 223, 231
Royal Wessex, 37, 61, 114, 176

S&DJR, 33, 34, 45, 116, 148-168
Salisbury, 13, 18, 19, 22, 23, 28, 30, 31, 39-41, 43-45, 48, 49, 54, 66, 74, 92, 97, 98, 100, 103, 104, 106, 107, 116, 123-129
Siemens, 17, 19, 22, 24, 53, 58, 86, 89, 100, 110, 117, 218-220, 225, 229, 230
Stagecoach, 13, 32, 53, 64, 65, 211, 212, 218, 223, 225
Swanage Railway, 177, 178, 231

Thameslink, 20, 212, 225, 226

Virgin, 160, 161, 224-226

'Warship' class, 49, 133
Waterloo, 10, 13, 15, 17, 19, 21, 24, 36, 37, 47, 53, 58-67, 69, 75, 82, 85, 87, 144, 206, 207, 212, 221, 225
Weymouth Quay, 16, 179
Woking, 18, 19, 21, 38, 51, 53, 58, 75, 80, 205, 207
Worting Junction, 19, 22, 39, 48, 66, 205, 228-230